AF717707

Stephen King

Stephen King

America's Storyteller

Tony Magistrale

PRAEGER

An Imprint of ABC-CLIO, LLC

A B C CLIO

Santa Barbara, California • Denver, Colorado • Oxford, England

Copyright © 2010 by Tony Magistrale

All rights reserved. No part of this publication may be reproduced, stored in a retrieval system, or transmitted, in any form or by any means, electronic, mechanical, photocopying, recording, or otherwise, except for the inclusion of brief quotations in a review, without prior permission in writing from the publisher.

Library of Congress Cataloging-in-Publication Data

Magistrale, Tony.
Stephen King : America's storyteller / Tony Magistrale.
p. cm.
Includes bibliographical references and index.
ISBN 978-0-313-35228-7 (hardcopy: alk. paper) — ISBN 978-0-313-35229-4 (ebook)
1. King, Stephen, 1947– —Criticism and interpretation. 2. Horror tales, American—History and criticism. 3. King, Stephen, 1947– —Film and video adaptations. 4. King, Stephen, 1947– —Characters—Women. I. Title.
PS3561.I483Z775 2010
813'.54—dc22 2009043306

ISBN: 978-0-313-35228-7
EISBN: 978-0-313-35229-4

14 13 12 11 10 1 2 3 4 5

This book is also available on the World Wide Web as an eBook.
Visit www.abc-clio.com for details.

Praeger
An imprint of ABC-CLIO, LLC

ABC-CLIO, LLC
130 Cremona Drive, P.O. Box 1911
Santa Barbara, California 93116-1911

This book is printed on acid-free paper ♾

Manufactured in the United States of America

Contents

Preface

This book undertakes the intriguing task of wrestling with several imposing questions. How do we account for Stephen King's enormous success both on best-seller lists and in movie theaters in light of a body of work that is so often critical of American life—its institutions, gender myths and relationships, and small-town communities? How do we explain the phenomenon of Stephen King, who is, on the one hand, an embodiment of the Horatio Alger story, rising from obscure poverty to the Forbes list of wealthiest Americans, and, on the other hand, a politically subversive writer? Is Stephen King merely another popular purveyor of horror—a *hack*, as some critics have insisted for years—or does he have something important to say about America, its past and its future direction? Is the culture that has embraced Stephen King as America's Storyteller, transforming him into arguably the most popular writer in history, reading him carefully enough?

Over the past four decades, Stephen King's movies and books have made him one of the most recognizable names on the planet. Certainly part of his popularity comes from his visualization of the dark side, feeding the Western world's postmodern fascination with indulging Gothic expressions in music and art. King's narratives, however, are also associated with describing very particular elements of America—its positive and negative group dynamics, its post-Vietnam identity, New England as a distinct regional place, to mention a few—especially for people reading them in other countries. Ten years ago, I was riding in a train from Paris to Augsburg, Germany. I shared the car with twenty or so high school students from Munich returning from a week spent touring the City of Light.

In casual conversation with several of the students sitting closest to me, I mentioned that I was an American and a professor of literature at the University of Vermont. After asking questions to ascertain where Vermont was located in the United States—was it somewhere near California, the universal surprise that Vermont itself is a state—my fellow travelers wanted to know about the courses I taught at UVM. When I mentioned my class entitled The Films of Stephen King, we immediately traversed both cultural and chronological differences. These teenagers didn't know much about Vermont, but they certainly had heard of Stephen King.

Each of my new friends had seen at least one Stephen King film, often bearing a different title in its Teutonic translation, and just as many had read some of his fiction—in English. I was not surprised to learn that *IT*, *Misery*, and *The Shining* were the most popular among them, and somewhat dismayed that none of these German children had even heard of *Apt Pupil*, King's mesmeric dark study that weds a fugitive Nazi with a not-so-innocent American blue-eyed boy. The point is that for many people around the world, Stephen King represents more than just a good Gothic scare; he is also synonymous—at least as much as the *Dallas* reruns dubbed on television and other ubiquitous elements of American popular culture, like Coca-Cola, that have found their way across the globe—with what they know of America and the extent to which they can identify with it. That said, how many Americans have come to view King in the same light: as a chronicler of contemporary culture, as much a sociologist of postmodern American life as he is a tremendously gifted storyteller?

Every artist is, at least in part, a product of his or her moment in time, even as that writer, if she or he is good enough, helps to define that era for future generations. Thomas Hardy's novels managed to capture the moment in which industrialization was transforming agrarian English life; Ernest Hemingway described the gap that existed between a generation of soldiers and artists who either fought in World War I or understood the cultural consequences attendant with millions dead and thousands maimed, and those who were insulated from the war's trauma; the British painter Francis Bacon captured on canvas the existential dread of modern man adrift in a universe where he is ultimately alone, bereft of God as well as a meaningful community of human others.

While Stephen King's universe is really not so far removed from any of the artists described above, for four decades he has worked incessantly to produce his own inimitable portrait of America at the end of the twentieth century and into the twenty-first. He has detailed the personal tragedies associated with divorce, alcoholism, and drug and child abuse. He has held a mirror up to our various prisons—those constructed with tax dollars and cement as well as the invisible ones that exist behind closed bedroom and kitchen doors that we ourselves create. For several decades now, he has been warning Americans about the degradation of the environment—most specifically, of the consequences that ensue from unholy alliances between the military and science, which in turn lead to dangerous experiments and the unleashing of nightmares. He has found a persuasive way to connect monstrosity with the loss of childhood vision, and to critique adults who have fallen out of touch with their imaginative capacities. Supernatural vampires and monsters may be the great popular attractions long associated with King's art, but at the heart of his best work is a deep-seated awareness of the very real anxieties about how Americans live and where we are going, as a nation and as individuals. More positively, he has also provided us with a range of unlikely friendships that mirror the success of the American melting pot, fusing the differences that typically separate race, class, age, and even worlds. In short, in the past forty years, Stephen King has supplied America with a national portrait. It is not always a flattering one, suitable for framing in the National Gallery or the White House, as it reveals our historical and cultural foibles and scars. But it also describes our transcendent, uniquely American survival instincts, fellowship, and acts of heroism from the least likely sources.

This book is concerned with defining the particular *American-ness* of Stephen King's fiction and films, from a biographical first chapter tracing his formative years and rise to the status of America's Storyteller, both in print and on Hollywood's big screen, to the second chapter's exploration of some of King's major influences: as a New England regionalist—profoundly shaped by his life in Maine—as well as his extensive reading of other writers both in and outside the horror genre.

Chapter 3 treats those various American social institutions—school, church, government, penal system, small-town communities—that reappear continually in King's fiction and function primarily to entrap and disempower individuals. The politically subversive nature of King's work is perhaps best exemplified in his constant equating of social institutions with prisons, and his consummate faith in the individual as superior to the groupthink of the community—particularly the small-town zeitgeist. Although rich in fantasy and speculation when envisioning the ravages of a post-apocalyptic future, King's work also employs the collapse of civilization and civilized values to construct a kind of laboratory for his characters to experiment in situations in which they must reinvent society and themselves.

Chapter 4 continues to stress the primacy of the individual in King's fictional universes, including both the real and the speculative, but it does so in terms of sexual choices and preferences. Using *The Stand* as an illustrative text among several others, the chapter explores various expressions of sexuality in King's art, as sexual behavior is often a barometer in his work to a character's moral baseline. If sexual deviance is the outgrowth of unrestrained impulse and expressions of fear and mental instability, conversely, people of good will in King's world tend to be affiliated with what the writer has defined as a "normative" (i.e., heterosexual and monogamous) sexuality.

Chapter 5 makes the case for revisiting arguably the single most important text in the King canon and repertory of film adaptations: *The Shining*. Entwining discussion of the novel with Kubrick's film and the televised miniseries, this chapter and the first part of chapter 6 explore all three *Shining(s)* and the various treatments of class, racial, and gender issues that have transformed these narratives into a highly relevant cultural critique of America, past and present.

The last two chapters in this book trace the most evolutionary aspects of King's work: his women characters and the career-long writing of *The Dark Tower*. In chapter 6, I examine the range of women characters that populate this writer's fictions and films—and their evolution from stereotyped peripheral helpmates and femmes fatales to individualized characters located at the center of his art. The trajectory of King's career includes a movement from early American road epics to a more circumscribed focus on domestic family life. Correspondingly, the road epics tend to be male-centered, whereas the later domestic narratives revolve around women caught in abusive relationships and struggling to define their own narrative voice.

The Dark Tower is the subject of this book's last chapter. The seven-volume adventure is best appreciated as an umbrella text encompassing the whole of King's fictional canon; it encapsulates and interfaces with many of the core plots, characters, and subject matter that King has configured over the course of his writing career. This chapter links the saga's main character, Roland Deschain, to images of American masculinity found elsewhere in King's work as well as in the construction of the American Western archetype. The chapter views *The Dark Tower* in keeping with King's tendency to blend genres, borrowing an admixture of identifiable elements from the American Western, the epic tradition, and the Gothic melodrama.

In the end, Stephen King's work remains as paradoxical in nature as the America he has been describing since *Carrie*. On the one hand, King would appear to be as fearfully conscious of the American urge toward institutionalization and conformity—in high schools, in small towns, in the blind trust of the government and its platitudes, and in our collective faith in technology and science—as were his fellow New Englanders, Thoreau and Hawthorne, a century earlier. On the other hand, King is also archetypically American in his adherence to the ideology of individualism. In so many King narratives his heroes are in flight from a corrupt and monstrous society. They possess the power and courage to leave these societies, but not the ability to change them. While King's faith in the moral supremacy of the individual (and in small groups of like-minded individuals) goes uncontested, these characters cannot effectively confront the surrounding forces of evil. Thus, the psychology of escapism becomes a central motif in Stephen King's canon, and it connects him directly to a core tendency that is inimitably American—from Thoreau's deliberate life in the woods, to Huck Finn's retreat to the river, to the lost generation of antiheroes in Hemingway, to the road-obsessed Beats. While he may have attained all the apparent trappings of the American dream in terms of financial wealth, multiple homes and cars, and celebrity status since declaring himself a writer, Stephen King has maintained a complex relationship with the culture that has now embraced him as its Storyteller. That relationship is the subject of this book.

Acknowledgments

I would very much like to acknowledge the assistance and contributions of many people and publications in the construction of this book. First, to my editors at Praeger—Suzanne I. Staszak-Silva, who first sparked my imagination with the concept of this book, and Dan Harmon, who took over when Suzanne left the company, and then shepherded the book through to publication—I am grateful and appreciative. Matthew Muller read selected sections of this manuscript and supplied always-trenchant criticism and advice. A truncated version of Chapter 4 was initially delivered as a conference paper at the Popular Culture Association. Thanks are also due to my family—my wife, Jennifer; sons, Christopher and Daniel; and our golden retriever, Goldilocks—for their generous willingness to share me with a demanding laptop. Finally, twenty-five years of teaching undergraduate and graduate students at the University of Vermont provided critical insights that have indelibly shaped, confirmed, challenged, and altered my understanding of Stephen King. My regret is that I cannot thank each of these students personally—there are just too many—but their sensitive and intelligent voices from classroom discussions and writing assignments resonate profoundly throughout this volume.

Chronology

1947 Stephen King born September 21 in Portland, Maine, second son to Donald and Nellie Ruth Pillsbury King.

1949 Donald King, father, leaves house on trip to store and never returns.

1954 Begins writing short fiction modeled after science fiction adventure stories and movies.

1962–66 Attends high school in Lisbon Falls, Maine.

1966–70 Undergraduate years as English major at the University of Maine, Orono (UMO). Meets future wife, Tabitha Spruce, also a UMO undergraduate. Works as a laborer in an industrial laundry.

1971–73 Marries Tabitha Spruce. Teaches high school English at Hampden Academy in Hampden, Maine; lives in mobile home. Publishes several short stories. Sells *Carrie* to Doubleday. Mother dies of cancer.

1974 *Carrie.* Moves with wife and daughter to Boulder, Colorado.

1975 *'Salem's Lot.* Returns to Maine and purchases home in Bridgton.

1976 Film version of *Carrie*, directed by Brian De Palma.

1977 *The Shining* and *Rage* (first novel to appear under Bachman pseudonym). Introduced to Peter Straub during three-month trip to England.

1978 *The Stand* and *Night Shift.* Writer in Residence at UMO. Teaches classes in creative writing and Gothic fiction. Uses later course to launch theories on the horror genre that will inform his study *Danse Macabre.*

1979 *The Dead Zone* and Bachman's *The Long Walk*. Concludes teaching duties at UMO.

1980 *Firestarter* and "The Mist." Buys current residence on West Broadway, Bangor. Kubrick's film adaptation of *The Shining*.

1981 *Cujo, Danse Macabre*, and third Bachman title, *Roadwork*. Receives Career Alumni Award from UMO.

1982 *Different Seasons* and fourth Bachman book, *The Running Man*, first volume of *The Dark Tower: The Gunslinger*. Wins World Fantasy Award for short story "The Reach" and Hugo Award for *Danse Macabre*.

1983 *Christine* and *Pet Sematary*. Film releases of *Cujo, The Dead Zone*, and *Christine*.

1984 *The Talisman* (coauthored with Peter Straub), *Eyes of the Dragon*, and fifth Bachman novel, *Thinner*.

1985 *Skeleton Crew*. Reveals "Richard Bachman" pseudonym.

1986 *IT*. Film version of *Stand by Me* based on King's novella, *The Body*.

1987 *Misery* (originally intended as a Bachman book), *Eyes of the Dragon, Silver Bullet, The Tommyknockers*, and *The Dark Tower: The Drawing of the Three*. Film release of *The Running Man*.

1989 *The Dark Half* (1.5 million hardcover copies—largest first-edition printing in publishing history). Film version of *Pet Sematary*.

1990 *The Stand*, revised and unexpurgated; *Four Past Midnight*. Film adaptation of *Misery*; Kathy Bates wins Academy Award for Best Actress. *IT* televised as ABC miniseries. Begins publishing essays and stories in *The New Yorker*.

1991 *Needful Things, The Dark Tower: The Waste Lands*.

1992 *Gerald's Game, Dolores Claiborne*. Film version of *Pet Sematary*.

1993 *Nightmares and Dreamscapes*.

1994 *Insomnia*. Film release of *The Shawshank Redemption*, nominated for several Academy Awards, including Best Picture. *The Stand* televised as ABC miniseries.

1995 *Rose Madder*. Film version of *Dolores Claiborne*.

1996 *The Green Mile*, published in six installments; *Desperation; The Regulators* published under Bachman pseudonym. Wins O.

Henry Award for "The Man in the Black Suit," as year's best short story.

1997 *The Dark Tower: Wizard and Glass*. Film adaptation of *Apt Pupil*. *Stephen King's The Shining* televised as ABC miniseries.

1998 *Bag of Bones*.

1999 *The Girl Who Loved Tom Gordon*, *Hearts in Atlantis*; *Storm of the Century* televised as ABC miniseries. Car accident hospitalizes King in mid-summer. Film version of *The Green Mile* is nominated for several Academy Awards, including Best Film.

2000 *On Writing*, *Secret Window*; *The Plant* (online publishing venture).

2001 *Dreamcatcher*, *Black House* (coauthored with Peter Straub, sequel to *The Talisman*).

2002 *From a Buick 8*, *Everything's Eventual*. *Rose Red* televised as ABC miniseries.

2003 *The Dark Tower: Wolves of the Calla*. Begins writing "The Pop of King," King's take on popular American culture, a monthly column for the magazine *Entertainment Weekly*. Wins National Book Award's Medal for Distinguished Contribution to American Letters.

2004 Last two volumes of *The Dark Tower* saga, *Song of Susannah* and *The Dark Tower*.

2005 Signs a deal with Marvel Comics to publish a seven-issue graphic comic series adapting *The Dark Tower*; *Faithful* (with Stewart O'Nan); *The Colorado Kid*.

2006 *Cell*, *Lisey's Story*. *1408* is released as a film.

2007 *Duma Key*, *Blaze* published as a Bachman book. *The Mist* released as Frank Darabont's fourth King film adaptation. Endorses Democratic presidential candidate Barack Obama. Marvel Comics publishes *The Gunslinger Born*, the first volume of a color comic book adaptation of *The Dark Tower*.

2008 *Just after Sunset*. King, Scribner's, and Marvel Comics reach an agreement for a color comic adaptation of *The Stand*.

2009 *Under the Dome* scheduled release.

2010 Scheduled release of *Ghost Brothers of Darkland County*, an original Southern gothic musical collaboration between Stephen King and rock musician John Mellencamp.

Chapter 1

The Writer's Life: A Stephen King Biography

Born September 21, 1947, in Portland, Maine, Stephen Edwin King—following in the astrological footsteps of fellow novelists Herman Melville and Leo Tolstoy—is a loquacious Virgo. Apparently, that was always the case even when a young Steve whiled away parts of deathless adolescent summers in 1959 and 1960 typing science-fiction stories and tales of mystery and suspense on his manual typewriter for mimeographed distribution to family and neighborhood friends. This may be one of those rare examples of a precocious child who knew exactly what he wanted to be when he grew up—and ended up so thoroughly achieving it, that he exceeded even his most ambitious dreams.

Stephen King has led an interesting life, especially for a writer. Since the novel *Carrie* began his reign of terror over the publishing world in 1974, he has become one of the most popular and widely recognized novelists of all time. Some estimates place the total number of Stephen King books worldwide at 300 million copies. King commentators have speculated that the only writers more popular than Mr. King were those who authored the Biblical gospels, and they had Jesus on their side. In the 1980s alone, King wrote seven of the top twenty-five fiction best sellers in America. His books have been translated into nearly every language. Last year on a visit to a bookstore in downtown Stockholm, I found three complete shelves containing many of his most recognizable titles translated into Swedish. Remarkably prolific, by the year 2004 King had averaged more than a book a year during three decades of publishing. Most of his novels and many of his short stories have been made into Hollywood films, and many people know King's work primarily through the movies.

Perhaps because of his best-seller popularity, his strong, plot-dominated narratives, his deftly drawn characters, or a combination of these elements, Hollywood discovered long ago that any Stephen King work is a bankable project; none of the 100-plus films from his literary canon theatrically released or televised in a miniseries format have failed to make money. As just a small example of his enormous financial clout, in 1995–1996 Stephen King placed #12 on the *Forbes* magazine list of the forty highest-paid entertainers. King was reported to have made $56 million that year, slightly less than Jerry Seinfeld ($59 million) or The Beatles ($130 million), but more than Mel Gibson ($28 million) and David Letterman ($27 million) combined. This is rarified company for sure, and the only other writer on the *Forbes* list who made more than King that year was Michael Crichton ($59 million).

Certainly every artist, mogul, and musical group whose talent was prodigious enough to merit an appearance with King on this list has his or her own remarkable success story, emerging from general obscurity and, in some cases, humble origins, to the riches and name recognition associated with fame. None of their stories, however, could possibly be more dramatic than the Horatio Alger tale of triumph that is Stephen King's biography. But we're getting ahead of ourselves. We need first to return to Stephen King, the man who spent many of his earliest years struggling mightily before that awkward teenage girl with telekinetic powers, a misunderstanding of her menarche, and an urge to attend her senior prom interceded and transformed King's world even more than her own.

Perhaps the single most important moment in King's childhood took place when he was merely two years old. His father, Donald King, a vacuum cleaner salesman and merchant mariner, went out one night to buy a pack of cigarettes in 1949, leaving his wife, Nellie Ruth, and two small sons at home. To borrow from the song "Hungry Heart" by Bruce Springsteen, one of King's friends and favorite musicians, his father went "went out for a ride and he never came back." The King family, never well off financially when Donald was part of it, grew more desperate still. The middle years of Steve's childhood were spent in Fort Wayne, Indiana, and Stratford, Connecticut, with frequent trips back to Maine to visit his mother's relatives. While King often reminds interviewers that the family always had food on the table and that his mother was a constant source of support and a welcome sense of humor, it is also clear that the King family moved around so much because they relied on financial help from relatives to make ends meet: "I guess in many ways it was a hard-scrabble existence, but not an impoverished one in the most important sense of the word. Thanks to my mother, the one thing that was never in short supply, corny as it may sound to say it, was love. And in that sense, I was a hell of a lot less deprived than countless children of middle-class or wealthy families, whose parents have time for everything but their kids" (Dyson 7).

Steve and his brother Donald may not have lacked for the essentials, but there wasn't much opportunity for leisurely extras. This is important to keep in mind, for King's strong blue-collar work ethic and respect for the working class was born in early real life struggles. (And never more in evidence than when I once asked him for the names of some of the best restaurants in Bangor, and King gave me three—all of them diners.) While generous to a fault, the successful adult has always remembered what it was like to grow up without much of a cushion. Instead of turning resentful, however, King learned the value of money and hard work—and these values are often imparted to his practical-minded, working-class heroes, such as Stu Redman, Red Redding, John Smith, Dolores Claiborne, and many of the Bachman protagonists.

EDUCATION AND EARLY WRITINGS

The Kings settled in Durham, Maine, when Stephen was eleven. He and his brother attended Lisbon High School, just northeast of Durham; Steve's years there were 1962–66. He was an average student and played tight end on the varsity football team: "My high school career was totally undistinguished. I was not at the top of my class, nor at the bottom. I had friends, but none of them were the big jocks or the student council guys or anything like that" (Dyson 10). Tall and awkward, overweight, with buck teeth and coke-lens glasses, King had personal insight into the cruelty of high school. As a sensitive child tortured because of his looks and sensitivity, "at times, particularly in my teens, I felt violent, as if I wanted to lash out at the world, but that rage I kept hidden. That was a secret place in myself I wouldn't reveal to anyone else" (Dyson 10). Over the years, King employed his art as a means for revisiting his personal sense of being a pariah in high school as well as his urge toward violent retribution. The majority of his adolescent protagonist-heroes, especially during the first half of his writing career, are cast from the mold of high school outcasts and lovable losers harassed by adolescent cruelty. The four boys at the crossroad of their youth in "The Body" as well as the Losers in the novel *IT* all suffer at the hands of oppressive fellow adolescents; one of the Bachman books, *Rage*, features a student who shoots his teacher and then takes his class hostage; and the main character of his first published novel, *Carrie*, is a scapegoat for all the other more popular and attractive female peers in her class. King has always had a soft spot for adolescent outsiders, possibly because he empathized personally with the level of cruelty they experienced as victims of their school's more physically powerful and popular students.

Thirty-three years after his own emergence from high school, King gave the keynote address at the annual meeting of the Vermont Library Conference in May 1999. In this speech, entitled "The Bogeyboys," he discussed the events that in the previous month had resulted in the massacre of students at Columbine High School in Littleton, Colorado. Although interested in the specifics of this tragedy, particularly in defining the influence of America's love of violence in the entertainment industry and the culture's easy access to guns, King also reminded his audience that the two killers, Eric Harris and Dylan Klebold, were examples of the failure of the American high school as an institution—its tendency to segregate students into winners and losers at an early age, and to judge them exclusively on looks and athletic talent. While he never excuses the violence of their response, King is extremely sympathetic to the torment both Harris and Klebold received from their peers that precipitated their turn toward bloodshed. Moreover, King's sympathy is couched in autobiographical terms, as he again drew from his own experiences both as a student and, later, as a teacher in high school:

> I remember high school as a time of misery and resentment. In Iroquois trials of manhood, naked warriors were sent running down a gauntlet of braves swinging clubs and jabbing them with the butt ends of spears. In high school the goal is Graduation Day instead of a manhood feather, and the weapons are replaced by insults, slights, epithets. The victims aren't always naked, and yet a good deal of the rawest hazing does take place on playing fields and in locker rooms, where the marks are thinly dressed or not at all. The locker room is where *Carrie* starts with girls throwing sanitary napkins at a sexually ignorant girl who thinks she's bleeding to death. I don't trust people who look back on high school with fondness; too many of them were part of the overclass, those who were taunters instead of tauntees. (http://www.stephenking.de/interviews/interview6.html)

It was at Lisbon High that he began to write seriously; he composed a series of stories, many of which incorporated science fiction themes. In 1964, for example, he produced a 3,000-word novel, *The Star Invaders*, which showed the influence of the science fiction pulp magazines that were popular during this era. After graduation from Lisbon, King enrolled at the University of Maine, Orono (UMO), primarily because the school offered him a full-tuition scholarship. Without such financial assistance he probably could not have afforded to attend college. Tabitha Spruce, who was also a student at UMO majoring in history, noted the level of King's student poverty: "Talk about going to college poor—this guy was going to college the way that people did in the twenties and thirties. He had nothing to eat, he had no money, he had no clothes; it was just incredible that anyone was going to school under those circumstances, and even more incredible that he didn't care. All he cared about was the education" (Winter 23). Looking back on his younger self from the dais after winning the National Book Award Medal for Distinguished Contribution in 2003, King described himself this way: "I had a bushy black beard. I hadn't cut my hair in two years and I looked like Charlie Manson. My wife-to-be clasped her hands between her breasts and said 'I think I'm in love' in a tone dripping with sarcasm" (King, National Book Awards Acceptance Speech). King never forgot what it was like to attend school under such hardships; for years he has provided undergraduate scholarships for financially challenged students to study at universities in Maine and several other states.

Always a voracious reader, college fed his appetite for books. As an English major, he took courses in creative writing, which rankled him because the cookie-cutter expectations of writer's workshops tended to stifle his imagination. Instead, King's most influential courses were in literature, where he studied many of the writers who would affect his own fictional prose in years to come: Thomas Hardy, Jack London, William Faulkner, Ernest Hemingway, Edgar Allan Poe, and Eldridge Cleaver. English departments in the late sixties were still pretty conservative places; before literary theorists and feminist scholars gave impetus to dismantling the canon in the 1980s and 1990s, English departments tended to view themselves as the custodians of high culture, the place where the classics were taught and the separation between high and popular culture was clear and rigidly maintained. In college, King fought this artificial designation, as he would continue to fight it as a writer throughout his career. He asked the English department at UMO to allow him to teach a course on popular American fiction that would include those writers—Shirley Jackson, John Farris, Ed McBain, and Don Robertson—who were as much responsible for King's development as a writer as were any of the dead white male classics revered in the departmental curriculum. With a tenured member of the department as the acting professor in the course, King taught Popular Literature and Culture at the University of Maine, the first time a class was offered in this topic and the first time an undergraduate served in the role of a professor.

King published several stories in college literary magazines, including versions of "Strawberry Spring" and "Night Surf," two tales that would be reprinted in his first collection of short stories, *Night Shift*. As an upperclassman, he also began submitting work to national magazines and periodicals; he sold his first short story, "Graveyard Shift," shortly after graduation, and finished writing *Sword in the Darkness*, a novel that would later be titled *The Gunslinger*, the first book of *The Dark Tower* series.

While at the university, King immersed himself in politics as well as literature, a response to the politically charged atmosphere that characterized many American campuses in the late 1960s. When he arrived on campus, a product of backwater America in a state with one of the smallest minority populations in the country, his politics were appropriately conservative and benign. He'd supported the presidential candidacy of Republican Barry Goldwater in 1964 and voted for Richard Nixon in 1968. At the university, however, King let his hair grow long, experimented with drugs, and identified—especially during his last two years as an undergraduate—with the Students for a Democratic Society's protest movement against the war in Vietnam and other American social ills. War protests and campus political life transformed King from a conservative into a noisy radical who led marches against the war and campus ROTC, and in support of left-wing causes and organizations. Few King scholars and readers appreciate sufficiently the extent to which both his fiction and his life have been influenced by the political consciousness that was raised during these formative years at UMO. Although his tone has become less strident and political issues are now often couched in subtexts and subtler contexts, the counterculture's blend of social activism, institutional distrust, and ethical outrage—the brew that helped to radicalize the young King—remains a distinct feature of his subsequent writings and personal life. Most Americans politicized in the sixties had by the seventies and eighties rejoined the mainstream establishment in order to make money and advance careers, but as will be documented in chapter 3, which deals with institutions and institutionalization in his fiction, King has held true to the political consciousness he developed as an undergraduate. In their adult years, Steve and Tabitha King have supported Democratic and progressive political candidates on both local and national levels. In 2007, for example, the Kings endorsed the presidential candidacy of Barack Obama, one of the most liberal politicians ever to run for this office. King has traveled all over the country, often at his own expense, to support community librarians and their battles against book censorship, traditionally instigated by rightist agendas, and conservative efforts to shape school curricula. As a long-time supporter of independent bookstores, King is reluctant to perform signings at chain superstores, claiming that they do not need his help to remain financially viable. In promoting his novel *Insomnia,*

King went coast-to-coast on his motorcycle, stopping only at independent booksellers. And perhaps most important of all, the Kings continue to provide financial support to community-based organizations that take care of Maine's less fortunate citizens. The Bath Family Crisis Services in Bath, Maine, was just one of many recipients of their generosity when the shelter for abused women and children received an unsolicited $50,000 donation one Christmas Eve (Beahm, *King from A to Z*, 19).

The university definitely enlarged King's political and intellectual scope, but it also confirmed his desire to be a writer; even before graduation he was thinking in terms of getting his work out into the world. By the time he was out of college, King had already amassed a substantial collection of rejection letters from New York publishers. While a student, King continued to write fiction, producing several early drafts of novels. Observers of his prolific canon have remarked on the tremendous output of fiction King managed to publish in the 1980s. Although always a prodigious writer, many of these books and stories were actually composed years earlier and then stored away until after King became famous. Two novels, *The Long Walk* and *The Running Man*, were both written when King was an undergraduate or immediately after his graduation, and both were eventually published a decade later under the pseudonym Richard Bachman.

During his senior year in 1969, King began writing a regular column for the university newspaper, *The Maine Campus*. The column was called "King's Garbage Truck" because one never knows about the contents of a garbage truck—sometimes it contains diamond rings and sometimes only junk. The collection of work King amassed for *The Maine Campus* reflected the eclectic title of his column: he wrote about films and books, the police, water fluoridation, birth control, baseball, and girls. Perhaps the one common element that connects his catholic ramblings is King's inimitable sense of humor; each article he wrote, regardless of its subject, contained elements of the writer's comic touch—through parody, satire, self-deprecation, and sometimes even verbal slapstick. The column also supplied an outlet for his emerging political perspective, specifically the antiwar movement and governmental abuses of power. The last column he wrote, on the eve of his graduation, is the darkest and best of the lot. King provides his readership with a somber announcement of the boy-man about to enter the "real world." Like so many American college graduates in 1970, King emerged less the optimist than the jaded cynic, less the patriot than the subversive skeptic. He wrote that his political views were "Extremely radical, largely due to the fact that nobody seems to listen to you unless you threaten to shut them down, turn them off, or make some kind of trouble." He announced that he had neither a "Favorite President" nor a "Favorite University Chancellor." His favorite films included a mix of highbrow and lowbrow cinema that would serve as a harbinger of his own fictional tastes throughout his career, ranging from *They Shoot Horses, Don't They?* and *Bonnie and Clyde* to *Attack of the Giant Leeches.* The writer saved his most scurrilous commentary for a bitter self-analysis and negative prognostication: "[Future prospects are] hazy, although either nuclear annihilation or environmental strangulation seem to be distinct possibilities. . . . If a seeker at his birth into the real world mentions 'changing the world with the bright-eyed vigor of youth,' this young man is apt to flip him the bird and walk out, as he does not feel very bright-eyed by this time; in fact, he feels about two thousand years old." It is worth noting that the entries constituting "King's Garbage Truck" have never been collected or published outside of their original venue, *The Maine Campus*, which still holds the copyright to King's essays. Several years ago, the University of Maine wanted to publish all of King's undergraduate writings in a single volume, no doubt hoping to capitalize on the writer's fame. But King asked his alma mater to forgo this venture, which they did, certainly out of respect for the wishes of their most famous alumnus, but perhaps also because King convinced them that his earliest published writing was exactly that: juvenilia that was often composed quickly to meet a newspaper deadline, and that it deserved to rest in peace.

THE REIGN OF TERROR

Perhaps the tone of King's last entry in his college column reflects the voice of a pre-graduation party hangover, or maybe the disguised terror of a graduating senior faced with the prospect of what to do next with his life, or maybe it is simply indicative of the pessimism of its era. Regardless of how we wish to interpret King's own self-prognosis, as deliciously ironic in light of his eventual fame or merely reflective of a dark hangover, upon his graduation the odds were overwhelmingly in favor of Stephen King's becoming just another shaggy-haired kid with a bachelor's degree in English finding his way to a job at an industrial laundry, or, if he were extremely fortunate, a teaching career at a small Maine high school. After marrying Tabitha in 1971, future prospects were definitely hazy, and King's own somber self-assessment began to appear prophetic. From 1971 to 1973, Stephen King, his wife, and their infant daughter Naomi and son Joe, two of their three eventual children, were living in a trailer; Stephen was teaching English at Hampden Academy in Hampden, Maine, while Tabitha was working at a local donut shop. The Kings did not have enough money to pay their telephone bill, and Steve was becoming concerned that he "was never going to be a writer of any consequence. I'd lie awake at night seeing myself at fifty, my hair graying, my jowls thickening, a network of whiskey-ruptured capillaries spiderwebbing across my nose—'drinker's tattoos,' we call them in Maine—with a dusty trunk full of unpublished novels rotting away in the basement, teaching high school English for the rest of my life and getting off what few literary rocks I had left by advising the student newspaper or maybe teaching a creative writing course" (Underwood and Miller 32). King came a long way in a very short period of time, literally transforming his life and family's, and in the process, the shape of the horror genre for certain, and, to a very real extent, the business of publishing fiction in America.

But the success of *Carrie* was an accident. The first draft of the novel ended up in the trash and was literally rescued by Tabitha, who noted something interesting in the plot of a confused and tortured female adolescent, and urged him to submit it to Doubleday, a publishing house that had already rejected him on four other occasions. The novel was accepted, and it sold a modest 13,000 copies in hardcover in 1974, but the paperback, purchased by New American Library, which sought to capitalize on the success of *The Exorcist* (1973), sold 2.5 million copies. Sales of the novel were further aided by the first film adaptation of a Stephen King work, Brian De Palma's 1976 movie that starred Sissy Spacek and Piper Laurie, who were both nominated for Academy Awards. De Palma's film version of *Carrie* managed to capture the slippery blending of horror and humor that is often a crucial—albeit elusive—element in a King text, and characterizes several of the most memorable cinematic adaptations of his work, such as *Stand by Me* and *Misery*.

Carrie not only signaled the start of "a career and not a hobby" (Dyson 20); it also commenced a long love affair between Stephen King and the movies. As of this writing, over one hundred films—both theatrical releases and made-for-television miniseries—have been produced based on King's writing. Most of his novels and many of his short stories have been made into films. Many of the world's major directors—Stanley Kubrick, David Cronenberg, Rob Reiner, Tobe Hooper, Brian Singer, and Frank Darabont—have produced excellent movies based on King narratives, and their films have also attracted a range of the most accomplished actors and actresses working in Hollywood today: Jack Nicholson, Tom Hanks, Morgan Freeman, Tim Robbins, Christopher Walken, John Cusack, Kathy Bates, and Rebecca De Mornay. The multibillion dollar industry represented by the cinematic side of King helps us realize that this writer is more than just a remarkably popular and readily recognizable cultural icon; it confirms his status as America's Storyteller, a versatile artist capable of producing narratives so compelling that they translate well into a variety of visual media. One hundred years from now, several of King's novels will likely endure—*The Shining, The Stand, The Dark Tower* series, the magnificent novellas in *Different Seasons*—as evidence of America's struggle with its own internal monsters at the end of the twentieth century. But it remains my belief that it will be the Stephen King film adaptations, maybe even more than the novels that inspired them, that will eventually crystallize into King's greatest cultural legacy.

King has acknowledged that over the years he has "developed a reputation in Hollywood as a 'bankable writer.' Castle Rock [productions] has had better luck than any one in decoding what it is that I do" (Magistrale, *Hollywood's Stephen King*, 7). What this writer does is to create memorable characters and highly visual, action-centered plots readily suited for presentation of the screen. However, even his best work has sometimes failed to translate well into film: *Pet Sematary* and *Dreamcatcher* are cases in point. While acknowledging King to be an immensely talented writer, some film critics are more focused than I am on the many clumsily adapted efforts to translate King to the big screen. Greg Smith, for example, cites the failure so often linked with celluloid adaptations of King's work and feels that King's reputation suffers as a consequence: "[T]he majority of films which have either been made using his works of fiction as models or that have been in some way or another connected with his name have been awful (in turn leading those who have not read his fiction to assume that it manifests a similar lack of quality)" (332).

It is impossible to imagine any writer, director, actor, or production company responsible for nearly one hundred films maintaining a consistent level of creative genius; thus, the King film canon includes regrettable efforts such as *Children of the Corn, Dreamcatcher, Desperation*, and *Maximum Overdrive*, work that never rises above the cheap frights, the undisciplined plotlines, and the bloodletting of B-grade horror. On the other hand, how many novelists, screenwriters, directors, actors, or production companies would not be ecstatic with the financial and artistic success of movies such as *Carrie, The Shining, The Shawshank Redemption, The Green Mile, Misery, Apt Pupil, Stand by Me*, and a handful of other titles that have now entered into the cinematic pantheon? *The Shining*, for example, after its 1980 release became one of Warner Brothers' top ten moneymaking films (Warren 145) and is always included near the top of every list of best horror films ever made. According to the Internet Movie Database and Allmovie.com, only *The Godfather*, as the most popular movie of all time, eclipses *The Shawshank Redemption*. As good a novella as "Rita Hayworth and the Shawshank Redemption" is, the book never attained the same cultural resonance as the film. In fact, the number of people who still do not recognize that the film version of Shawshank is a close adaptation of a Stephen King narrative always impresses me.

Hollywood's obsession with Stephen King throughout the 1980s, averaging between two or three film adaptations per year, provided the writer with an international name recognition that helped to catapult King into the best-seller stratosphere. The success of films such as *Stand by Me* also attracted a mainstream audience of readers who didn't typically buy horror. The money allowed the Kings to quit their jobs and focus their attention on writing (Tabitha is also a novelist, primarily of adolescent fiction). *The Shining* (1977) became King's first hardcover best seller, and everything else that he has published since has spent anywhere from six to forty weeks on the best-seller lists. In a list of the top twenty-five fiction bestsellers of the 1980s compiled by *Publishers Weekly*, King had seven titles, and for one week in the mid-1980s King had seven different titles on *The New York Times* Bestseller List simultaneously (in his office on Florida Avenue in Bangor, King has a framed enlargement of the *Times* list hanging on a wall behind his desk). As the writer was forced to acknowledge, "I have grown into Bestsellasaurus Rex—a big, stumbling book beast that is loved when it shits money and hated when it tramples houses. I started out as a storyteller; along the way I became an economic force" (Beahm, *Stephen King from A to Z*, 20).

The "economic force" that he attained in the 1980s allowed the King family to move into a historic home on Broadway Avenue, a street near the center of Bangor where the profits of former timber barons from the nineteenth century built rambling mansions. Constructed in 1856, the King house contains twenty-three rooms and, from the front, maintains a classic Victorian edifice. But from the side the dwelling swells out like the self-metastasizing Rose Red, stretching far and deep into the property like a suburban airplane hangar housing an indoor swimming pool, a library, and a movie theater. The King family also owns a summer home in western Maine and a winter residence in Florida.

During the 1980s King dominated the publishing industry; he published *Firestarter, Cujo, Different Seasons*, three books in *The Dark Tower* series, *Danse Macabre, Pet Sematary, Eyes of the Dragon, Christine, Misery, IT, The Tommyknockers, Skeleton Crew, The Talisman*, and *The Dark Half*. In addition to his publishing better than a book a year throughout this decade, Hollywood released an average of two King film adaptations or more per year, and the writer emerged from all this as not merely a literary juggernaut, but a cultural phenomenon as well. His audience demographic defied any kind of generic recognition; his fiction attracted adolescents and their parents, people who are normally not readers of novels and college professors. And in the process, King's influence on a generation of young writers and filmmakers became undeniable. His recurrent interests in religious fanaticism, governmental conspiracies that unleash various plagues to threaten the continued existence of humanity, and child abuse, for example, are much imitated in post-King horror art and have afforded other artists avenues for probing America's unhealthy underside.

What the Beatles were to rock music in the 1960s, Stephen King was to horror fiction and film in the 1980s; the influence of both helped to transform their respective genres. "The early eighties was a boom time in horror," editor Jeanne Cavelos observed in 2002, "with the number of books being published quickly rising to ten times what it was a few years before (mainly due to Stephen King's influence)" (Guran). Both the Beatles and King additionally mirrored the larger spirit of their respective times: the Beatles embodied the optimistic Age of Aquarius, while King's sobering portrait of life in the eighties reflects a post-Vietnam/Watergate malaise, the bitter collapse of the American dream into nightmare. In his study of American Gothicism, *Nightmare on Main Street*, Mark Edmundson argues convincingly that the Gothic fictions of writers such as King offer a necessary counterpoint to the national optimism with which the country generally identifies. The culture can handle only so much faith in the American Dream and the promise of universal equality when these ideals are undercut by the social realities of poverty, racism, class separation, and governmental abuse of powers; over the years, King's canon has served to remind us of precisely where America has failed to measure up to its reputation. As King himself maintains, "my work underlines again and again that I am not merely dealing with the surreal and the fantastic but, more importantly, using the surreal and the fantastic to examine the motivations of people and the society and institutions they create" (Magistrale, *Second Decade*, 15).

From 1977 to 1984, King decided to publish five novels under the pseudonym Richard Bachman. The reason for this choice was simple enough: curiosity to see if his fiction could fly without his brand-name help mixed with the disturbing appreciation that the name Stephen King was beginning to saturate the entertainment market. Although many of the Bachman books were written when King was just beginning his career as a writer, none of them are easily dismissed. Moreover, their themes frequently resonate with the plots of novels published under his name. The Bachman books are about people disenfranchised of power on several levels: personal, familial, and societal. The core protagonist is a male, highly frustrated, to the point of desperation, with a propensity toward violence and a certain unhealthy fascination with fame. In his book *Stephen King as Richard Bachman*, Michael Collings summarizes the naturalistic qualities that give shape to these texts: "No one can finally do anything. Characters become enmeshed by social pressure, politics, the external environment; they can no longer control themselves, their actions, or the actions of others" (17–18). The suicidal impulse that to a greater or lesser extent shapes the behavior of all these protagonists is driven by the emptiness of their personal lives and the quest to somehow transcend their anomie by becoming the center of local and/or national attention.

The Bachman novels also offer a bleak portrait of the American government and its deluded citizenry. Often employing grisly game shows featuring life-and-death contests for the participants, the state employs television, a medium meant to distract a poor and potentially volatile mass public, to redirect pressure away from the government's daily acts of ethical misconduct. Thinly disguised in a futuristic setting, the novels highlight the very real dangers that were threatening American civil liberties in the era of Jesse Helms and Ronald Reagan. The Bachman books thus represent a real distillation of the political disenchantment noted throughout King's undergraduate years, and they embody the spirit of the nineteenth-century naturalist writers, particularly Frank Norris and the late Hardy, that King read and admired as a student. The Bachman novels were more strident in their tone, more pessimistic and dystopic than most of the work King was publishing at the same time under his real name. It was as if the Richard Bachman pseudonym gave King license to vent his darkest misgivings about America and human nature in general: "When I put on my Bachman hat, I feel everyone starts at 'Go' and there's no guarantee of a happy ending. It's tremendously liberating; Bachman doesn't have a conscience, he's not afraid to say things that I may be afraid to" (Dyson 44). But it was King's name that brought Bachman sales and fame: *Thinner*, the title of the last novel published under the pseudonym, sold 28,000 copies when Bachman was the author and 280,000 copies when it was revealed that King was its author (King, "Why I Was Bachman," ix). The Richard Bachman pseudonym has continued to haunt King even after it was exposed in 1986; ten years later, in 1996, King published a "twinner" novel—two books about the same characters ostensibly authored by two different writing personae. The Stephen King novel was entitled *Desperation*; the more violent Richard Bachman novel was called *The Regulators*. In 2007 King once more resurrected Bachman as the author of the novel *Blaze*.

As his reign of terror developed momentum into a serious economic and cultural force throughout the 1980s and 1990s, King tended to focus more attention to writer-protagonists and their efforts to cope with sudden fame. King described this interest in 1989: "What I have written about writers and writing . . . has been out of an effort to try and understand the ramifications of being a so-called famous person, or celebrity. What does it mean when somebody who is a novelist is invited to appear on 'Hollywood Squares'? I am trying to understand these things" (Magistrale, *The Second Decade*, 11). *IT, Misery, The Dark Half, Bag of Bones*, and *Lisey's Story* are all novels that feature celebrity writers who share with their creator many of the drawbacks that attend popular acclaim. *Misery*, the story of a writer kidnapped by his "number one fan," who then forces him to produce a novel that fulfills this fan's obsession with her favorite literary character, is an extreme version of the issue that shadows all of his writer-protagonists, as well as King personally: how to balance the creative impulse with a rabid fan base that often in its obsession with its favorite author fails to respect basic perimeters of privacy. King has been stalked, threatened, sued, and had his house invaded by overzealous and sometimes psychologically unstable fans; he has been forced to place surveillance cameras under the eaves of his home in Bangor; his telephone is unlisted; he has paid guards who watch over his property; and he has hired one secretary whose job is to handle the enormous amount of mail he receives daily. As a celebrity figure, he appears to share more in common with movie and rock stars and professional athletes than with other, more anonymous, famous writers.

In the early 1980s I attended the International Conference for the Fantastic in the Arts when Stephen King was the guest of honor. King's attendance was kept secret from the Fort Lauderdale population in the hope that he could avoid being mobbed, and just enjoy the conference. Somehow word got out by the last day that Stephen King was a guest at the hotel and had agreed to do a two-hour book signing; hours before the signing took place, the line of people who queued up, hoping to have their books inscribed, stretched from the hotel's main ballroom, through the lobby, into the parking lot, and down the sidewalk for about half a mile. King recognizes that his popularity is the engine driving his literary success, but, at the same time, the years have taught him about the dark side of celebrity—and this insight has managed to scare the very person who has made a career out of terror: "America has developed this sort of cannibalistic cult of celebrity, where first you set the guy up, and then you eat him. It happened to John Lennon; it has happened to a lot of rock stars.

But I wish to avoid being eaten. I don't want to be anybody's lunch" (Dyson 31). I think it is impossible for most people to comprehend, much less identify with, the larger-than-life phenomenon that is Stephen King's life. While walking down Church Street in Burlington, Vermont, with me in March 1999, King wondered aloud, not at all disingenuously, why so many strangers felt the need to point him out and stand and stare. Even as late as 1999, his fantastic success still sometimes rendered him somewhat dazed and confused.

The dramatic results of overnight fame and money change people. We have all heard stories of those who have won lotteries and contests that suddenly transform average men and women into instant millionaires. Unprepared for such bounty, these lucky men and women, instead of investing their winnings with a sharp tax accountant, immediately quit their jobs, begin to purchase everything in sight, indulge needy friends and scheming relatives they never knew they had before, and often develop serious drug and alcohol addictions. For those who don't eventually sober up from their good fortune, the fortune either kills them or dries up before too long and they are left with only the lingering bills and staggering memories. How many Hollywood stars and professional athletes have become lost forever in a miasma of partying and decadence that reflects a life without discipline and limits? As fortune's shining star continued to shed its brightest light on Stephen King during the 1980s, the kid who went to college with only a single pair of blue jeans could now legitimately compare himself to John Lennon—both in terms of wealth and celebrity—and was worried enough about the cost of fame that he wrote novels about its dark side. Accordingly, by the mid-1980s, a problem with drugs and alcohol that had clearly originated in college became serious enough to require King to make a choice. He had always been fond of beer and pot, especially as aids to help him write and to garner the courage to help a generally shy man speak in front of huge public forums, but his financial status was now such that he could afford harder drugs as well, such as cocaine—the drug of choice during the 1980s for those who could afford its steep price tag. So many of King's characters, especially his males, share their creator's own struggle against alcohol and drug dependency, and I will have more to say about this issue in the chapter on *The Shining*. King's family forced him to the test: his drugs or his marriage, which was more important to him? He made the decision to go into rehab, and he now often acknowledges that Tabitha saved him from a path of certain self-destruction. After completing his detoxification program, King has been alcohol- and drug-free since 1988. Cigarettes are his last remaining addiction, and King isn't sure he will ever be able to give them up completely.

DEFINING AND EVALUATING THE CORPUS

Throughout the 1990s, King continued to put novels and collections of short stories into print at the rate of about a book a year, and Hollywood continued to keep pace with his output. King's work during the 1990s, however, differed from the more ambitious books published earlier in his career. The early novels are large, epic in their narrative scope, and they revolve around recognizable genre themes (sometimes conflating two or more in a single text): horror, dystopian technology, epic fantasy, and the journey quest. *The Shining, The Stand, The Talisman,* and *IT* are fictions that present a macrocosmic view of postmodern America, providing the reader with a journey to the center of a post-Watergate heart of darkness. King's epic propensities are never more strongly evinced than in *The Stand, The Talisman, The Dark Tower*, and *IT*, texts that weave a vast historical, mythological, and social matrix into a journey quest.

In contrast to this macrocosmic examination of America frequently considered from the off-ramps of its interstate highway system, the books that were published in the 1990s show evidence of King's ability to produce highly circumscribed, tightly wrought narratives bearing few of his earlier epic tendencies toward narrative and thematic expansiveness. If *The Shining* and *The Stand* can be likened to epic sagas played out on a big screen to accommodate their involvement with history and dramatic social dynamics, then books such as *Misery*, *Dolores Claiborne*, and *Gerald's Game* are more like classic Greek dramas presented on a circumscribed stage, employing a consistent scenic backdrop and a small cast of characters, and performed in front of an intimate audience. In addition to being generally shorter and more compact, the work published in the 1990s also tends to include a more realistic and sympathetic treatment of women. I will have more to say about King's gender renderings in chapter 6, dealing with his fictional females, but suffice it to say that, if the first half of King's literary canon can be read as an accurate and potent rendering of Everyman wandering amid the wastelands of postmodern America, the novels that followed throughout the 1990s tend to focus more on representations of the American Everywoman and her disgruntling domestic life.

In light of these differing emphases that can be said to distinguish roughly the two halves of King's prolific career, it is worthwhile to speculate about their effect on the writer's popularity, specifically as translated into book sales. The length of time each of his novels has spent on *The New*

York Times Bestseller List provides an interesting and accurate barometer for distinguishing those novels that constitute roughly the first half of his publishing output from work that was published after *Misery*, the novel that constituted essentially the first of King's "domestic fictions." The ten novels that were published during the decade from *The Shining* (1977) to *Misery* (1988) remained on the *Times* Bestseller List an average of 31.4 weeks. Each of his published narratives from *The Shining* to *Misery* maintained a minimum of 23 weeks on *The New York Times* list; most retained their place on the list longer—for example, *Firestarter*, 35 weeks; *IT*, 35 weeks; *Misery*, 30 weeks. In contrast, none of his books published in the decade after *Misery* remained on the list longer than 23 weeks, and most were on it for a much shorter period—for example, *The Dark Half*, 19 weeks; *Dolores Claiborne*, 14 weeks; *The Regulators*, 14 weeks. From the release of *The Tommyknockers* (1988) to *Wizard and Glass* (1997), the eleven novels published in this decade averaged 19.8 weeks on the *Times* Bestseller List. The 11.6-week difference per book on the Bestseller List that separates these two publishing decades in King's career reveals much about what King was writing during this time as well as how he was being marketed. These deflated sales statistics were partly responsible for King's contentious decision in 1997 to abandon an eighteen-year publishing relationship with Viking and to sign on with Scribner, the house that continues to publish his work as of this writing. King believed that Viking failed to market, promote, and package his books sufficiently to boost sales figures that, as we have seen, reached a plateau during the 1990s.

There are, however, probably several other ways to interpret this sharp fluctuation in sales, one being that *The New York Times* statistics underscore the market's saturation point for a writer who published at least a book a year for each of the past three decades. But it is also possible that this dramatic shift in volume sales, far more than being a consequence of inadequate packaging and promotion, reflects King's laudable efforts to challenge himself as a writer by composing narratives that are not neatly categorized into the horror-fantasy genre. The subtext of *Misery*, after all, has often been read as King's protest against fans disgruntled with their favorite author's evolution into other genres. The books of the 1990s are not similar in subject matter to the narratives that originally established King's reputation in the 1970s and 1980s as the master of the macabre. The *Times* statistics may reflect the disappointment of a large segment of the King readership that expected from him a consistency in genre and style of fiction. Ironically, while the books published in the decade of the nineties tended to be more "mainstream" in their subject matter—focusing on domestic situations, race, and gender issues—because of King's firmly-established reputation as a popular male horror novelist, his audience base did not enlarge as a result of promotion by Oprah Winfrey's book club or inclusion on college women's studies syllabi (as it legitimately should have been).

The nineties also witnessed several theatrical releases of excellent cinematic adaptations of King's work. *Misery* (1990), *The Shawshank Redemption* (1994), *Dolores Claiborne* (1995), *Apt Pupil* (1997), *The Green Mile* (1999), *Stephen King's The Shining* (1997) and *Storm of the Century* (1999) arguably represent the best of Hollywood's efforts at translating King into celluloid. Not only were these films incredible successes financially; they also brought King the kind of critical recognition that his own fiction seldom garners. *The Shawshank Redemption* was nominated for seven Academy Awards and won two Golden Globes; *The Green Mile* was also nominated for several Academy Awards, including best picture, while Kathy Bates won both an Academy Award and the Golden Globe in the Best Actress category for her work in *Misery*.

However, the process of becoming America's Storyteller—on paper and on celluloid—has sometimes weakened King's reputation in the eyes of the academic world. Yale professor Harold Bloom has been a steady voice of churlish meanness and narrow-mindedness in his relentless attacks on King's merits as a writer, denouncing him as an illustration of the dumbing down of American culture: "I cannot locate any aesthetic dignity in King's writing; his public could not sustain it, nor could he. . . . King will be remembered as a sociological phenomenon, an image of the death of the Literate Reader" ("Introduction" 3). Professor Bloom's dismissal of King's work and cultural influence, incidentally, has not stopped him from publishing and cashing royalty checks for several edited books with Chelsea House Publishers that analyze King's fiction. The sheer number of these books alone indicates the range of criticism that King has inspired from the academic community. Moreover, the fact that the Chelsea House volumes on King are included in the same series with other canonized writers such as Faulkner and Shakespeare is further illustration of the self-undermining of Bloom's categorical dismissal of King. (Indeed, at the risk of sounding as aggressive as Professor Bloom himself, Bloom's books are edited poorly—with egregious citation errors and multiple spelling mistakes—and obviously hastily assembled by his Yale graduate students. They are clearly efforts to capitalize financially on King's popularity, and are thus, ironically, more of an indication of the "death of the Literate Reader" than anything ever published by Stephen King himself.)

Bloom's disparaging comments, regrettably, have echoed throughout the musty halls of high school and college English departments, literary and film journals, and book reviews of his novels since the onset of King's rise to fame. Despite what the growing cottage industry of King film and literary scholarship has had to say about King's importance as both a sociologist and an artist, his enormous popularity and his clear emphasis on the primary importance of the story itself as superior to writing style have doomed him to utter dismissal or faint praise at the hands of the literary establishment. Moreover, King has never been one to curry favor with the literati; he has been vocal in voicing his dissatisfaction with book reviewers and critics who read his work badly or not at all; and though he is himself a careful and voracious reader, he has no patience for weighty fictions centered on densely plotted and overly complicated stylistic prose renditions, such as those found in the novels of Toni Morrison, or the "academic novel" with its salacious English department intrigues: "If you take a situation from John Updike or Saul Bellow . . . you would begin by casting a character as a teacher at a university. This professor would come home early one afternoon to find his wife having it off with the gasman. How would that make this character feel? To tell you the truth, I couldn't give a shit" (Magistrale, *The Second Decade*, 3). Whatever the merits of the criticism that has been leveled against him, the worst it has accomplished is to keep King's work from being taught in classrooms across America. This is regrettable for so many reasons, but mostly because it keeps an accessible and interesting fiction writer from students who might find in his stories a reason finally to enjoy reading. From there, critical inquiry might somehow become as much or more of a meaningful and relevant activity for these students (and some of their teachers) than forcing them to memorize yet another soliloquy from Shakespeare's *Julius Caesar*.

King may not be the greatest prose stylist to publish in the English language, but he is, indisputably, one of the greatest storytellers ever to employ the language. And when the audience consists of barely literate, visually oriented young people, whose attention spans have been conditioned by too many video games and hundreds of hours of television channel surfing rather than books, King's stories pose at least a viable alternative to the typical high school English department curricula currently in place across most of America. It was in light of these pedagogical concerns and King's enormous popularity among young people that several iconoclastic high school English teachers organized a 1996 weekend conference addressing many of the issues related to the reading and teaching of Stephen King's fiction in the secondary school classroom. The proceeding volumes from this conference, *Reading Stephen King: Issues of Censorship, Student Choice, and Popular Literature*, discussed topics ranging from deconstructing the high school literature curriculum, to King and the at-risk student, to King's novels, libraries, and the topic of censorship.

I suspect that few English teachers have actually heard of *Reading Stephen King*, but the fact that this volume was published by the National Council of Teachers of English, one of the major governing organizations for high school English teachers, is nonetheless an apt reflection of the impact that Stephen King continues to exert on contemporary American culture and the potential of his work to challenge traditional notions of literary canonicity.

The combination of being pigeon-holed in the academically disreputable horror genre, his popularity, his wealth and celebrity status, the fact that his novels are often overwritten and could benefit from the hand of a steely editor focused on taming and condensing his expansive prose, and the sheer enormity of his canon made King suspect as a *serious* writer for many literary critics and English teachers in the 1980s and 1990s: "Once you sell a certain number of books, the people who think about 'literature' stop thinking about you and assume that any writer who is popular across a wide spectrum has nothing to say" (Dyson 38). But during the 1990s, the permutations of King's two-decade-long celebrity, literary skill, and success in Hollywood also began to bring some of the accolades that serious writers covet. With the collapse of a uniform curriculum in university English departments across America, professors began teaching courses in popular culture and film and the rise of the popular novel, and they included texts formerly excluded from the curriculum, such as those authored by racial minorities, women, and genre writers. Starting in 1990 and ongoing since, King's essays and short fiction began appearing regularly in *The New Yorker*, arguably the best literary magazine in the world; in fact, one of the magazine's staff writers, Mark Singer, published a long profile of King, "What Are You Afraid Of?" in the September 7, 1998, issue. In 1996 King won the prestigious O. Henry Award for the demonic story "The Man in the Black Suit," which was also first printed in *The New Yorker*. But his most prestigious recognition to date occurred in 2003, when he received the National Book Awards' annual Medal for Distinguished Contribution to American Letters.

As expected, Harold Bloom and his fellow cultural elitists were outraged, but in the eyes of many others—fans and critics alike—such recognition was long overdue. As the poststructuralist revolution in literary theory began to find proponents in graduate schools (who would replace a wave of retiring high school and university English teachers in tenure-track positions throughout the 1990s) willing to deemphasize the separation between popular and serious fiction and to focus critical attention on the interdisciplinary nature of cultural studies as a legitimate academic discipline, King has become the subject of numerous books and essays, of PhD dissertations—both in the United States and abroad—and literary conferences where he is treated as a figure who has bridged the gap between low and high culture. Indeed, the specious divide separating popular literature from serious literature was a major aspect of King's acceptance speech for the National Book Award: "I've tried to improve myself with every book and find the truth inside the lie. I salute the National Book Foundation Board, who took a huge risk in giving this award to a man many people see as a rich hack. . . . Giving an award like this to a guy like me suggests that in the future things don't have to be the way they've always been. Bridges can be built between the so-called popular fiction and the so-called literary fiction" (King, National Book Award Speech). In discussing the remarkable achievement that this bridge represents, critic Brian Kent posits that King "has carved out a sizable audience of scholarly-academic readers, while maintaining and expanding his popular appeal. For while his heart may be with that huge popular audience, his mind often lands him in academic terrain, in terms of his own awareness of the standards and skills around which university English departments cohere" (40).

His appeal to academics was, by way of illustrative example, very much in evidence at the Popular Culture Conference in Atlanta in 2006. On the program were *five* separate sessions (featuring three to four presenters per session) devoted to analyzing King's films and fictions, as well as a roundtable on the last day of the conference where all the King panelists engaged in lively scholarly discourse about his work. As King concluded in his National Book Award speech, "Honoring me is a step in a different direction, a fruitful one, I think. I'm asking you, almost begging you, not to go back to the old way of doing things. I hope that the National Book Award judges, past, present and future, will read [popular] writers and that the books will open their eyes to a whole new realm of American literature. We can build bridges between the popular and the literary if we keep our minds and hearts open" (King, National Book Award Speech).

Stephen King has always been a literary gambler. He takes chances in his fiction—crossing and creating hybrid genres, exploring innovative narrative designs. In 1996 he undertook a publishing gamble, releasing the novel *The Green Mile* in six installments separated by about six weeks per installment. "I want to stay dangerous, and that means taking risks. That is part of the excitement of the whole thing, though—at this point I'm driving through thick fog with the pedal all the way to the metal. It's like a novelistic striptease" (Dyson 43). Unique as this venture was to contemporary American publishing, King actually modeled his experiment after the nineteenth-century tradition of the serial narrative. Victorian writers such as Dickens and Dostoevski were paid by the word and published their novels initially in periodicals, one installment at a time. As a result, their readers awaited the publication of subsequent installments with great anticipation. Dickens's popularity was such that his American readership actually waited on the docks of New York for boats from London bringing copies of the British publication bearing chapters of his novels. King rekindled the idea in 1996, certainly in no small measure because *The Green Mile* was such a compelling read, with each volume of about 100 pages selling in excess of a million copies. By August 1996, when the last installment of the book appeared in bookstores across America, King had six paperback bestsellers on *The New York Times* list at the same time.

Over the years, King has experimented with other unorthodox publishing ventures. He has structured recent contracts with Scribner's unique to the business, asking for less money up front in advances and more in royalty payments contingent upon how many copies are sold. He has been willing to sell the rights to his fiction to filmmakers for a dollar. He likes having his work adapted to film, but he also asks for 5 percent of the gross distribution and the ability to have a say on the choice of director, the cast, the quality of the screenplay, and other aspects of production. He has prereleased a select number of volumes in the *Dark Tower* series with publisher Donald M. Grant before issuing the respective novels for mass distribution with his New York publisher. The Grant books are handsomely illustrated and bound and probably are as much as testament to King the bibliophile as they are a business favor to Mr. Grant.

King has also tried online publishing, bypassing his publisher and selling his writing directly to his fans via the Web. In 2000 Steve asked readers to pay voluntarily for downloading installments of his novel *The Plant*, promising that he would continue writing the book if they would be honest enough to pay for it. The experiment eventually failed because, by Part 4 of the six-part novel, only 46 percent of the people who downloaded installments had actually paid for them. In 2009 "N.," one of the stories included in his 2008 collection *Just after Sunset*, was turned into an original Web video series in collaboration with Marvel Comics; in 2007 Marvel released *The Gunslinger Born*, a lavishly illustrated color comic book adaptation of selected scenes from *The Dark Tower*, and in 2009 its companion volume *The Long Road Home*. King is currently considering a YouTube video to accompany release of his novel *Under the Dome*. In conclusion, the publishing business has brought King tremendous wealth and fame, but his best-seller status has also allowed him to have his own inimitable fun playing with multimedia adaptations of his work and redesigning the model with which New York publishers typically conduct business.

On June 19, 1999, Stephen King met personal horror literally head on. While walking facing traffic on a rural highway near his summer home in

North Lovell, Maine, King was struck and seriously injured by a vehicle driven by Bryan Smith, a man with a history of multiple vehicular infractions, including several counts of driving while intoxicated. Distracted by his dog searching for hamburger in the backseat cooler, Smith's Dodge hit King and knocked him thirty feet into the air. King landed in brush and by some miracle of fate just missed striking his head on a large rock. He was rushed by helicopter to a trauma center hospital in Lewiston where he was treated for a compound fracture of his leg, a right knee reduced to "so many marbles in a sock," a shattered hip, pelvis, and four broken ribs, a punctured lung, chipped spine, and head injuries serious enough to require dozens of stitches and render him unconscious. On the way to the hospital, King's lung collapsed and he realized that he was "actually lying in death's doorway." Smith pleaded guilty to a driving-to-endanger charge and received a six-month suspended sentence. At the time of Smith's sentencing, King chided prosecutors for making a deal that did not include jail time and did not permanently revoke Smith's license. A little over a year later, in September 2000, Smith took his own life at his home in Maine.

King's physical recovery was long and arduous; his psychological rehabilitation was equally traumatic. In the month after his accident he underwent "five marathon surgical procedures that left me thin, weak, and nearly at the end of my endurance." He was placed on a medicinal cocktail that interfered with his sleep and eating habits. He wondered if he would ever walk again without the aid of crutches or a cane, if he would ever feel the urge to write again. On June 19, 2000, King published "On Impact," a gripping essay in *The New Yorker* that detailed the accident and his subsequent recovery. King describes himself, lying in the woods, legs mangled and semi-conscious, confronting his assailant, who explained that he wanted "some of those Marzes bars they have up to the store." In spite of his pain and obvious terror, it occurred to King "that I have nearly been killed by a character out of one of my own novels" (78). The accident left America's Storyteller dispirited and incapacitated, but five weeks later he found his way back to the computer and the start of his recovery in the resumption of his writing career.

King writes an average of four hours every day except his birthday, Christmas, and the Fourth of July. Writing for him has always been more than just a hobby or a vocation; if it were merely this, his financial status might have ended his literary career long ago. Instead, writing is an activity that keeps Stephen King whole, psychologically balanced; it is a means for exorcising his personal demons. So once again the connection to his art brought Stephen King a reason to push forward with his life. Like Paul

Sheldon, whose story in *Misery* eerily parallels King's own accident and recovery, the imaginative act of entering "the hole in the page" is a kind of narcotic that lifts the writer out of himself and to another place. As he concludes "On Impact": "For me, there have been times when the act of writing has been an act of faith, a spit in the eye of despair. Writing is not life, but I think that sometimes it can be a way back to life" (85). Stephen King has made a life for himself out of his writing. Although he has lately wondered publicly if he may have run out of things to say—if it might be time to stop, to retire, find something else to do with his time—it is clear that King and his art share a kind of marriage. His eyesight is growing steadily worse, and King fears that in the next few years he may lose it completely. But even should this occur, no one should imagine Stephen King's blindness compelling him to give up his daily writing any more than Beethoven's deafness deterred him from composing music. For an artist like Stephen King, the pleasure of finding the truth inside the lie is a lure that ultimately transcends all other preoccupations.

Chapter 2

Tracing the Influences: Regional and Literary

In a conversation with Stephen King that took place a few years ago, I made the mistake of asking him why he continues to live in Bangor, Maine. After all, I thought naively, Bangor is at best a sleepy town that rolls up its streets on most Friday nights soon after ten o'clock. Additionally, I reminded him that he could afford to reside anywhere in the world, so why Bangor? King took me in with a look that suggested he had just swallowed some particularly offensive species of bug—indeed, that perhaps I myself was a member of that insect species. His response was a sardonic, "Now, just where would you have me live—Monaco?"

Aside from providing me with a well-deserved lesson in humility, this little anecdote actually reveals a great deal about Stephen King—the man, the writer, and the most famous citizen of Bangor, Maine. As noted in the preceding chapter, Stephen King has spent almost his entire existence in Maine. He recently purchased a winter residence on the west coast of Florida, and he has traveled extensively both in this country and in England, but his life and, most importantly, his *psychic space* remains Maine-haunted. In an interview I conducted with King in 2003, he told me that when he and Tabitha graduated from the University of Maine, Orono, they faced a decision on where to move. The Kings both agreed on the importance of staying in Maine, but Tabitha wanted to go to Portland, a coastal town, while Steve was committed to Bangor, located dead center in the middle of the state. "I wanted to go to Bangor because I thought that Bangor was a hard-ass, working-class town . . . I thought that *the story*, the *big* story I wanted to write was here . . . and I didn't want to be in Portland because Portland is a kind of yuppie town" (Magistrale, *Hollywood Stephen*

King, 3). Portland is a city that over the years has benefited from a steady influx of tourism, its upscale downtown commercial district, its scenic locale on the edge of the ocean, and the University of Southern Maine; in a final analysis, Portland probably has more in common with quaint California seaside cities such as Santa Barbara or even Monterey than it does with the rest of Maine. Among other New England towns, Portland is more appropriately compared to Burlington, Vermont (both town populations hover around 70,000 when their universities are in session) than it is to Bangor. The latter is, indeed, "a hard-ass working class town," a smaller version of Buffalo, or perhaps Utica, New York. Its history is rust-belt industrial, and with the exodus of manufacturing and textiles to cheaper plants in the American South and overseas, Bangor, like Buffalo and Utica, has known its share of hard times.

Listening to King ruminate about Bangor is a little like eavesdropping on one of its elder citizens; he speaks of its geography, its history, its mythology with an easy intimacy—and most of all with a sense of respect for the city's gritty survival instincts. Bangor is where the Kings call home, so there naturally exists a sense of prejudicial loyalty to the place, but over the years the city has also shielded King from the curious throngs of fans and paparazzi who descend—typically during the summer months—looking for memorabilia associated with America's Storyteller. Like most New Englanders, Bangor natives tend to be close to the vest, reluctant to gossip with strangers and, more specifically, to supply even the most innocuous tourists with much information about King's West Broadway residence, his workplace on Florida Avenue, or his daily habits in the city. In a culture that maintains a love/hate relationship with its celebrities, as likely to devour them as they are to worship, the decision to remain in Maine may have been unconsciously self-protective. In the relative wilderness of Bangor, especially as, say, compared to Hollywood, King and his family were able to avoid the less attractive aspects of being famous in America, either through pesky tabloid fodder or through active stalking and death threats of the deranged. King certainly gets his fair share of disturbing personal interactions and posts, but I think he would be the first to acknowledge that the situation would be worse if he didn't live in Maine. Had the Kings chosen to relocate in a place such as Monaco, they might have felt compelled to take up residence in one of that municipality's many gated mansions or communities; in Bangor, by way of contrast, all the King children attended the city's public school system and Steve has always felt comfortable taking his dogs on walks into the center of town. The inhabitants of Bangor, at least those with whom I have spoken over the years, are justifiably proud of their favorite son, his civic generosity, his success and fame, and the fact that he still has not forsaken them or their town for Monaco.

King certainly has done his part in helping Bangor to stay afloat financially and culturally. Each fiscal year, the Kings, through the auspices of the Stephen and Tabitha King Foundation, donate at least 10 percent of their pretax income to various organizations, and the majority of these charitable causes are local. In 1992, for example, Stephen King, an avid baseball fan, built a $1.2 million Little League ballpark for the city that is used for the Bangor high school team as well as a minor league franchise affiliated with the city. Each year, he spends another large sum of money to maintain its pristine upkeep. The Kings provided over $2 million to renovate the Bangor Public Library as well as funds to maintain the famous opera house in the center of the city. To benefit the Bangor Symphony Orchestra, bids were solicited from charitable contributors for the opportunity to appear as a character in a future King novel or short story. A pediatrics unit at Eastern Maine Medical Center, equipment for the Bangor Fire Department, music teachers for rural Maine schools, gym facilities for the Bangor YMCA, undergraduate scholarships for financially challenged students to study at universities and colleges in Maine and several other states—the list of community-based projects funded by the King family is a long one. And for at least the last two decades, Stephen King has insisted that before he would sell the rights to one of his novels or short stories to a Hollywood producer, the contract had to stipulate that the film would be shot somewhere in Maine, unless the setting of the film absolutely dictated otherwise. He chose to do this for at least two reasons: his desire to maintain the Maine atmosphere that is such a palpable presence in so much of his fiction, and the hope that an infusion of Hollywood cash might help alleviate some of the poverty that characterizes those parts of Maine unaided by tourism and second-home real estate taxes.

KING'S MAINE: STATE OF PLACE, STATE OF MIND

To a very real extent, the various invented Maine locales—Castle Rock, Haven, Jerusalem's Lot, Little Tall Island, Chamberlain—found in King's fictional universe are all connecting points on the road to Derry, the epicenter of small-town evil on King's geo-literary map. The landscape of Derry, the city featured so prominently in *IT* (as well as in *Insomnia*), which ultimately came to constitute the "big story" King had in mind when he moved his family to Bangor at the start of his literary career, forms a simulacrum with Bangor: "Eventually, at least in the geography of my mind, Bangor became Derry. There is a one-to-one correlation between Bangor and Derry. It's a place I keep coming back to" (Magistrale, *Hollywood's Stephen King*, 4). If the reader were physically to juxtapose a city map of Bangor with the fictionalized landscape of Derry, several interesting correlations would present themselves almost immediately. Not only does the overview of Bangor resemble Derry in size and topography, but there are several actual structures that appear on both topographies: the Standpipe water tower, the Paul Bunyan statue, the Bangor Auditorium/Derry Civic Center, the Barrens—an open tract of land running diagonally through both Derry and Bangor—the public library, the interlocking system of canals, and the rivers (the sewers in Derry empty into the Penobscot, the name of the river that essentially bisects both Derry and Bangor). There is even a Derry Mall that is located just outside the city limits of the town, just as the Bangor Mall is a short drive away from the center city.

If we were to establish some generalizations about the landscape of Stephen King's fictional kingdom, we might safely begin by recognizing that he appears far more interested in small-town rural American life than with metropolitan American urban centers. No doubt reflecting his own choice of homes and lifestyle—a summer home in Center Lovell, Maine, the main house in Bangor, and a winter residence outside Sarasota, Florida—King's novels and stories are typically set in small towns that are seldom larger than Bangor. When he does write about larger cities—Lud/New York in *The Dark Tower*, Las Vegas in *The Stand*, for example—it is invariably with a jaundiced critical eye; his cities take their place alongside Dante's infernal city of Dis, as they are self-poisoned, tortured, and dystopic places that represent the worst elements of Western capitalism gone amuck: greed, violence, poverty, corruption, visceral power struggles among psychotic individuals. This is not to say that he is less critical about small-town America, however. If Bangor is the inspiration for Derry, then it appears that Durham, Maine, the place where King spent most of his adolescence, may be the model for Castle Rock. Castle Rock, Haven, and Derry are all places where evil thrives in King's narratives because most of the neighbors and civic-minded citizens lack the moral courage to stand up to tyrannical figures such as Leland Gaunt in *Needful Things* and Andre Lenoge in *Storm of the Century.*

King is as much a chronicler of small-town American life as Sherwood Anderson in *Winesburg, Ohio*, Ernest Hemingway in the Nick Adams stories, and Mark Twain in his tales of towns at the edge of the frontier. The compulsion toward a supernaturally motivated groupthink, a concept that begins as early in King's canon as the townspeople-turned-vampires in *'Salem's Lot* and continues to inform much of the

Castle Rock novels, typically results in the inability of King's rural inhabitants to initiate difficult moral choices; instead, they surrender in a zombie-like abandonment of individual will and volition to the dictatorial force of supernatural corruption centered in a charismatic demonic male stranger. This figure enters the town either to manipulate its citizens for his inimitable agenda and amusement, or to drain, vampire-like, its psychic resources in service to his infernal agency. The vampires that eventually take over 'Salem's Lot and the psychic siphoning that occurs in *The Tommyknockers*, for example, merely exaggerate the homogeneity already in place in the towns themselves; the progressive degeneration of individuals into a spiritless mass of barely conscious undead underscores the moral vacuity of the community itself—a spiritual malaise that existed long before whatever respective monster settled in.

King seems to understand intuitively that the small-town Maine environment is capable of destroying individuals because of its encrusted isolation, pressures to conform, and lack of compassion. The fictional towns that dot his fictional landscape share characteristics particular to small Maine communities. There is a secretive and protective shell that surrounds most native New Englanders, especially when compared to the surface hospitality of the Midwest or the South, and the reader would do well to remember that Maine is the most New England of all the states. Perhaps these observations can be attributed to the closed, insular societies that make up American small-town regional life anywhere; or it may just be the interminable winters that force neighbors to keep to themselves in the Northeast's fierce semi-arctic climate, a place where, as Selena St. George observes at the end of the film version of *Dolores Claiborne*, "it's cold even when it's warm." The winter climate affects more than just those six calendar months where it dominates regional conversation and consciousness and provides partial explanation for the frosty reception strangers and neighbors alike often receive at the hands of Maine natives.

King's view of Maine and New England is always complex and variegated; on the one hand, his regionalism recognizes the limits inherent in his fellow natives—their tendency toward a punitive groupthink behavior. But at the same time, he has also carved out many of his most memorable characters from the New England personality's fierce streak of independence and dignified humility. Were it not for the heroes and heroines who also emerge from King's small Maine universe, possessing humane values that remain constant in the face of the mass corruption surrounding them, one could argue that the misanthropy that typifies small town life in King's fiction reaches its nadir in his portraits of large cityscapes; they are both violent and fallen places that offer little moral hope. But heroism in King's universe nearly always commences in small-town humility. I'll have more to say about this construction in the next chapter, but it suffices for now to acknowledge that the survival of the individual is dependent upon carrying out moral choices on King's ethical continuum. Common men and women with few pretensions, King's Maine natives are capable of summoning an independent resolve sweetly tempered by a vested stake in the survival of some semblance of a social fabric. Characters such as Ben Mears and Mark Petrie (*'Salem's Lot*), Mike Anderson (*Storm of the Century*), Dolores Claiborne, Frannie Goldsmith (*The Stand*), the Losers Club (*IT*), Trisha McFarland (*The Girl Who Loved Tom Gordon*), and John Smith (*The Dead Zone*) are confronted with situations that both torment and threaten their psychological reserve, but due in no small part to their obstinate streak of Yankee independence, they stand up to the various evils—supernatural and otherwise—that invade their towns. At the same time, though these characters are all forced into situations where they must separate in varying degrees from the corrupt social world around them, they still seek solace from like-minded individuals—even if this requires that they move someplace else.

One of the greatest legacies of Stephen King's canon will be his portraits of end-of-the-century men and women struggling to endure in an America that is slowly rotting from the inside out, surrendering whatever elements of decency and virtue it once possessed and facing the decidedly contemporary moral vacuum created by an out-of-control technology. King has written well and often about the consequences of a cell-phone-computerized-television-saturated-overly-armed-and-surveillanced drug-addicted culture, and the anomie that haunts postmodern America. Although we are drunk on a dazzling array of new communication devices, King reminds us in so many of his books that we don't appear to be communicating with each other very well. Perhaps this is a main reason the writer still remains a citizen of Bangor, clinging to the nostalgic possibilities of small-town America. At least in Castle Rock, Little Tall Island, and Derry there exist those few individual exceptions to the pervasive alienation that characterizes the larger spiritual malaise symptomatic of postmodern America. As we will trace in greater detail in the next chapter, King has always placed his faith in the survival skills of the individual rather than the group; he adheres to a faith in the human potential to endure and retain moral values even as dysfunctional social institutions and the relentless urge toward conformity deathlessly challenge these virtues. And it is likewise certain that King believes these values most likely reside in the individual hearts and minds of simple-hearted Mainers—men, women, and children who resist and confront the general corruption of Castle Rock, Little Tall Island, and Derry to carve out their own self-determined identities. King essentially affirms a fundamental American archetype and myth: that the American has always possessed the potential to rise above the corruption of the past. But in King's world independent survival is most often rooted in the bedrock of small-town New England values—in his mind, perhaps one of the last outposts for realizing a modern version of Jean Rousseau's uncorrupted noble savage. In his early but still highly relevant essay, "Beyond the Kittery Bridge: Stephen King's Maine," Burton Hatlen, one of the novelist's influential college English professors at the University of Maine, perhaps defines most succinctly the bifurcated vision I have been describing in the last two pages: "Maine as the last refuge of the honest, independent frontiersman, and Maine as a place where people are so closed in upon themselves that all sense of community vanishes, thus permitting the horrors of the night to leak in . . . Maine is kind *and* cruel" (59).

I am not the first to recognize the landscape parallels that exist between the fictionalized worlds created by Stephen King and real-world Maine. Several local newspapers, including the *Boston Globe*, have featured photojournalist essays comparing these two topographies, and several years ago a Harvard graduate student wrote her PhD dissertation on this very subject. George Beahm published an entire book, *Stephen King Country*, as a photographic journey to the places that inspired the fictional settings for several of King's major novels. Each of these critics has tried, with varying degrees of success, to view King primarily as a regionalist writer, finding parallel juxtapositions between scenes from King's work and actual places in Maine. Beahm describes this fictionalized landscape as a surreal environment, "shifting from the real world to unreal world, where everything that's familiar becomes increasingly unfamiliar, as if the landscape is literally metamorphosing . . . there are parts of Maine where you could get lost and never be found" (*King Country* 98). In *Gerald's Game*, the seclusion of the Maine woods contributes to the terror Jessie Burlingame experiences while handcuffed alone in her cottage, and it is also the reason she nearly dies there: there is no one around to rescue her or hear her screams for help. Beahm's point about the uncanny manifesting itself in the Maine landscape is evident in the appearance of Raymond Jobert, the hovering "space cowboy" who is one part Peeping Tom and one part homosexual sociopath (which might explain why he leaves her tied to the bed), whose nocturnal visits to Jessie leave her and the reader wondering for half the novel about his very corporeality.

Even the supernatural creatures that have become signature features of King's horrorscape within the popular imagination are often Maine inspired. The Wendigo in *Pet Sematary* is a monster that owes its origins to regional Native American lore and the heavily wooded landscape of the Northeast. In this novel, King melds the Indian myth of a trickster figure with the harsh winter climate that is hostile to human habitation and survival. The ancient Wendigo emerged as an element of Native American folklore to serve as a metaphor and a warning for Indians; its restive cannibal spirit wandered the forest and haunted the nightmares of men highly susceptible to cabin fever and the consequences of a shortened winter food supply. King's novel updates this fear by having the Wendigo prey on modern human tragedy and grief rather than the ancient dread of starvation and the urge toward cannibalism, but the novel's power still resides in a restless supernaturalism that exists beyond the human capacity—among both the primitive and the civilized—to understand or contain. As such, the novel bridges the temporal and cultural gaps that distinguish Maine past from Maine present in creating a monster whose hunger transcends historical distinctions.

The narrative also ends up speaking to those universal elements that define the human condition and bring all men together in pity and outrage: the survival urge in the face of nature's indifferent cruelty, and the design of fate that seems in active opposition to this urge. Most of *Pet Sematary* appropriately capitalizes on that period unique to the Northeast: late autumn slipping daily into deep winter, where falling temperatures and the desolate landscape make it feel as if all of nature bears a genuine antipathy to anything human: "The wind was sharper, colder, quickly numbing his face. Never in his life had the stars made him feel so completely small, infinitesimal, without meaning. He asked himself the old question—*is there anything intelligent out there?*—and instead of wonder, the thought brought a horrid cold feeling" (114). The novel's plot hinges on the cruelty of Maine's climate and the dark secrets residing in its landscape, as both occupy signature roles in thwarting the best intentions of Jud Crandell and Louis Creed. Mary Lambert's direction of the film adaptation unfortunately descends into a parody of evil Chucky the child monster, but before it does so, it manages to capture in several notable scenes the bleakness of an encroaching Maine winter.

Those of King's narratives not set in Maine still frequently maintain some semblance of the place. The fierce snowfall that surrounds the Torrance family at the Overlook Hotel in *The Shining*, or the deathless winter that Paul Sheldon must confront along with his long rehabilitation and effort to dodge his tumultuous relationship with the psychotic Annie

Wilkes in *Misery*, may take place somewhere in the Rocky Mountains of Colorado, but it is clear that the length and the severity of the season that King describes in these narratives owe something to his native Maine experience. In fact, Annie is acutely susceptible to seasonal mood disorders; her violent and self-destructive tendencies are sometimes cued by the same climate conditions that have saddled Maine with the highest per capita suicide rate in the United States. And, too, the vast sense of space that demarcates both these novels—a land with human habitation limited to small-town clusters and the occasional visiting writer—also reminds us of Maine.

It is no accident that single mom Wendy, her son, and the Overlook's former head chef retreat to the refuge of a lakeside camp in Maine after the devastation that takes place in *The Shining*; the same movement back to Maine concludes *The Stand* as well. This palpable sense of space is what enabled Rob Reiner in the film version of *Stand by Me* to feel comfortable setting Castle Rock in the Pacific Northwest instead of King's state: a similar bifurcated view of nature as pastoral (hills instead of mountains) and confrontational (bogs filled with slimy leeches) informs both places. Although the disturbing short narrative "The Raft" takes place on a lake forty miles outside Pittsburgh, the isolation of the lake itself, its frigid waters, the plot's focus on the season's inexorable movement from summer into winter, and the aqua-monster that devours the four college students who decide to take a late season swim in its waters are again reminiscent of a physical environment that could just as likely be found in Maine with its many secluded lakes. King has spoken at length about the importance of his native state as an influence on his writing: "If I decide I don't want to be in Maine for a story, my mind always seems to take me back there. If I am in Iowa or Nebraska, it is a place that is flat and empty. A place where I can still recognize a similarity to Maine. So place comes through, and place casts its own weight over whatever you are writing" (Magistrale, *The Second Decade*, 10). It is in light of the "weight of place" that *Duma Key* and "The Gingerbread Girl" emerge as exceptional oddities in King's canon. Set in the tropical locale of Florida and emphasizing sand and sea over snow, these two texts reflect the new address of King's winter home in Sarasota, and thus appear almost absurdly out of place, like a palm tree planted in Bangor, in the larger context of King's Maine-dominated work.

King's books and stories have been so strongly shaped by Maine's physical and civic environments that it is impossible to imagine separating landscape from personality, climate from theme. Hatlen discerns in King's Maine writings a "powerful ambivalence . . . and out of this ambivalence has emerged a distinctive vision of human beings and their relationships to one another and to nature" (50). Hatlen defines this "ambivalence" as central to comprehending the Maine experience: that it is a place that embodies the pastoral ideal in its refuges of seclusion at the same time that this ideal is called into question by the "darkness" that is therein revealed. He stresses both the physical and spiritual "darkness" that lurks beyond the small towns, deep into the woods and into the souls of the human natives who spend too much time alone fighting the cold. "Indeed," Hatlen concludes, "how many writers before King have so clearly delineated the hard, self-destructive streak that we find in so many Maine people? Edwin Arlington Robinson maybe—but I can't think of anyone else" (57). Rather than invoking a chamber-of-commerce, pastoral relationship with the Maine landscape, King typically draws upon a nature that is hostile and savage, an environment where malefic energies—both real and supernatural—reside in secret in those deep dark woods.

INTO THE MAINE WOODS: *THE GIRL WHO LOVED TOM GORDON*

Hatlen's fine essay is necessarily limited in its argument only to the fiction King published up to and including *Cujo* (1981); his thesis on King's ambivalence toward Maine becomes all the more perceptive when it is applied to the Maine-haunted novels that would follow: *Pet Sematary, The Body, IT, Dolores Claiborne, Gerald's Game, Bag of Bones,* and especially *The Girl Who Loved Tom Gordon*. Of all King's narratives, *The Girl Who Loved Tom Gordon* arguably captures best the writer's misgivings toward the Maine environment. We are provided a relentless portrait of the forest that makes the landscapes of "Hansel and Gretel" or "Little Red Riding Hood," the acknowledged inspirations behind King's narrative, appear, well, like those of a fairy tale. The novel's nine-year-old intrepid main character, Trisha McFarland, is beset by every manner of wild thing that calls the woods home—from bugs to a huge black bear—when she wanders away from her mother and brother to go to the bathroom and gets lost: "Moving her hands slowly and carefully, Trisha examined herself. She isolated at least a dozen stings. Her back felt all scraped up and her left arm, which had absorbed most of the damage during the final part of her slide, was a net of blood from wrist to elbow. Not *fair*, she thought . . . the woods were filled with everything you didn't like, everything you were afraid of and instinctively loathed, everything that tried to overwhelm you with nasty, no-brain panic" (56).

In some ways, Trisha is a younger version of Jessie Burlingame in *Gerald's Game*. Both females find themselves alone in the woods and must construct a barrier to encroaching madness while at the same time designing a plan for self-rescue. Jessie's quasi-hallucinatory figure of Raymond Jobert is revisited in the shape-shifting black bear that stalks Trisha in the second half of the book. In her semi-hallucinogenic state brought on by fatigue, fever, and starvation, the bear metamorphoses into a supernatural embodiment of the woods itself, a shifting composite of nature's faceless and aggressively malevolent spirit. King begins *The Girl Who Loved Tom Gordon* with a sentence that parallels closely William Blake's famous portrait of the tiger as a fearful product of a misanthropic god: "The world had teeth and it could bite you with them anytime it wanted" (9). However, while the lamb, its sweetness meant to counterpoint the random wrath of the tiger—"Did he who made the Lamb make thee?"—tempers Blake's description of a hostile universe, King's forested environment provides no such relief for Trisha. In fact, for most of the novel, the reader discovers that the natural world, with its unrelenting dark corners and sharp teeth, essentially provides a mirror to Trisha's domestic situation: recently divorced parents—an alcoholic father, embittered mother—and a self-absorbed brother who is dedicated to punishing them all. She is therefore equally lost in both places, appropriately referring to herself as "The Invisible Girl" (22).

King's portrait of the northern section of the Appalachian Trail where Trisha gets lost is far removed from any pastoral idyll. And similar to most of King's other Maine main characters, Trisha is cast in a situation that nearly destroys her. But the child, even at nine, also possesses many of the self-reliant virtues that King extols in his native Mainers. Though Trisha has her moments of self-pity when she weeps herself to sleep, she also refuses to give up; she and the reader discover that her mind is even more resilient than her bruised and emaciated body. She measures her rations, meager as they are, carefully; she finds edible berries and fiddleheads in the woods; she seeks shelter from thunderstorms; she keeps hope alive. Most important, her faith is sustained and she is distracted from her plight by the same source that has performed a similar task for Stephen King and millions of other New Englanders over the past century: Trisha loves the Boston Red Sox.

In particular, Trisha establishes a highly personal bond with her favorite player, a real-life Red Sox reliever named Tom Gordon, whose work she continues to follow throughout her ordeal in the woods on her Walkman radio. In 1998, Gordon pitched the Red Sox and recorded forty-four saves—forty-three of them consecutively, an American League record. Unfortunately, Gordon never again pitched so well; he soon after left the Red Sox organization, pitched for the rival Yankees, and eventually exited major league baseball inauspiciously. But in 1998, this pitcher was the workhorse in the Red Sox bullpen—the go-to guy. His legacy provides Trisha with an example of self-determination that sustains her own self-resolve to continue to find a way out the woods. Gordon sets an example for her in his job as a closer: coming in late in the game, often when the contest is still very much in jeopardy, to try and seal the victory. While the child feels abandoned by her family—in comparison to her obsessive thoughts centering on Gordon, her parents and brother seldom linger long in her consciousness—and in the throes of nature's hostile grip, Gordon serves to close many of her anxieties, a reminder of a safe place beyond the woods. He is also a surrogate father figure who replaces the image of Trisha's biological father self-pityingly immersed in the throes of divorce and alcoholism, while likewise anticipating the fairy tale arrival of the male hunter who, late in the novel, completes Trisha's rescue.

Before the Red Sox broke the infamous "Curse of the Bambino" with a World Series victory in 2004, five years after the publication of *Gordon*, they were baseball's lovable losers, a talented team that played with great heart, but typically destined to be thwarted in the late innings of big games. As King remarks in the Postscript to the novel: "God may be a sports fan, but He doesn't seem to be a Red Sox fan" (223). This is the Red Sox history that has nonetheless managed to endear itself to Trisha and her creator; a gritty team whose reputation garnered respect because of its refusal to quit despite the onerous curse associated with the franchise. One could certainly argue that prior to their championship in 2004, the Red Sox shared much in common with Bangor, Maine: hard working players without pretensions and stuck with loser reputations. The Tom Gordon figure that emerges in King's and his heroine's imaginations embodies the same humility, courage, and work ethic that are always characteristics associated with the writer's New England heroes and heroines. As a real-life player, Gordon gave his best in each of his many outings, and he always acknowledged a power that was greater than himself. Moreover, Gordon serves in a special role for this terrified little girl: unlike her biological father, Tom Gordon never lets Trisha down—and even "speaks" to her through her imagination throughout the ordeal, always providing sound advice and soothing encouragement. At the end of the novel, after Trisha is finally rescued, fatherhood and Tom Gordon are inextricably linked in Trisha's exhausted mind, as the girl drifts off to sleep safe in a hospital bed, but only after first supplying her father with Gordon's signature victory salute—his right index finger pointed toward heaven—"closing her eyes on his understanding" (219).

Gordon is ultimately reminiscent of the Jim figure in Mark Twain's *Huckleberry Finn*, an older black male who serves as the protector and moral educator for a vulnerable young white child. The bond that Trisha establishes with Tom Gordon is not the first time King has employed this type of black-white relationship: readers will find it repeated in *The Shining* and *The Talisman*, and in slightly altered forms in *The Stand* and *The Green Mile* as well. It is fascinating that a novelist so adept at providing a vast array of fictional personalities is clearly compelled to revisit this singular type of racial relationship in so much of his writing; in fact, so wedded is this concept with King's work, that three of the above King novels are cited in the *Wikipedia* encyclopedia entry for "Magical Negro." Several critics have taken King to task for this construction, arguing that he has perpetuated a racist myth of the "Magical Negro," a black man whose sole purpose is to rescue and guide a lost white character. In assessing John Coffey's character in *The Green Mile*, for example, Heather J. Hicks declares that it is "an amalgam of racist stereotypes" (37). The complaint that critics such as Hicks, Sarah Nilsen, and Brian Kent ("Christian Martyr or Grateful Slave?") have with King's "Magical Negroes" centers less on the writer's intention to create African American characters that are nurturing and stable—and thus interestingly linked to his Maine heroes and heroines—and more on their one-dimensionality.

In creating blacks who are long-suffering and whose reasons for existence are primarily defined via their service to white characters, these critics argue that King undercuts whatever liberal spirit may have inspired their creation and, ironically, produces racist stereotypes that lack both independence and individuality, characteristics that are always associated with his Maine heroes and heroines. I will leave it to others, however, to pronounce judgment on King's racial sensibilities; I wish to point out only that whatever deficiencies are inherent in the writer's construction of the "Magical Negro" figure, they are at least in part fueled by his regionalism. As a Mainer, King's exposure to blacks has been necessarily limited; throughout the past century, Maine has remained the whitest state in the union, and has thereby necessarily restricted King's exposure to black people throughout most of his life. So once more we witness evidence of the influence of Maine on King's writing, and always as a decidedly ambivalent presence.

INSIDE KING'S LIBRARY: LITERARY INSPIRATIONS

Burt Hatlen's essay provides fine starting points for considering King's plethora of literary influences and his position as a writer working from a tradition that includes artists as diverse as Nathaniel Hawthorne, Stephen Crane, Frank Norris, Theodore Dreiser, Edwin Arlington Robinson, Bram

Stoker, and William Faulkner. Although limited by space concerns in pursuing these individual correspondences, Hatlen was probably the first at least to cite each of these literary figures in connection with King, as so much of King's fiction can be read as either a direct literary homage to his encounters reading these earlier writers or as a demonstration of the influence of the literary genres they represent, including the Western, the Gothic, and naturalism. One need only pursue the index of King's nonfiction treatise on the horror genre, *Danse Macabre*, to recognize that King is a voracious reader (and movie watcher) and that, furthermore, Hatlen's list is indeed only a starting point. At various places in King's canon, I have observed allusions to each of the following authors, to greater and lesser degrees, and they remain the core literary figures to which King keeps returning: the Bible, J. R. R. Tolkien's *The Lord of the Rings*, the medieval tales of King Arthur, Shirley Jackson's "The Lottery" and *The Haunting of Hill House*, Robert Browning's *Child Roland to the Dark Tower Came* (which I will discuss in chapter 7), Edgar Allan Poe's short stories and "The Raven" (see Magistrale and Poger, *Poe's Children*, 93–111), H. P. Lovecraft's tales, Twain's *Huckleberry Finn*, Robert Louis Stevenson's *The Strange Case of Dr. Jekyll and Mr. Hyde*, the novels of Charles Dickens and Thomas Hardy, and the poetry of William Carlos Williams and T. S. Eliot.

These are the "highbrow" literary sources that if persuasively presented would undoubtedly stun a vast majority of English teachers who stubbornly maintain that King is only a "lowbrow" fiction writer. The point worth noting here is the fact that King has always been a serious writer who has sharpened his craft from his careful appreciation of the masters in fantasy, horror, and mainstream fiction that preceded him. For example, the importance of Tolkien as an inspiration for *The Stand, The Talisman,* and *The Dark Tower* seems to me unequivocal. All the themes that accompany the construction of the heroic quest are present in these King narratives: the journey itself, the interaction with strangers along the way, the surprise dangers, the moments when despair threatens to derail the quest, and the learning (moral) curve associated with successful completion of the quest. Both Tolkien and King borrow from the epic tradition in their journeys to Mordor and the Dark Tower respectively, and the ease with which Tolkien blends elements of reality with those of fantasy appears to have had a pronounced influence on King. King's excursions into the fantasy genre often center on alternate worlds that are entered through cosmic doors and portals. Once placed in this alternate world, King's characters likewise confront magical creatures and supernatural occurrences. Perhaps the major distinction between Tolkien and King is that the fantasy universe of Middle Earth is just as likely to enchant as it is to terrify—the bounty of the Shire provokes just as powerful a poetical effect on the reader as Mordor's vast doom. King's fantastical geography, on the other hand, is harsher, more likely to resemble Mordor than the Shire; his alternate universes are dystopian in design and effect. It is also worth pointing out that King's epic travelers, who are often small boys out on their own or journeying within a group of friends far from home, come to resemble closely Tolkien's Hobbits: painfully human in their limitations and longings, but also capable of summoning great courage in the face of overwhelming obstacles and circumstances.

As in the *The Lord of the Rings*, constructions of good and evil in King's epic fantasies are clearly demarcated. Michael Stanton points out that in Tolkien (and King), "Good is relatively weak and divided because it is free; Evil by contrast seems strong because its forces are united—though they may be in chains. But a turning point comes, very late. The tendency of Evil, because it is strong and composed partly of pride, is to over-reach and injure its own cause" (16). It is possible to recognize the importance of this maxim in the acts of Sauron and Saruman when the War of the Rings breaks out in Tolkien, as well as in the choices that Flagg and the Crimson King make, reflecting their will to dominate in *The Stand* and *The Dark Tower*, respectively.

The Stand borrows heavily from Tolkien's epic, but so does King's seven-book series *The Dark Tower*. Most obviously, there are several encounters between the heroes questing for the Dark Tower and various ambassadors of evil that are in service to the Crimson King and his minions. And each of King's volumes builds and then culminates, as does Tolkien's saga, in epic battles that literally shake the foundations of his invented universe. King's band of heroes is as much inspired by Tolkien's overwhelmed Hobbits and men as they are by the noble knights of Arthur's Round Table, and both tomes are peppered with moments of deception, betrayal, and acts of selfless heroism. The narratives of Mid-World, as rendered in *The Dark Tower*, owe much to Tolkien's Middle Earth, in terms that suggest the Fellowship of the Ring linking the Hobbit boy-men to Roland and his own adolescent *ka-tet*, Cuthbert and Alain, and, in later books, Jake, Susannah, Eddie, Oy, and Callahan, as well as in the rendering of a fantasy realm that is more reminiscent of the Middle Ages. Human beings invested with the duty to serve others in need are called into battle against larger-than-life forces that are a curious amalgamation of dilapidated technologies and medieval supernaturalism. For example, *Wizard and Glass* melds the same dystopic vision of a technological wasteland on the verge of reanimation (the Citgo oil patch that will be used to power the leftover war technologies of a distant, self-destructive past civilization) we find in *The Stand*, with Tolkien's sense of the rich mystery, myth-making, and allegorical potency of fantasy. Although Tolkien's epic is not directly referenced by Roland's tale-within-a-tale, it is clear that King borrows from *The Hobbit* and *The Lord of the Rings* in its telling: the Big Coffin Hunters in *Wizard and Glass* (as well as the robotic wolves who ride horses in *The Wolves of Calla*) are merely King's versions of the orcs and subhuman miscreants that labor soullessly in the service of Sauron; Sauron himself, identified as a sleepless eye that watches and seeks, is one of the models for the despotic John Farson/Crimson King, who is similarly a disembodied evil presence in the narrative and likewise adopts Sauron's restless eye as his flag; the allegorical nature of a small group of good innocent boys embattled against a larger army of evil further suggests the connection to Tolkien. In both sagas, each writer seeks to create a mythology and language unique to the invented worlds. Although King's sense of song, historical mythology, and inventive diction is not as complex or as richly multilayered as Tolkien's, Roland Deschain understands that teaching his *ka-tet* about the history and rituals of Mid-World is nearly as important as investing them with the fighting skills of a gunslinger.

However, King's most blatant borrowing is his use of the glass orbs that radiate tremendous energies at the same time as they provide their owners with visionary prophecy. Like Tolkien's one ring that controls the others, the major battle that takes place in *Wizard and Glass* is for ownership of the pink glass ball, the "one representing the nexus-point of the Beams" emanating from the Dark Tower (437). Just as Frodo is seduced and drained of his will by the ring he bears to Mordor, Roland and Rhea are corrupted by the supernatural power of the pink orb: "Because they're alive and hungry. . . . One begins using em; one ends up being used *by* em" (438). King adds references to other transcendent balls throughout *The Dark Tower*, most notably in *The Wolves of Calla*, where Black Thirteen emanates its own compulsive energies drawing both good and evil to its command. And while it may not be capable of rendering its owner invisible, as is the case with Tolkien's ring, Black Thirteen can open doors that connect Mid-World to our own. Importantly, the powers of Tolkien's ring and King's glass balls become corrupting obsessions for the human and nonhuman in both narratives; this serves to underscore one of the central moral maxims in both epics: evil calls to evil and forces it to serve a narrow design that is a constant threat to the stability of the Mid-World–Middle Earth.

If Tolkien serves as the great model for the epic fantasy quest that influenced King so profoundly in *The Stand* and *The Dark Tower*, Shirley Jackson's fiction epitomized the haunted-house tradition to which King added his own inimitable contributions in *'Salem's Lot, The Shining*, and

Rose Red. Her classic short story "The Lottery" was an obvious shaping influence for the decision the town of Little Tall Island must make at the conclusion of *Storm of the Century*, while *The Shining* and *Rose Red* were written, at least in part, as homages to Jackson's classic haunted-house novel, *The Haunting of Hill House*. On several occasions in *Danse Macabre*, Stephen King discusses the merits of *Hill House*, referring to its disturbed protagonist, Eleanor Vance, as "surely the finest character to come out of th[e] new American gothic tradition" (268). Because Hill House may serve as a highly personalized metaphor for Eleanor's guilt over improperly caring for her mother, the reader is never sure if this guilt is projected onto the house, or vice versa. Thus, when spectral activity does occur, it is the most subtle and benign of occurrences, particular to and a mirroring of the feminine psyche of Eleanor herself. Not only is its supernaturalism centered on Eleanor exclusively, but it is also of a variety that unnerves rather than terrifies, unsettles rather than sets the women running. King modeled his own haunted houses after Hill House as a place with psychic properties that draw human psychics to it, but he also upped the ante by supplying both Rose Red and The Overlook with the ghostly energies of a hyperkinetic fun house.

Hill House is a novel that invites and nurtures the contemplative; *Rose Red* was written as a teleplay to service an essentially visual experience. *Hill House* slowly builds tension that is never relieved, not even in the anticlimactic car crash that may result in Eleanor's death. *Rose Red*, on the other hand, is a made-for-TV roller coaster ride. There are more characters, so there are more scares and more shocking deaths. When the ghosts manifest themselves at Rose Red, they are neither in doubt, as they are at Hill House, nor subtle in their haunting. While *Hill House* is fraught with tension and ambiguity (e.g., how much of the haunting is real? how much in Eleanor's head? why is it occurring?), *Rose Red* possesses very little tension; it is not slow in building up to anything; its ghosts are well-known entities; they set out to do violent and aggressive damage from the moment the house becomes a featured presence. These two texts are ultimately examples of 1990s horror excess versus 1950s psychological tension. *Rose Red* might have been a more successful production had it been more like Jackson's novel: subtler in the slow building of tension and pace.

This is often the case in King's art: he begins with an established literary trope—the haunted house inherited from Shirley Jackson and the line that connects her to James and Poe, replete with psychic investigators—and then fashions his own distinct adaptation, often modifying and hyperbolizing the trope to the point where it no longer much resembles the original inspiration. King thus invests the quiet supernaturalism at work in Jackson's novel with a psychic power that always borders—and frequently crosses over into—chaos. Indeed, the Overlook explodes in the novel and televised versions of *The Shining* precisely because the place loses control over its own spectral energies. Similarly, Rose Red springs to life in the most ostentatious manner possible—activating fountains and statuary, elaborate blooming flowers, dramatic deaths through second-story stained glass windows, the metastasizing of the building itself. The level of its fun-house eccentrics is never in doubt even if the focus and rationale behind its hauntings are.

There's a psychic energy contained in Rose Red and The Overlook that far surpasses whatever animates Hill House, even as Jackson's house was the prototype. The latter's manifestations are always linked to Eleanor and her relationship to her family. But there are many moments when the reader is not sure if this focus is real or in Eleanor's head. The voice of the child that she hears in chapter 5, for example, is not heard by Theodora. The novel gradually funnels toward Eleanor exclusively—the other three characters appear less and less central to the text, becoming more like bystanders to Eleanor's inner struggle. This is why it becomes harder to distinguish how much of Eleanor's haunting is self-induced. Hill House is in the tradition of haunted houses that are psychically aligned with specific female protagonists—for example, *Northanger Abbey, The Turn of the Screw, The Yellow Wallpaper.* Eleanor may be "disappearing into this house" (200), but the house may just as likely be disappearing into Eleanor. The novel is more about Eleanor's mental breakdown than it is about a supernatural haunting; this is a book about a haunted psyche. In *Rose Red*, there is no single psyche at the center of the haunting. All the psychics inside simply serve as a collective jumpstart to reawakening the house's spectral power; the house then takes over completely, *independent from them.* Psychology professor Joyce Reardon claims that "Annie is the key to Rose Red," but the house appears capable of being animated by any human presence—as Bollinger's disappearance before the psychics' arrival would indicate. In the end, Rose Red is more like the Overlook Hotel and the Amityville House than Hill House insofar as it is self-generated and self-contained: the house dictates to the humans, not the other way around. Unlike Hill House, Rose Red is a highly active presence, it haunts indiscriminately regardless of whoever enters it. Rose Red features a random victimization of humans: from the workmen who are murdered to lady visitors from the historical society. The house possesses a consciousness unto itself that sometimes appears unrelated to its human prey. In fact, Rose Red may be animated just as much by a pre-existing evil that existed a priori to the house's construction (innocent workmen are mysteriously killed), as it is by the history of its principal owners, the Rimbauers, and the sins of father Rimbauer.

I am certainly not the first King scholar to recognize this writer's debt to Shirley Jackson and other literary sources. One of the earliest essays discussing King's literary roots, Ben P. Indick's "King and the Literary Tradition of Horror and the Supernatural," traces King's inheritance back to H. P. Lovecraft and influential British gothic writers from the nineteenth century. Other scholars (Strengell 55–57 and Winter 50–51), as well as my own work (*The Second Decade* 37–46), have discussed in varying detail the connections King shares with Hawthorne. Indeed, in keeping with the earlier sections of this chapter, King's descriptions of his native Maine and his close scrutiny of character, tradition, and the clash between civilized values and the wilderness find their closest points of comparison in the writing of his fellow New Englander. Mary Jane Dickerson has written convincingly about the parallels that connect King's novels, *IT* in particular, to those of William Faulkner—a writer King first read as a college undergraduate but whose novels continue to resonate in King's. These correspondences exist on the narrative level—their creation of texts that feature a literal splicing of past into present—as well as in the mutual construction of a mythology of place: the interconnected historical eras, families, and regional geography of King's Maine finds its antecedent in Faulkner's Yoknapatawpha cycle chronicling his version of the "myth of the South." Like Faulkner's work, the fictional cycle unifying King's Castle Rock microcosm often features families, characters, and events from one book that are referenced again in later books; certain plots are likewise dependent on events that have transpired in earlier narratives. For example, the haunting presence of Frank Dodd, the Castle Rock serial rapist-murderer in *Cujo* who merely haunts the perimeters of this novel, reappears in a much more substantial role in *The Dead Zone*. Dick Hallorann, the Overlook's head chef in *The Shining*, makes a brief appearance as a young man in *IT*; and Father Callahan, the disgraced priest from *'Salem's Lot*, returns to King's universe in *The Dark Tower*. Jeanne Campbell Reesman's "Stephen King and the Tradition of American Naturalism in *The Shining*" and Brian Kent's "Canaries in a Gilded Cage: Mental and Marital Decline in *McTeague* and *The Shining*" discuss another individual King text, *The Shining*, in light of the tradition of American naturalism, suggesting that Jack Torrance's fate closely resembles those of characters trapped in the mechanistic universes of Frank Norris, Thomas Hardy, and Jack London. Indeed, King has often acknowledged his debt to the naturalist school: "The books that influenced me the most when I was growing up were by people like Thomas Hardy, Frank Norris, and Theodore Dreiser. All those people of the naturalistic school believed once you pull out one rock, it's sort of a relentless slide into the pit" (Underwood and Miller 79).

The Hardy connection to King is an especially intriguing one, as Hardy's sense of humans operating in a fated world that is often outside their ability to control finds echoes in most of the Bachman novels, *Cujo, The Shining*, and *The Stand*, among other King texts. The night when Roland and Susan Delgado meet for the first time in *Wizard and Glass* is also reminiscent of the country atmosphere that suffuses Hardy's Wessex novels. The two young people, on uniquely different missions, coincidentally run into one another on a dark road on the outskirts of town. Although their lives are moving in entirely different directions—Susan, her virginity confirmed by the loathsome witch Rhea, is on her way back to a future as Mayor Thorin's mistress and his mother surrogate; Roland, serving the Affiliation, who is sent by his father to avoid possible conflict in his home town of Gilead, is about to encounter more conflict than his father could ever have imagined—the two fall immediately in love with one another and their destinies are hereafter entwined. As in *Tess of the D'Urbervilles* or *Far from the Madding Crowd*, Hardy's novels are full of similar chance encounters between innocent young people walking through meadows, down country roads, or attending county fairs who are destined to have their fates intertwine. Moreover, these coincidental moments alter the destiny—or *ka*—of both the individuals involved and the larger narrative that includes them; from this point on, their fates are irrevocably linked together. What often appears to be a chance meeting that occurs between strangers—the incident where Angel Clare accidentally encounters the pretty maids from the dairy farm and carries them, one at a time, across the muddy stream to protect their white Sunday dresses from getting dirty in *Tess of the D'Urbervilles* is a case in point (this is the moment when Tess and Angel fall in love)—foreshadows their future life together and serves to shape the larger narrative that embraces both characters. When Roland and Susan encounter one another in the chapter "A Meeting on the Road," both recognize the importance of maintaining self-restraint: Susan's "position is a delicate one" (138) and, because of it, at all future meetings the two must act as if they are strangers encountering one another for the first time. As in Hardy, however, human passion is not so easily self-controlled, and neither Roland nor Susan can keep their feelings for each other secret for very long, even at the risk of their mutual self-destruction.

There is much more work for scholars to pursue in finding further connections between King and his literary ancestry, but the job has clearly begun, as several of the aforementioned King scholars have established important correspondences. Inspired by their efforts, I wish to conclude this section by highlighting one more Kingly influence that has yet to be explored: the writings of Ernest Hemingway. In *The Art of Darkness*, Douglas Winter references Hemingway's early impact on King, dating back to the latter's undergraduate classes in American literature at the University of Maine (236–237). This would roughly correspond to the writing of the earliest Bachman books, *Rage* and *The Long Walk*. Consequently, it is not surprising that the young author's initial novels should bear important similarities to Hemingway. George Dawes, King's protagonist in *Roadwork*, even claims literal kinship to Nick Adams (a "cousin from Michigan"), who is the central character in many of Hemingway's short stories, when Dawes seeks information about the use of firearms early in the novel (*Roadwork* 335). Not only is King-Bachman interested in setting stories within the same arena of sport that so fascinated Hemingway, he also reflects the somber existentialism that dominates Hemingway's vision. As is the case throughout Hemingway's canon, the basic philosophical premises from which all the Bachman protagonists proceed are that man is lost in his world, that society will strip him of his dignity and independence if he follows its rules and rituals, and that ultimately human beings are responsible for picking their way from moment to moment to create meaning in their lives. The sporting arena is the place, for both Bachman and Hemingway, where one's masculinity is tested and defined. But as with Jackson's *Hill House* influence on King, the latter translates sport in the Bachman books into a more grotesque metaphor than Hemingway ever employed: a televised life-and-death struggle within a suffocating, class-based political subtext.

But it is not just in the early Bachman King where we find literary and philosophical correspondences that parallel Hemingway's. The sense of the individual alone and at odds with an environment that is actively opposed to his or her survival is a central theme found in both writers. The post–World War I pessimism that informs Hemingway's most important books closely resembles the inheritance of the post-Vietnam King. Both writers emerged from eras chastened by governments that had fought wars under the respective guises of protecting Christian civilization and halting the evil growth of communism. Both writers learned that the platitudes of governments, like those of religion, were convenient rationalizations used to justify killing other men and sacrificing yourself. Consequently, the alienation and reevaluation of societal values that burden Jake Barnes in *The Sun Also Rises*, Frederic Henry in *Farewell to Arms*, and Nick Adams in the short stories are similar to the existential void that confronts the major characters in *The Stand* and the Bachman books.

The "Hemingway Code," which provides his characters with a means for coming to terms with fluctuating social realities and death as the universal constant, is likewise present in King's fiction and, not surprisingly, constitutes a similar list of required values. The way of the hero in both fictions is not through subscription to abstract ideals and an outmoded value system to which naïve others maintain allegiance—patriotism, God, imposed definitions of masculinity, morality, etc.—but a rule for life that the hero has made for himself. This is why King's and Hemingway's heroes are men of few words (think of Stu Redman and Jake Barnes, as examples). They understand that rhetoric can be used to coerce and deceive, that verbiage cheapens and falsifies the facts of life itself. In accordance with their codes, the hero must establish his own set of values by facing life courageously and by acting honestly in terms of this reality. Thus, the primary attribute of the hero in both Hemingway and King is honest courage; he cannot pretend that people or situations are other than they are, because to do so is to risk disaster inside and out. Along the way, the hero may be able to provide assistance to others—and he does so out of the recognition that all men and women share a similar fate in a universe that offers no assurance before and beyond the grave. But in lending such assistance, the hero must be careful not to become entrapped in some other person's value system. For above all else, the heroes in Hemingway and King are core existentialists condemned to be free—they must act, and action is always preferable to passive acceptance—in a way that reflects self-control and a refusal to give in to fear. In each of these writers' fictions, the hero seeks to impose his will over the forces outside himself: chaos, death, passivity, the unknown, fear itself.

This is typically why King and Hemingway heroes are usually found alone or acting in very small groups. As we will detail further in the next chapter, dealing with institutions and institutionalization, too much involvement with the masses leads to groupthink and the surrendering of individuality. In this way especially, King and Hemingway can be viewed as archetypical American authors: they view with profound skepticism any attempt to strip the individual of his responsibilities to himself, whether in the politics of a small town, the bedroom, the battlefield, or a life-threatening televised game show. This is precisely the reason that Hemingway distrusted Marxist ideology his entire career, and it also explains why evil ideologies in King's work rely so heavily on the surrendering and suppression of individual freedoms. In both fictions, life can only be endured if a man's will is maintained, if he controls himself and his environment, and if he maintains a separate place for this control apart from the collective will of others.

At the same time that King's fiction shows evidence of his appreciation of modern mainstream literature, from Jackson to Hemingway, and classic horror/fantasy art from Poe to Tolkien, he would be the first to point out that many lesser-known and less-respected writers were equally as important to shaping his craft, and that the entire argument regarding "high" and "low" literary endeavors is probably a barometer that indicates more about the person making the distinction than it ever does about the distinction itself. "When I went to school my important creative writing work was done through paperbacks that I read as a child," King acknowledged in a 1980 interview; "I went to school with John D. MacDonald and learned about character from Ed McBain" (Underwood and Miller 78). MacDonald and McBain are both authors of very popular hard-boiled detective fiction novels; not surprisingly, there are elements of the detective writer throughout King's canon, and not just as models for character development. *The Dark Half, Needful Things, Dolores Claiborne,* and *Secret Window, Secret Garden*, among other titles, either contain actual detectives who emerge as central characters in the narratives or function on a narrative level as detective stories wherein the reader must "solve" a mystery in the course of the narrative's unfolding.

King's reading, in other words, tends to parallel his writing temperament, capable of addressing a literate academic audience while still maintaining a strong popular appeal. Indeed, just as we might discuss the importance of William Carlos Williams's poetry, particularly his epic poem *Paterson*, as a source for the urban microcosm that King creates in *IT*, any scholar or student seeking to understand the narrative design of King's short stories, especially his earliest tales, would want to examine a generous sampling of the many teleplays Rod Serling and Charles Beaumont wrote for the 1960s television show *The Twilight Zone*. King would have encountered their short, half-hour excursions into the uncanny as a teenage nascent writer.

King's first collection of short stories, *Night Shift*, published in 1976 and gleaned from various magazine publications years prior to the assembling of this collection, demonstrates strong similarities to stories that appeared on *The Twilight Zone* and its later serial companion into the televised bizarre, *The Outer Limits*. He acknowledges the tremendous impact they had on his imagination in *Danse Macabre*: "*The Outer Limits* was, perhaps, after *Thriller*, the best program of its type ever to run on network TV. Purists will scream nonsense and blasphemy; that not even *Thriller* could compete with the immortal *Twilight Zone*. That *The Twilight Zone* is damn near immortal is something I will not argue with" (220). Less centered on inhuman creatures of monstrosity than decidedly human monsters, *The Twilight Zone* tended to rely heavily on twists at the end of the show that would produce strong morality lessons, featuring characters that needed desperately to confront their pride or avarice, and learn something of value about themselves as a consequence. *The Outer Limits*, contrastingly, tended generally to be less didactic and sentimental, and more deeply committed to the genre of science fiction; it inherited the tradition of the nameless thing from space descended to earth that was a staple of the creature features from the 1950s drive-in movies.

The tales in *Night Shift* show the influence of both these television shows. The same narrative dynamic established in *The Twilight Zone* episodes can be traced in tales such as "Battleground," "Strawberry Spring," "The Ledge," "Quitters, Inc.," "Last Rung on the Ladder," and "The Man Who Loved Flowers." Each of these short tales is conceived so that the main character is in a situation that is bizarrely uncomfortable. Most similar to the *Twilight Zone*, the King stories tend to feature a dramatic turnabout, a surprise conclusion rendered quickly and meant to shock and unnerve reader and protagonist alike. The typical protagonist finds himself in a compromising situation—for example, out on a high-rise ledge facing the gangster husband whose wife he is in love with or, in another tale, narrating a series of brutal serial murders on a college campus—and then must confront an awful reality: in order to keep his lover and his own life he must walk around the thin ledge of the building, and, in the second example, that the campus serial murderer reveals himself to be the first-person protagonist of the story. All of the aforementioned tales could easily be converted into *Twilight Zone* teleplays, and indeed many of them eventually were adapted to film for George Romero's collection of King shorts, *Creepshow* (1982).

Monster figures (often from space) or infernally animated machinery, more likely to have made an appearance on *The Outer Limits* rather than the more human-centered *Twilight Zone*, emerge as the central characters in "I Am the Doorway," "The Mangler," and "Trucks." The people who are trapped in these tales are always less interesting than the special-effect monsters that threaten them, and *The Outer Limits* was the first show on television to bring these hideous plants and machines into American family rooms. As King remembers the series: "Each episode had to have some sort of monstrous creature that would make an appearance before the station break at the half hour. In some cases the [monster] was not harmful in and of itself, but you could bet that before the end of the show, some outside force—usually a villainous mad scientist—would cause it to go on a rampage" (*Danse Macabre* 221). Some of the stories in *Night Shift* show the pronounced influence of *The Outer Limits* and represent King's initial efforts in the science fiction genre; a story such as "Trucks" would eventually inspire later novels such as *Christine* and *From a Buick 8*, while "I Am the Doorway" points the way toward novels such as *The Tommyknockers* and *Cell*.

Like many of the episodes of *The Twilight Zone* written by Serling and Beaumont, the earliest of King's stories often conclude with O. Henry-like endings that, as Joseph Reino accurately observes, "though momentarily pleasurable to millions of unsophisticated readers (who are only concerned with what horror 'finally happens') have been justly censured by perceptive reviewers" (102). On the other hand, these narratives, like the early efforts of televised horror, demonstrate, respectively, the growing pains of an emerging artist and of an artistic medium. As King became a more accomplished short story writer, later collections of tales, such as *Nightmares and Dreamscapes* and *Everything's Eventual*, for example, are more illustrative of King's versatility as a writer and consequently less derivative of the initial narrative design, regardless of how interestingly rendered, of early horror television. Like his novels, his later stories grew in their level of sophistication, relying less on surprise, telegraphed endings or O. Henry-like moral renderings. Little surprise, then, that later King stories would garner great praise for the writer along with the accumulation of notable awards—"The Reach" winning a Hugo Award in 1982 and "The Man in the Black Suit," first published in *The New Yorker* magazine, taking the prestigious O. Henry Award for the year's best short story in 1996.

Any attempt to trace the literary influences behind the work of Stephen King would be remiss not to at least mention the importance of the Bible. In several interviews King has indicated that it remains one of the greatest sources for his writing. Although King is not overtly religious—his narratives are actually highly critical of most organized religions and fundamentalist zealotry in any form—he often employs biblical references to underscore and enrich his own plotlines. *The Dead Zone* and *The Green Mile*, for example, feature Christ figures as main characters, and *The Stand* and *The Dark Tower* may be read both as allegorical confrontations between the forces of good and evil and as quasi-religious quests to find meaning in a post-apocalyptic world. The narratives are, at least on one level, best appreciated as an amalgamation of Christian epics that include *Beowulf*, medieval romances (such as *King Arthur's Tales*, *The Romance of the Rose*, and *The Divine Comedy*), and works by Tolkien and C. S. Lewis. King's own epic quests, and I would include *The Talisman* and *IT* along with *The Stand* and *The Dark Tower* within this specific designation, are similar insofar as they all seek to sustain hope in the face of evil's efforts at negation. The saving of a post-apocalyptic America or Roland's Mid-World is a fundamentally redemptive design, and though Roland and his *ka-tet*, like the citizens in Boulder, Colorado, initially appear far removed from Christ figures, they also recognize that their journey to the Tower and the collective effort to reaffirm human society (from its most underdeveloped forms found in imperiled Mid-World border towns to twentieth-century Manhattan itself) and carry on life are intricately tied to the salvation of others. Further, the efforts of these small groups are sustained only because of faith—that the Tower exists and can be refortified, that the human race is worth continuing, and that there is a White power that continues to animate the universe—that endures beyond the realm of rational expectations or the probable. Evil overwhelms and strains the credibility of all these quests, and the individuals undertaking them suffer distractions and self-doubts; yet their respective errands into the dark wilderness all bear fruit: they do succeed. In each of these quests, faith supersedes doubt, and goodness triumphs over the powers of destruction.

King's fiction has been profoundly affected by nonfictional sources as well, such as the psychoanalysts Freud and Jung, literary critic Leslie Fielder's recognition of white and black character alignments as a response to the fear of women in his seminal work *Love and Death in the American Novel*, and Joseph Campbell's mythological archetypes. All these sources are immensely valuable to any informed discussion about King's canon (see Magistrale, *The Second Decade*, 3–6), but Campbell's interpretation of the call to adventure, heroic rites of passage, and the transformation of the hero in the completion of the cosmogonic cycle as outlined in *The Hero with a Thousand Faces* is absolutely crucial to understanding the purpose of the journey-quests found in King's narratives. King establishes the connection unequivocally in this interview statement, in which he discusses the value of *The Hero with a Thousand Faces*: "I was introduced to Joseph Campbell by Peter Straub several years ago. . . . *Hero* is a wonderful book, and it definitely had some affect on me" (Magistrale, *The Second Decade*, 3).

Campbell posits that epic adventures rely on similar patterns of exposition: a hero leaves home to venture forth into battle against forces that are greater than himself in "a distant land, a forest, a kingdom underground, beneath the waves, or above the sky; it is always a place of strangely fluid and polymorphous beings, unimaginable torments, superhuman deeds, and impossible delights" (58). As a result of surviving the challenges encountered in these exotic places, what Campbell names "the passage of the magic threshold" (90), the hero is reborn—enlarged and emboldened—and he uses the confidence gained from his experiences to "break through personal limitations [and] the agony of spiritual growth" (190).

From here, his powers often serve as a source for renewing the society he symbolically represents, assuming the role of Christian figure of redemption to counter the loss of spiritual potency that often has rendered his world into a waste land: "Stated in direct terms: the work of the hero is to slay the tenacious . . . dragon and release from its ban the vital energies that will feed the universe" (352). The transformation of the hero, then, is defined in dual contributions: the salvation of the world he willingly sacrifices his life to protect, and the inner changes that take place in the hero himself, pushing him "into depths where obscure resistances are overcome, and long lost powers are revivified, to be made available for the transfiguration of the world" (29). *The Dark Tower* epitomizes the working out of Campbell's paradigm in King's work with Roland and his *ka-tet* in the roles of transformative epic heroes, but it is likewise possible to trace its mythopoetic influence informing both the collective quests and the personal growth that occurs to the boy-men in *The Body, IT,* and *The Talisman* as well.

This chapter has highlighted several of the more pronounced literary inspirations behind King's work. Were this volume more narrowly focused, we might also explore some of the major cinematic and musical influences on the writer's work as well. King's chapter on "The Modern American Horror Movie" in *Danse Macabre* signals the scope of his appreciation of horror movies, highlighted in his discussion of classics such as *Psycho, The Haunting,* and *The Amityville Horror,* all films that preceded King's own contributions to the haunted house archetype in *'Salem's Lot, The Shining,* and *Rose Red,* in addition to lesser-known fare such as *The Giant Spider Invasion* and *Them,* early science-fiction horror films that shaped King's construction of the monster(s) in *IT.* As with his literary influences, the movies that fired King's imagination are an eclectic lot, including several genres that are striking because they are so far removed from horror and sci-fi fantasy. In chapter 7, dealing with *The Dark Tower,* we will more thoroughly examine King's epic in light of the tradition of the American Western; the *ka-tet* gunslingers and the severely violent episodic adventures that climax in various border towns on the cusp of civilization and the frontier are direct descendants from the cinematic legacies created by Sam Peckinpah and John Sturgis (as well as the Western's Italianate variants, such as *Fistful of Dollars, The Magnificent Seven,* and *The Good, the Bad, and the Ugly,* filmed by Sergio Leone). Further still removed from what is typically associated with horror and science fiction, I don't know of a contemporary novelist writing in the past half-century who has done more to revivify the prison genre than Stephen King. *The Shawshank Redemption* and *The Green Mile* certainly fit within the category of the Hollywood male buddy film, but they are also highly evolved prison narratives (Mary Findley's essay on *Misery* advocates its inclusion as a King prison movie as well) in the tradition of *Papillon*, *The Great Escape*, and *The Collector*.

Many of King's storylines have also been enhanced through allusions to the ubiquitous rock and blues music he listens to and that so often finds its way into his narrative texts. *The Body* (*Stand By Me*) and *Christine* rely so heavily on the popular music of the fifties and sixties that it is impossible to imagine either functioning without their myriad musical allusions. Bruce Springsteen and John Mellencamp, two of King's favorite musicians, write songs about the types of men and women that frequently populate King's fiction; they are tributes to average folk who find a way to endure personal tragedy, oftentimes even managing to triumph over the consequences of cosmic cruelty. The Ramones, Blue Oyster Cult, and The Doors, on the other hand, provide the pounding soundtracks and brooding lyrical poetry that are appropriate audio backdrops to accompany many of the apocalyptic visions that emerge from King's darkest fantasies and alternate universes.

There still exists a tremendous opportunity for King and cultural studies scholars to catalogue a broader range of popular culture—visual and musical confluences in particular—that King has incorporated into his work, for they are as varied and frequent in their occurrence as they are crucial to an overall appreciation of King's career contribution. And this influence works the other way as well: a whole generation of graphic illustrators has grown up reading King's novels. *The Dark Tower* collection (particularly the vibrant paintings of Steve Stone) and Marvel Comics adaptations are just two of the many examples of King's fiction inspiring contemporary artists and graphic illustrators. Like Poe before him, King's highly visual prose has always served as an inspiration to visual illustration. Additionally, the range of King's influence on other writers and other multimedia artists is emerging as an issue worthy of research. At this point in time, I know of no scholarship that has begun the interesting job of tracking these relationships. Turning my attention next to defining other aspects of the Stephen King universe, however, I reluctantly leave that challenging task to someone else.

Chapter 3

Institutions and Institutionalization: Evil's Design and Heroic Rebellion

Midway through the *The Shawshank Redemption*, Ellis Boyd "Red" Redding suggests that the reason Brooks, a former inmate in the prison, committed suicide shortly after being paroled, was his inability and lack of desire to adapt to a new life on the outside. "These walls are funny," Red posits, "First you hate them. Then they grow on you and you can't live without them." In both the film adaptation and King's novella, we realize that Red is not just referencing Brooks's problem, but likewise his own fear of a life beyond penitentiary walls. In preparing for his surprise escape, Andy proposes that Red, when he is finally paroled, should join him down in Zihuatanejo, Mexico, but Red doubts himself and his survival skills anyplace outside of Shawshank, the location where he has lived his entire adult life and in which he has unwittingly acclimated: "I couldn't get along on the outside. I'm what they call an institutional man now.... I wouldn't know how to begin. Or where" (71). For Red and Brooks, if not for Andy, the outside world is scary and unpredictable; the inside world of the prison, although isolating and oppressive, is at least familiar and comprehensible.

The prison is just one example of an institution in King's universe. But it remains a dominant image that is likewise linked to and encompasses other institutions throughout his fictions and films. Nearly every institution that appears in his canon—high school, organized religion, corporations, the government (on all levels of its operation), the small-town community, the workplace, and even many marriages and the nuclear family itself—typically operates as a prison without walls. There are precious few instances where King treats any of these cultural and societal institutions favorably. Like Red's incarceration at Shawshank, King's characters frequently find themselves in social dynamics that not only limit their freedom but also create stifling environments that threaten their very definitions of selfhood.

THE METAPHOR OF INSTITUTIONALIZATION

The narratives of Stephen King are not merely excursions into a world that never was and never could be, but also a serious social fiction. The latter comprises a commentary on, and a critique of, postmodern America's value system—our politics, interpersonal relationships, our most revered and trusted institutions. His work describes a particular matrix in time; it bears a direct association with significant aspects of American culture and the types of human relationships it has engendered. The social influences that helped to shape *The Mist* and *The Stand*, two of the best examples to illustrate this dimension of his work, are tantamount to casting a cultural context for King's entire canon. There are a few attempts to escape in *The Mist*, but eventually the majority settles in to an understanding that the supermarket is their only safe refuge against the flying creatures. In the film, the horror of *The Mist* begins with the command: "There's something in the mist. Close the door." This is the first sign that the characters in the supermarket are imprisoned. Although they are trapped for only a short period of time in the supermarket, the employees and shoppers in *The Mist* devolve to basic human instincts, and in their daunting predicament display traits similar to those of typical convicts: breaking up into exclusive groups, one of them exhibiting signs of institutionalization that Red describes after years of penal incarceration.

Two important features underscore the connection between *The Shawshank Redemption* and *The Mist*. In an interview that King gave to *Time Magazine*'s Gilbert Cruz in 2007, he responded to Darabont's assertion that in *The Mist* he finally broke out the mold of only directing prison movies written by Stephen King. King disagreed, and supplied a wry correction: "It's still a story about people in prison. They're just in prison in a supermarket." Second, just as Warden Norton in *Shawshank* employs a perverted interpretation of Christianity as justification for his oppressive regime in place at the prison, in *The Mist* a version of fundamental Christianity again is used as a force for ensuring that people conform to a single behavioral norm. The customers inside chose either to escape or to become institutionalized to a single mindset. Inside the supermarket we see that the religious zealot, Mrs. Carmody, preys upon the fears of the people trapped inside, convincing many of them that the monsters outside are evidence of some kind of divine retribution, and that salvation is possible only in following her dogmatic biblical interpretation of these bizarre events. She operates from a position of religious fanaticism that believes God is demanding human sacrifice, and as both novella and film unfold, more and more people begin to side with her, essentially submitting to religious institutionalization. The individuals trapped inside the grocery store eventually split into two main groups, those on the side of Mrs. Carmody and those who support David Drayton. Her insistence on a collective level of compliance parallels the action of the military that originally unleashed the monsters. As such, Carmody and the American military represent dangerous versions of institutionalization—both establish power from fear and then use it as a means for intimidating and controlling those who are unable to cope with the situation.

In both *The Stand* and *The Mist*, the American government and its military are portrayed as divorced from the American people and operating without conscience. Through its ill-advised scientific weapons experimentation, the military almost succeeds in destroying the world. It is clear that King has a certain level of cynicism toward most scientific advancement, and his doubts challenge some of the most basic tenets of classical liberalism. The same bureaucracy responsible for the misadventures in Vietnam and Iraq has turned its vast resources and attention toward complicating and endangering the lives of private citizens. In both *The Stand* and *The Mist*, as well as others that appear throughout his canon, King's governmental representatives and political agents are either directly responsible for releasing the dual genies of science and the supernatural, or bear culpability for heightening already dangerous situations in their misguided efforts to cover up mistakes, in their denial of responsibility, and in their failure to help citizens cope with the aftermath.

In Frank Darabont's 2007 film adaptation of *The Mist*, the powerful indictment against the military government—in terms of both its Faustian compulsion to explore beyond the known barriers of quantum physics and its unconscionable efforts to keep secret what is consequently unleashed upon its unsuspecting citizen-victims—that King provides in his original novella is given greater depth and immediacy. Two of the soldiers who participate in the Arrowhead Project, the secret military installation that manages to crack open an inter-dimensional barrier separating our world from a Lovecraftian collection of aggressive flying reptiles, commit suicide in the back room of a rural supermarket. Although the soldiers never do divulge the purpose of the Arrowhead Project, their suicides are meant to underscore the larger culpability and shame the government bears. Additionally, there is a third soldier who is on the verge of deployment to Iraq in the next few days. The mob inhabiting the supermarket, urged on by the biblical authority of Mrs. Carmody, sacrifices him to the creatures that lurk in the fog. The deaths of the three soldiers appear particularly significant as a political subtext to the film. Their suicides and murder take on additional meaning in the context of how most Americans had developed severe misgivings about the course of the Iraq war at the time of Darabont's film production.

After initially being misled by the false intelligence that assured anxious Americans in a mood for retribution following 9/11 that there were weapons of mass destruction ready to be deployed against the nation, the Bush administration and its military allies in the Pentagon not only relied on this false information in their rush toward war, but also continued to lie to themselves and to the American public footing the cost in lives and dollars about the degree to which this war was a total misadventure. The end result has left the majority of Americans highly skeptical of their government, not because they didn't believe that Saddam Hussein was an evil dictator, but because their own government never provided an honestly stated or persuasive political justification of this war. The Bush administration lied to the American people in order to justify a war that is only related to 9/11 and the threat of terrorism insofar as it created a greater level of instability in the Middle East, provided evidence to the rest of the world that the United States is as much a danger to peace as is Muslim terrorism, and added further justification for Islamic fundamentalists around the world to establish solidarity with Osama Bin Laden and his call for a universal jihad against America.

In Darabont's version of *The Mist*, the soldiers in the supermarket are essentially held accountable for war crimes; they become scapegoats who accept blame for the misguided efforts of their political and bureaucratic superiors. Their choices of death are also notable, as the two men elect to hang themselves, ironically paralleling Saddam's form of execution for war crimes committed against his own people in Iraq. The fact that these soldiers choose to kill themselves in exactly the same manner is further evidence of the degree to which they have become institutionalized: rather than tell their fellow citizens about what is happening or repent their role in it, their deaths reflect the narrow groupthink of the military. Whether it is associated with nonexistent weapons of mass destruction or methods of torture employed against the purported enemies of America, governmental silence is viewed as patriotic. In contrast, the truth behind the lie of silence is somehow distortedly aligned with an individual's act of subversion—and again we are back to a discussion of the dogmatic groupthink that so often finds its way into King's formulations of evil. The last soldier, who dies at the hands of his fellow citizens in *The Mist,* might best be interpreted as a sacrificial payback reflective of the collective fury Americans felt in 2007 after being deceived for years by a government and a military that has demanded collective compliance (from both Congress and the American people) for a war that was always more about oil and Israel than about curtailing terrorism and fostering Iraqi independence. The flying monsters in the mist should not, therefore, be viewed as separate from the monstrous actions of the government that released them. The mist itself becomes a metaphor for the U.S. government's effort to obfuscate and hide the truths of Iraq and the scientific machinations of the Arrowhead Project from its people, as well as the country's willingness to invest the military establishment with an undeserved blind trust.

The film's ironic and tragic ending, differing strongly from the open-endedness of King's novella, again reflects the sober futility of the Iraq war, as David Drayton murders his little group of four, including his young son, rather than have them sacrificed to the creatures in the mist. He gets out alone to face the flying monsters only to discover that his heroic actions were inappropriately premature: the military arrives minutes later, too late to save the day, but anxious to clean up the mess it is responsible for having created. Unlike the horror films of the 1950s, to which *The Mist* pays homage, the military is not invested with the trust of its citizenry, and it does not provide a solution to the problem it has created. The film's conclusion suggests that the nightmare unleashed by the American military will not be contained until it has destroyed the very things Americans value most deeply: the lives of American soldiers, their families, the economic stability of the nation that went into great debt in order to finance this war, and the collective faith of those who were misled into believing in the government's justifications for going to war.

Throughout the King universe, there is a possibility for anything and everything to become a prison. In his canon, various evil incarnations share a similar mode of operation: the demand that others relinquish moral choices, surrender independent thought, and abandon individual conscience. Like Henry Thoreau, another independent New Englander who worried that America was on the verge of "cultural institutionalization," there is enough of the classic Yankee American in Stephen King to insist that following a dogmatic groupthink results in the abnegation of personal identity and self-determination. In *Civil Disobedience*, Thoreau laments the proliferation of his own version of institutionalization that results in the sacrifice of the individual's independence and free will. Thoreau employs language that is a nearly perfect parallel to the conformance rituals that occur in the corruption of Jerusalem's Lot, Little Tall

Island, and Derry: "There is but little virtue in the action of masses of men. . . . The American has dwindled into an Odd Fellow—one who may be known by the development of his organ of gregariousness, and a manifest lack of intellect and cheerful self-reliance" (116–117). Thoreau was perhaps the first to remind us about the social dialectic that separates "gregariousness" from "intellect" and "self-reliance." Red's similar theory of institutionalization can be seen to extend well beyond the perimeters of actual concrete walls, as King's characters often find themselves confronted with the demand to conform to values and expectations that are imposed upon them.

In King's narratives, evil manifests itself as a monological presence. Whether in the shape of a religious fanatic, the fascistic authority of Annie Wilkes, Andre Linoge, Randall Flagg, the Crimson King, and Warden Norton, or the societal conformity dictated by the Tommyknockers and It, evil thrives in a controlled and highly ordered world where individual men and women have for whatever reasons surrendered their independent moral conscience. The first of these groupthink manifestations to occur in King's fiction can be traced back to the high school institution in *Carrie*. In the role of the outsider, and thereby linked to traditional forms of monstrosity found throughout the horror genre, Carrie is the center of unwanted attention from the other girls in the school. Led by the vicious Chris Hargenson, whose hatred for Carrie is so extreme that it borders on mental illness, the girls in the school band together to humiliate their ostracized classmate. Chris enforces this group identification—notice that she never acts alone—in attacks against Carrie because the latter represents a threat to a code of feminine behavior and appearance that Chris so fully inculcates. As the Queen Bee in the high school, Chris demands total adherence from the other girls in serving the group will. When Susan Snell makes the deliberate decision to think for herself and tries to provide Carrie with a second chance at having a life in the school, Sue is immediately exorcised from the group and, by the end of the novel and film, isolated and bereft of all her friends, becomes another tortured version of Carrie herself. The novel and film couldn't be any clearer in their reactionary messages: straying from the groupthink results in the destruction of the individual.

But what is most discomforting in this dark study of high school rituals, acceptance codes, and exclusionary practices is that Carrie is trapped between her mother's obscene religious fundamentalism, where all women are doomed to carry the sin of intercourse as the ancestors of Eve, and the high school girls, led by Chris, where women are doomed unless they adhere to the proper trappings of contemporary femininity. In both cases, women are refused their individuality and the opportunity to choose behavior for themselves. Only after Carrie agrees to play the game according to Chris's rigid code of female identification—e.g., wearing makeup, putting on a tight dress and high heels, showing cleavage, becoming the prom girlfriend to a popular boy, learning how to control the flow of her menstrual cycle—does she open the door to finding acceptance in the school. The "Plug it up" chant of the girls in the locker room is more than just a means for tormenting Carrie: it is their own ironic acknowledgment that to be a female means to have the body under control at all times, to repudiate its natural rhythms, and to conform to the cultural behavior codes of other women. Even the "good mother" in this text, the gym teacher Miss Collins, insists that Carrie must become part of the oppressive gender system encoded in the school, and she does her best to initiate Carrie into feminine bondage by instructing the girl on what to wear and how to act in a feminine manner. In other words, Mrs. White's oppressive code of conduct at home is mirrored in the high school's definition of appropriate feminine hygiene and behavior, and Carrie is not accepted into the group—and even that acceptance finally proves ephemeral, thanks to Chris, whose memory of any code violations is relentless and unforgiving—until she acknowledges her otherness and renounces it.

King's malefic incarnations are devoid of courage and imagination; they subsist in closed, self-contained systems that refuse to compromise their empowerment. Evil in King's fiction is always fascistic; it tries to make its knowledge the *only* knowledge, usually through violent persuasion. It manipulates, restricts, and silences opposition. And most often the narrative itself, while projecting such a consciousness, is appropriately reduced to a single authoritarian voice. In *Carrie*, *'Salem's Lot*, *The Body*, *Needful Things*, *The Stand*, *The Mist*, and *IT*, among many other examples, evil is represented in the community collective united with the malefic avatar—a monological merging of speech, thought, and action. Correspondingly, these forces of evil, whether supernaturally incarnated or merely human, can exert control over individual men and women only because of their own capitulation, which Red labeled as "institutionalization." Whether out of fear or just the inability to fight conformance with the group mindset, institutionalized men and women in King narratives are imprisoned by their own loss of self-confidence and willing subjugation to another's power, a force that might be limiting in what it demands, but is nonetheless greater than themselves.

The imposition of a single community mindset is imperative to understanding fictions such as *'Salem's Lot*, *Storm of the Century*, *The Tommyknockers*, *The Stand*, *IT*, *Needful Things*, and *The Dark Tower*. Each of these texts features a central figure of evil—typically a demonic male who comes from outside the community—who tries to impose his supernatural will over the denizens of a small Maine town. In the course of the narrative, this demonic figure sets in motion a confrontational dynamic among the town's citizens wherein they are pitted against one another in service to the design of the evil outsider. Anyone who disagrees with the groupthink of the whole is subject to censorship and, more than likely, violent death. This is why silence is the common thread that connects individual illustrations of collective groupthink in these various novels. As we will see later in this chapter, what differentiates King's heroes from those characters who have become institutionalized is their refusal to remain silent, and their corresponding effort, either alone or in concert with a small group of rebels, to fight the synergy of indifference and conformance.

Sometimes, as in *The Tommyknockers* and *'Salem's Lot*, the town's inhabitants are themselves transformed into identical monstrous creatures; the figure of the zombie vampire in *'Salem's Lot* becomes a symbol of the town's loss of individuality and conformance to Barlow's greater will, and the mindless citizens of Haven reflect the influence of the alien consciousness in *The Tommyknockers*. The individual members of each town are respectively drawn to, and shaped by, the evil generated by the Marston House and the spaceship in the woods. As in one of King's favorite films, George Romero's *Night of the Living Dead*, the towns' citizenry become the walking dead who have sacrificed their reason, vision, and courage for inclusion in a group identity.

In *Storm of the Century*, a single group mindset is a consciously made choice tyrannically imposed at the risk of destroying the entire island. Little Tall Island's citizenry selects a utilitarian course of action that saves their town at the expense of a single child and his family. The decision to give Ralph to Linoge reflects an unspoken bond of corruption between the town and its mysterious stranger. A societal groupthink is at work in Little Tall Island's inability to recognize the insidious nature of Linoge's demand. The island's decision to doom a child instead of taking the more difficult and potentially lethal stand against Linoge's manipulation is an indication both of its inability to rise above the personal limitations of individual citizens that Linoge continually exhorts (as if to say to the town: you are all corrupt already, so what's one more act of malfeasance) and of their collective unwillingness to undertake difficult moral choices. What is at work in *Storm*, as well as in the other narratives mentioned above, is a collective version of institutionalization: the town's citizens are unwilling to think beyond their own personal safety or to entertain complicated issues that threaten the imposed status quo; when faced with a difficult challenge, they choose the expedient solution, and then go on with their lives without belaboring the consequences of their choice.

Only Mike Anderson, the hero of this teleplay, is willing to become a pariah in his refusal to capitulate to Linoge's scheme. His choice preserves his independence, but it comes at the expense of his place in the community. By the end of the miniseries, the island's central citizen—its constable, easy-credit grocer, voice of calm and rational assurance, good Samaritan, and civic conscience—is unable to continue living among his neighbors. He uproots himself and moves to the other side of the continent, where he begins a new life, a symbol of his rejection of the island's mass corruption. As we will see illustrated in other examples later this chapter, King applauds Anderson's moral independence; it evokes the civil disobedience of Henry Thoreau's enlightened "majority of one" (121) rather than surrendering to the moral cowardice of the town itself. In *Storm*, King insists that even though the small-town Maine environment is sometimes capable of producing heroic individuals, most often it destroys the majority because of its socializing pressures to conform.

In the novella *The Body* and its film version entitled *Stand by Me*, we see further evidence of a small-town cultural groupthink that is in opposition to the protagonists of the tale. As in *Storm*, all four of the young male protagonists are affected by boundaries set up by their families, their economic and social status, and rigid conceptions of masculinity. Castle Rock itself establishes a caste system that is difficult to escape; when you are born into the town's blue-collar institutionalization, rising above it is like trying to transfer out of shop classes into college prep coursework in high school. The youth of the town rarely escape to reach a successful, much less fruitful adulthood, and instead remain trapped in hopeless, dead-end jobs—yet another version of the prison. The four boy protagonists learn fast that once the authorities type-cast an individual child—either because of family history, or grades, or economics—the likelihood of escaping the predetermined category is akin to running away from a speeding locomotive. The Castle Rock adults all behave in a similar manner, and their attitudes toward the four central characters in the narrative are similarly horrific. Dysfunctional family life, especially overt violence and the silent abuse of indifference between fathers and sons, and older brothers and younger ones, is a major theme in the text and it affects all of the protagonists to a greater or lesser extent. The plot may revolve around the quest to view Ray Brower's crushed body, killed while picking blueberries along the train tracks, but it is clear that the entire population of Castle Rock is dead—dead to their fellow citizens, dead to their own children.

Gordie Lachance suffers from an inversion of the favorite-child syndrome, fading so far into the background of his grieving parents' lives that he feels he has become the "invisible boy" and, because of his father, becomes convinced that he should have been the one to die rather than his older brother. Chris Chambers's father is a quasi-criminal and a drunk, and despite his son's obvious intelligence, integrity, and leadership qualities, the boy is unfairly stereotyped because of his father's reputation. Perhaps the most evident case of a parentally induced imprisonment is expressed through Teddy and his warped, obstinate idealizations of his abusive, mentally unstable father, a man even the disturbed Milo labels a "Loony." Teddy's destiny, along with Vern's, is directed by their families' economic and social station. Vern follows in the path ordained for him—getting married right out of high school, picking up a laborer's job, and settling down to the routine in a town similar to Castle Rock. Teddy tries to make something of himself, but he ends up doing time in a literal prison. As a result of where they came from, neither boy has ever been given the opportunity to aspire to a better or at least a different kind of life.

While Teddy and Vern show the effects of Castle Rock's understated institutionalization, Gordie and Chris manage to break free of the walls that surround them and to realize the dream of social mobility. The ending of the film establishes the visual divide between those who will endure and transcend the Castle Rock prison and those who will be institutionalized by their adversity: Vern and Teddy go off in opposite directions while Chris and Gordie continue walking together, essentially leaving behind the other two boys.

As much as these four boys struggle with ill-fated solutions, they also experience the most basic and universal of life transitions: the loss of innocence, coming of age, and confronting the expectations of gender. The loss of innocence and their emergence into adolescence are temporary prisons that appear painful and unjust, but will over time prove transitory; the performativity of gender and the social value placed upon it, however, proves less escapable. Ace and his gang of miscreants constantly emasculate the four friends verbally, and Gordie is particularly vulnerable in his choice to deviate from the expected norm by not playing football and aspiring to become a writer. The confrontations the boys experience strongly parallel Dufresne's encounters with Bogs and the other rapists in Shawshank Prison. While Gordie manages to escape the institutionalization of Castle Rock, it is clear that Vern and Teddy do not. Furthermore, although he appears to join Gordie in breaking free of his class restrictions and graduating law school, the town's penchant for aggressive action over verbal negotiation also reclaims Chris in the end, who is killed in his effort to break up an altercation between two strangers. Chris's death comes to parallel that of Brower's, insofar as both symbolize the waste of human potential through the powers of institutionalization that so often dominate King's narratives. Brower is destroyed by the train, which symbolizes the industrial hard-heartedness of Castle Rock (Magistrale, *Hollywood's Stephen King,* 40), and Chris is killed by the violent tendencies interminably linked with Ace and his gang.

A central thesis of King's magnum opus, *IT*—that an entire town can become an institutionalized landscape dominated by a collective groupthink—surely owes its origins to *'Salem's Lot* and *The Body.* But unlike these earlier texts, the historical sweep of *IT* makes the novel's level of institutionalization a more pervasive indictment. Over time, the monster that is It has come to exist in a collusion with the town of Derry, more specifically, the adults of Derry. The human inhabitants have become so accustomed to the avatar of It's evil, Pennywise the clown, that they no longer even see him on his quest to ravage the town's children. Indeed, Pennywise's actions merely reflect the town's general indifference toward its children. As in *The Body,* kids are abused by their parents throughout *IT*—from Eddie Kaspbrak's mother-induced asthma to Alvin Marsh's barely repressed incestuous urge directed at Bev. The extent of childhood oppression, as Mike Hanlon observes, is excessively high in Derry, indicating that there are certain social conditions in concert with a convenient group institutionalization in this town that make child abuse the norm rather than an aberration, and criminal activity an acceptable community event. Whenever any act of violence or cruelty occurs in Derry (usually orchestrated by Derry's adult males), Pennywise is present to celebrate it, to participate in it, and to reap the power accrued from the act itself. When the Bradley gang is slaughtered in the center of town in a *Bonnie and Clyde*–like ambush, Pennywise is a member of the righteous mob, emptying her own bullets from a smoking rifle (653). Similarly, when the Black Spot is torched by a legion of local racists, the clown is there in the guise of a giant bird of prey, "big bunches of balloons tied to each wing" (470).

King's supernatural manifestations of evil are often symptoms of urban decay. In a November 6, 1986, address at the University of Maine, King acknowledged that *IT* specifically owed much to William Carlos Williams and Charles Dickens insofar as "the novel is an epic poem of the city as an organism." Derry, Little Tall Island, Castle Rock, Haven, and 'Salem's Lot are all sick little places where citizens cooperate or foster relationships with monstrous paranormal figures. These supernatural avatars simultaneously embody the worst elements of the resident adult human citizens (child abuse, violence, oppressive institutionalism) while also forming a parasitical relationship with the town itself. Each time Derry experiences evidence of its "unusually high rate of every violent crime we know of" (504), Pennywise reemerges from the Barrens to stalk Derry's children, suggesting that the town's thirst for blood activates Pennywise's own thirst. Derry's collective evil—and its refusal to confront these acts legally or morally—suggests that Derry and Pennywise share a reciprocal corruption: that the monster is the town, and the town is the monster. The fact that the Derry adults are unable to see Pennywise and the various manifestations It assumes (even the blood in Bev's bathroom remains invisible to everyone except the children) is a sign that King wishes us to view Derry's citizenry in league with the monster and, just as importantly, separated from their children, who are able to see It. Derry has simply come to accept the existence of Pennywise as its avatar—the price for conducting business—so perhaps that is why the monster remains essentially an invisible presence for its adult citizens. In return for helping the town to thrive financially, It devours Derry's future, a price that appears to reflect the town's general antipathy. Derry's adults profess a love for their progeny, but aside from imposing an early evening curfew, there are no concrete examples of adult panic or concern surrounding the loss of so many young people. Indeed, the adults in this novel are most conspicuous in their collective silence and willful failure to become involved even when criminal acts occur in the streets just outside their homes. Derry embodies the institutionalized behavior that tolerates and perpetuates various social pathologies elsewhere in King's canon. In Derry, however, the vast level of apathy and self-corruption King describes in other novels is narrowed and concentrated in one city, and it has been festering for decades.

ENTER THE HERO

Against these backdrops of individual and organizational institutionalization, King pits heroic men and women who are typically working-class people devoid of supernatural powers and struggling to figure out how to survive the enormity of evil that confronts them. As discussed in the preceding chapter, J. R. R. Tolkien has long been a favorite writer for Stephen King, and there is little doubt that the meekly resourceful hobbits Tolkien created in *The Lord of the Rings* serve as influential prototypes for the modern American heroes in King's fictions and film. These brave individuals are resourceful but ordinary; they are tested to the point of their ultimate endurance; and usually they emerge from the test as better human beings. They find themselves pitted against the various institutions that appear throughout the King canon: the prison bureaucracy, religious zealotry, government-sponsored oppression, and the school system—all the structures of the American social environment that threaten individuality with groupthink behavior and mass conformity. The various "hobbits" found in King's fiction distinguish themselves by virtue of their rejection of the status quo. Although overwhelmed by the various examples of institutionalization that they must confront, these men and women not only find a method of survival, but also manage to vanquish whatever oppressive system has overwhelmed others.

If the force of the monster in *IT* is best summarized as a unity between townspeople and the malefic avatar It, then the unique voices and experiences of the Losers form a viable alternative to evil's self-enclosure. Jeanne Campbell Reesman argues that individuals who band together in small democratic and participatory groups to counter evil's despotic monarchies generally triumph in King's fiction. In her analysis of self-survival in *IT*, she argues: "Repeated confessions, telling and retelling of events, remembering and sharing—all telling is important to the group. All important decisions to act are henceforth made in dialogue" ("Riddle Game" 165). While the monster It creates a monological voice that echoes through Derry's history and the groupthink of the adults who participate in like-minded acts of violence and oppression, the childhood heroes in the Losers' Club communicate with one another in a way that emphasizes the uniqueness of their individual experiences, the plurality that composes their alternative vision, and their commitment to resisting the town's social ethos by helping each other and Derry's other imperiled children. In doing battle with the monster, the minds of adults are brought back into dialogue with the minds of children. Ironically, the children that It seeks as prey are the ones who possess the will and power to destroy the destroyer. Stan Uris commits suicide and thus is the only one of the Club who does not make it back to Derry for the second battle. Unlike his friends, Stan is unable to talk about his fear, to face it and share it verbally; his silence links him to It and propels him toward self-destruction. All the Losers have something, some personal talent or attribute, to contribute that helps to defeat the reductive energies of the monster. It's urge to appropriate and institutionalize thought is countered by the Losers' efforts to keep a sense of otherness alive as a mark of resistance. In the "Epilogue—Bill Denbrough Beats the Devil (II)," Bill Denbrough, who becomes one of the heroes in this book by overcoming a stutter to find his own voice, which helps to vanquish the monster, muses as he prepares to depart Derry: "Children I love you. I love you so much. . . . *Be true, be brave, stand. All the rest is darkness*" (1087). His sentiment is more than a fitting coda to a novel about children, their unfailing love for one another, and the threat of encroaching darkness; it is also the spirit of resistance—the exhortation to *stand* against oppression—that animates the whole of King's efforts to thwart institutionalization.

Heroic characters exist all through King's universe, so the examples I discuss here merely illustrate a consistent narrative pattern that has held true throughout the writer's career. The prototype for the King hero is arguably Andy Dufresne from *The Shawshank Redemption.* Although Andy is probably better educated and employed than the majority of King's blue-collar heroes and heroines, he still shares much in common with them. There is a strong element of the independent New Englander in all these characters. Andy stands out from the other prisoners around him, asserting his humanity while others succumb to institutionalization, at the same time that he undermines the corrupt authorities that run the prison. As the typical King hero, Andy is unassuming, humble, smart, and patient. Most of all, however, he is best defined in terms of his indomitable spirit. After decades of doing time for crimes he did not commit, Andy gives up neither his desire for freedom nor his personal humanity. Andy's subversive acts force him to spend more time "in the hole" enduring solitary confinement longer than any other prisoner at Shawshank. He becomes a target for The Sisters and for years endures their homosexual assaults. And while he has every reason to become cynical and embittered because the system so terribly failed him, instead of turning inward toward self-pity and despair, he channels his anger and prodigious energies outward, electing to help others instead. Several men receive their high school equivalency diplomas because of his dedicated tutelage; he builds the Shawshank library and saves Red from capitulating to institutionalization. As a prisoner who witnesses the complex web of illegality that is orchestrated by Warden Norton, Andy is acutely aware of how corrupt social pressures encroach on individual integrity. So, while he seeks solidarity with his small group of friends, Dufresne also resists conformity. In spite of the close bonds he maintains with the prisoners he helps, Andy is clearly distinguished from the rest of the prison population. Red tells us he had "a walk and a talk that just wasn't normal around here . . . like he had on an invisible coat that would shield him from this place." Maybe it is his level of intellectualism, surrounded as he is with high school dropouts, evinced in his personal preferences for chess over checkers, wall posters of Einstein over Betty Boop, fiercely independent film starlets over sports legends. In the end, Andy's distinctiveness, his individuality, never results in an air of elite superiority—except when he calls Bogs an "ignorant fuck" and Warden Norton "obtuse"—and both these men deserve their put-downs. Andy's self-confidence transcends the need for ostentation and insulates him from the conforming forces at work on the other prisoners at Shawshank. He fights fiercely against the pressures of institutionalization in order to remain honest, brave and forthright, and in the end his values triumph over and bring down the systemic corruption at the prison.

What gives Andy the ability to endure and remain positively focused, in contrast to other long-term prisoners, notably Red and Brooks, who are overwhelmed by the pressures of institutionalization? Perhaps the most important asset that Andy Dufresne possesses is the power of hope. He refuses to sacrifice his individuality or the individualities of other prisoners in the face of a penal system that demeans and dehumanizes the incarcerated, turning them into numbers who must "ask permission before taking a piss." In the film version of *The Shawshank Redemption*, director Frank Darabont helps to illustrate this character trait through the metaphor of music. Andy's love of Mozart is meant to contrast with the deadening silence that typically characterizes the interior atmosphere of his cellblock. Further, while Andy spends two weeks in the hole for refusing to "turn off" *The Marriage of Figaro* as it soars over the prison public address system, Red is afraid to play even a note on the new harmonica Andy presents to him after one of his parole hearings. Andy recognizes that music is more than just the beauty of sound, and thus stands in direct contrast with the gray sterility of prison life. Music is also a subversive expression, something inside "that they can't take away from you." Red has allowed the institution to take his music, as well as his spirit, away from him. In the only scene in which Red and Andy argue in the film, Red, mirroring his own level of capitulation to institutionalization, insists that he gave up playing the harmonica when he went to prison because "it didn't make much sense in here." Andy offers the rejoinder that in jail is where music "makes the most sense" because it represents transcendence and the sustaining of individual character: it is a reminder of "something inside that they can't get to, that they can't touch. That's yours." As illustrated in the scene where Mozart floods the prison yard, music cannot be confined behind walls or be pushed into boxes. Like the quest for human freedom, it is not easily regulated or suppressed. Andy is the music that eventually tunnels under the walls of Shawshank and back out into the world.

In Darabont's film, after receiving parole and the awareness that he's "not going to make it on the outside," Red chooses to follow Andy's path, literally and metaphorically, to a stone wall in a Maine meadow. When he arrives there, a harmonica begins to play softly in the background as Red seeks "that black piece of volcanic glass in a Maine hayfield" (98) pointing the way to a more positive future that Andy has left for him to find. The background notes from the harmonica are important because they illustrate the final triumph of music and Andy's worldview over Red's and Brook's suicidal impulses. Additionally, the stone wall where all this takes place is an allusion to Robert Frost's "Mending Wall"—Andy references Frost's work in both the novella (98) and film—a poem that is also about the forces of institutionalization that separate men from one another. In Frost's poem, two neighbors work to replace the individual stones in a wall that demarcates the legal perimeters of their respective properties: "on a day we meet to walk the line/And set the wall between us once again." Winter frost has broken apart the wall that separates the property lines dividing the men physically, but the narrator of the poem also comes to see it as an opportunity to knock down the walls that separate them metaphorically. His opinion that "Something there is that doesn't love a wall" parallels Andy's sentiments toward Red in insisting that men have the potential to establish meaningful connections to one another, even to the point where race and class differences can be surmounted. Red's level of institutionalization, on the other hand, finds its voice in Frost's neighbor's somber retort that "Good fences make good neighbors." Both the poem and King's text state the difference between living a life of isolation from other men, or realizing the bond that men might share with one another; it is the difference in choice, finally, that is stated so forcefully in Andy's resonant phrase, "get busy living, or get busy dying."

When Red crosses the border into Mexico, he is not merely "breaking parole" and thus committing another crime against the state; he is also breaking free of the same conventions that have restricted the neighbor in Frost's poem, who "moves in darkness . . . / Not of woods only and the shade of trees." Frost's neighbor "will not go behind his father's saying," an indication that his negative thinking is in part the result of being trapped in the past. Red's institutionalization is likewise the product of years of "walled-in" oppression, isolation, and the steady erosion that "hope is a dangerous thing." Andy, in contrast, never loses hope; this is the "shield" that Red first noted while watching Andy walk through the prison yard. The magic of *The Shawshank Redemption* is that this shield is transferable—it passes from Andy to Red (and then to the reader/viewer)—and it is the most persuasive representation of what the word "redemption" means in the title.

Institutions and institutionalization in Stephen King's universe underscore the death-in-life status of men and women who have lost hope and surrendered to despair. The zombie-like routines of the vampire-citizens in *'Salem's Lot* parallel the mindless group moral atrophy in *Storm of the Century*. Against these forces of soullessness, King pits individuals who, like Mike Anderson, maintain their individuality while also recognizing the need for other people. These heroes and heroines are invested with a resiliency that is akin to true religious faith; in fact, they are the most spiritual characters in King's world. The forces of institutionalization effect a passive insanity (even when the result is aggressive violence) upon those who are its victims. Scattered across King's landscape is a plethora of writers—both private and professional—who share at least one thing with their creator: they view writing as a means for establishing self-control in a universe where madness always threatens to reign. In contrast to the single groupthink and group-voice that characterizes his most institutionalized characters, King's heroes and heroines are the most verbal characters (or at least they are learning to find their voice along with their independence). The many writers in King's fiction are associated with this group. They have, as King noted in an interview with me, real "powers. They are the only recognized mediums of our society. Our job, basically, is to create the possibility of making people believe the unbelievable—the suspension of disbelief" (*The Second Decade* 11).

In his essay on the role of writing in King's novella *The Body*, Leonard Heldreth argues that "writing succeeds for Gordon because it offers control over experience. . . . Writing permits a systematic formulation of the plan or world view and provides the means for keeping it before not only the author but all his readers" (72–73). King reaffirms this point in the interview he gave to *Playboy* magazine in 1983: "Writing is necessary for my sanity. As a writer, I can externalize my fears and insecurities and night terrors on paper. . . . And in the process, I'm able to 'write myself sane,' as that fine poet Anne Sexton put it" (Underwood and Miller 44). The social institutions and the forces of institutionalization enumerated throughout King's canon rely on the persuasive power of social conformity and self-abnegation. But what underlies the severity of this measured control is a disturbing element of insanity, a fascistic madness born from excessive discipline and oppression. The reader need only consider a few of the major purveyors of an institutionalized worldview in King's fiction—Annie Wilkes, Warden Norton, Randall Flagg, the Crimson King, Leland Gaunt, Andre Linoge, Greg Stillson, Mrs. Carmody, the Tommyknockers, the U.S. military—to note a similarity of behavioral traits that are finally reduced to the same thing: a demand for conformity so rigid and relentless that it crosses over into the realm of madness. Their need for ultimate control over other people and situations is more than just unhealthy—it signifies a breakdown in their communication skills, their inability to tolerate divergent thought, and their incapacity to function in a social context. This is true for all of King's evil despots to greater or lesser degrees. When we finally encounter the Crimson King in the last book of *The Dark Tower*, he is violent red lashing out in all directions. When Patrick erases his body, the King's eyes remain—crimson fury crossing over into madness. There is simply no compromising with King's evil avatars; although they often masquerade, like Linoge and Flagg, as the last magicians of rational thought, or as upstanding Christians and socially respectable prison wardens, their true status is that they are violently disturbed sociopaths far removed from any definition of reasonable conduct. King's description of institutionalization as it occurs in *The Tommyknockers* makes the connection between such oppressive dominance and madness explicit: "Their two minds: the human one and the alien one. Always there came a point where the becoming might degenerate into madness—the madness of schizophrenia as the target minds tried to fight the alien mind slowly welding them together . . . and then eclipsing them. This was the time of necessary acceptance" (237).

King's writer-protagonists represent the counterpoint to this dark condition that is so often in league with an infernal supernaturalism. The one exception to this thesis is really no exception at all: Jack Torrance in *The Shining* is a writer whose abrogation of his mind and spirit to the powers at the Overlook Hotel is paralleled in the loss of his desire to write. In fact, it is possible to trace Jack's descent into the collective groupthink of the ghosts at the Overlook in terms of the loss of his desire to write. When he chooses to abandon efforts to write his play in the novel, Torrance loses the release that "let something out of him that might otherwise have swelled and swelled until he burst" (48). Kubrick's film rendition highlights this same loss in the reductive repetition of the "All work and no play makes Jack a dull boy" manuscript, perhaps deliberately punning on the fact that Jack's loss of control over his writing will result in "no play" as well as a "dullness" of effect produced in page after page of the same mechanical cant. Jack is initially seduced by the idea that the hotel is a subject worthy of inspiring his greatest written composition, when in reality his creative energies are siphoned away as he becomes institutionalized into the Overlook's spectral bureaucracy. In Jack's case, writer's block indicates the onset of psychosis.

In contrast to the madness that is always attendant to a uniform groupthink in King's world, other writers in his canon are endowed with tremendous imaginative capacities. Like the child-savants found in King's early novels, his writers are also distinguished from conventional adulthood by virtue of their subversive independence, romantic optimism, and active conscience. As early as the novel *'Salem's Lot,* King proposes that to contravene institutionalization an individual must possess enough imaginative freedom to resist the groupthink—only then do avenues for freedom become recognizable and evil vulnerable. At the end of this novel only a writer, Ben Mears, and a child remain untouched by the uniform vampiric energy that has taken over their town and turned its citizens into the passive-aggressive agents of Barlow, the head revenant. Their dedication to resisting Barlow and the other vampires is rewarded by survival. Other writer-protagonists occupy similar heroic status throughout the King canon. From Bill Denbrough in *IT*, to Thad Beaumont in *The Dark Half*, to Scott Landon in *Lisey's Story*, the writer's job is to reassert selfhood and independence in the midst of conforming behavior and self-destruction. Without the power of his craft, Paul Sheldon in *Misery* could never have survived his sentence as a prisoner in Annie Wilkes's farmhouse penitentiary; similarly, Jessie Burlingame's truest moment of transcendence in *Gerald's Game* comes not in her release from Gerald's handcuffs, but in the act of writing to Ruth Neary, in communicating her experience rather than continuing to repress it and thereby remaining in bondage because of it.

Throughout the novel *Misery*, Paul Sheldon must confront the urge to capitulate to the madness that surrounds him as a prisoner inside Annie Wilkes's world. It is not just that Sheldon is trapped in a rural farmhouse during an interminable winter recovering from a car accident and the inflicted wounds from his tormentor; he is also victim of Annie's internal horrors: a psychopathology that is out of both their abilities to control. In the face of Annie's oppressive madness Paul has only his art—the craft of storytelling—as his weapon. It is a skill that he has taken for granted; it has brought him a very comfortable living as a famous novelist, but he has stopped challenging himself as an artist. In some ways, the author of the Misery Chastain books has fallen asleep at the typewriter—he keeps writing the same book in the same genre featuring the same characters and following a similar plotline for each best seller. Although his work has made him an affluent and famous writer, Paul Sheldon has willingly slipped into an institutionalized state—he knows that his fame and fortune have been purchased by rewriting the same essential plotline—and it takes the raw violence of Annie's oppressiveness to sober him while reawakening his survival skills. Like Warden Norton or Andre Linoge, Annie would have "her pet writer" follow her instructions to the letter—from rebirthing her favorite literary character to joining Annie in a suicide pact. Like the vampires in *'Salem's Lot*, Annie is a kind of rural vampire: she sucks out Paul's inspiration and creativity in order to fashion a self-enclosed world. For much of the novel Paul must submit to her worldview; it is not so much escape that he contemplates as suicide.

Reflecting its place in a post-feminist world, the novel inverts the traditional male villain/besieged female prototype: the story's female character is no mere passive maiden but rather the agenda-setter. Like the masculine monsters that precede her throughout the history of the gothic novel and the horror film, Annie is a female version of the gothic villain-monster, and her aggressive impulses are frequently aligned with masculine images of rape, as when she forces Paul to swallow pain medications or silences him when outsiders on the property are searching for Paul. Conversely, Paul assumes the role of the traditional romance heroine: like Miranda in John Fowles's *The Collector*, Paul is kidnapped and held against his will, bound to his bed, is forced to placate his captor with language that will not offend, and is reliant on her for food and medicine. But whereas Miranda is sacrificed to the will of her captor, a victim of her own femininity, Paul is able to triumph over the subjugation that is imposed upon him. The creation of her art offers Miranda no real opportunity for salvation or transcendence in her time of need. Sheldon, on the other hand, uses his art to escape the bondage that eventually kills Miranda.

As is often the case in King's texts, the novel features a dynamic struggle for power, and in the course of the narrative, as Paul regains his authorial prowess, the reader witnesses a slow shift in this dynamic; Paul's skill as a storyteller triumphs over Annie's sadistic need for controlling every aspect of their relationship. His art, in other words, poses a counterbalance to Annie's madness. It staves off the darkness long enough for Paul to recognize the importance of his freedom and his desire to break from the institutionalized condition that has Annie trapped within and would likewise have him remain there as well: "He wondered in a dull sort of way how close he was to going insane" (226). Through his self-discipline and mental toughness, but most of all through the inspiration afforded by his writing talents, Paul reconnects to the only certainty that has ever existed in his life: the stability born "through the hole in the page" via the act of writing (310). By commencing a new novel that holds Annie in the same death grasp in which she holds him, Paul buys time to strengthen his broken body and the opportunity to thwart Annie's indomitable will. Like any successful artistic challenge, he learns how to create meaning out of personal suffering, triumph out of despair.

In this sense, then, King inverts the clichéd romantic stereotype of art as the product of madness. Instead, as King's *Playboy* interview suggests, the art of writing is a means for attaining sanity and avoiding the madness of institutional uniformity. Despite the loneliness necessitated by its creation, writing is ultimately a means of connection to others; it is thus aligned with Andy Dufresne's acts of selflessness to other men at

Shawshank, his love of music, and his commitment to freedom and independence in the face of forces that would strip him of his selfhood. The writer's magic is a similar sort of liberation. Like the escape hole in the wall of Shawshank prison that becomes Andy's "pipe dream" all the way down to Mexico, the "hole in the page" that Paul Sheldon falls into while reawakening the powers of his craft stands in the face of King's oppressive institutions and the negative energies of institutionalization.

Chapter 4

Sex with Consequences: Sexuality and Its Discontents

Stephen King's universe contains ample evidence of free will at work; characters flourish or perish primarily because of choices they make. John Smith makes a conscious decision to thwart the political career of Greg Stillson, Louis Creed elects to revisit the Micmac burial site to bring his son and wife back from the dead, and Andy Dufresne makes up his mind to "get busy living" by disappearing through a tunnel under the bowels of Shawshank prison. More often than not, in the King universe free will and moral choice are solidly within the individual's purview. As Carroll Terrell points out in his discussion of the religious implications in *The Stand*, "This confirmation of the power of light over the power of darkness allows for free will as Harold Lauder, the bright boy of the book understands. He may go with the light or the dark, but whatever he does, he agrees with Jean Paul Sartre, that he's condemned to be free" (146).

In the choice of good or evil, how King's characters respond to the issue of personal sexuality is often the clearest indicator of a man or woman's true nature. People of good will in his canon tend to gravitate toward sexual relationships that mirror their personalities: nurturing, open, and responsive to others. Correspondingly, the sexuality of evil is sterile and isolating. When King's characters are seduced by the corruption of what the writer tends to view as a warped sexuality, it is symptomatic of moral failing. Once they succumb, they eventually forfeit their identities and the ability to control their own destinies. In contrast, characters who manage to forge sexual unions that do not rely upon the oppression of someone else tend to create happier and more heroic lives.

In the *Playboy* interview published in 1983, early in his career, King was remarkably candid on the subject of sex, acknowledging his own personal conservatism which, in turn, will be seen to inform his fiction as well: "I think I have pretty normal sexual appetites, whatever the word normal means in these swinging times. . . . There's a range of sexual variations that turn me on, but I'm afraid they're all boringly unkinky" (Underwood and Miller 45). As a purveyor of horror art, King is professionally disposed toward speculating on worst-case scenarios: What happens when the government loses control over its germ warfare program? What happens when substance abuse addictions or obsessions with power grow beyond the individual's ability to regulate? And what happens to sexuality when it expresses itself outside the guiding strictures of love? This last question must be viewed in light of what the writer deems a "normal sexual appetite"; as deviant sexual practices become more frequent and intense in each of King's books, the participants' affiliation with evil becomes correspondingly stronger. In King's world this means that sex performed without the blessing bond of heterosexual love is always lascivious and malefic, while the capacity to control lust and violence—that is, maintaining sexuality as a means for the expression of love—is related to the ability to resist evil and choose good. The fall from innocence in King's universe is not simply the loss of physical virginity, for King has very clear demarcations regarding sexuality. Innocence is in fact affirmed in normative heterosexual relationships. By contrast, those characters that participate in "alternative sexualities" usually mark their fall from grace through deviant sexual expression. Once this fall occurs and a character is marked with deviance, the effects usually prove fatal, morally and mortally. The severity of King's judgment here might be tied to his career-long association with the Gothic, wherein transgressions against the status quo—particularly sexual transgressions—result in horrific consequences; or perhaps it is the influence of the writer's strong Methodist upbringing, or the ambiance of New England Puritanism with which King has lived nearly his entire life. A combination of all these factors, in addition to his own forty-year monogamous marriage, invariably translates the sexual behavior of his fictional characters into spiritual barometers. And nowhere is this moralistic paradigm more in evidence than in the unexpurgated edition of *The Stand*.

FREE WILL AND SEXUAL CHOICE IN *THE STAND*

When we first encounter Glen Bateman, arguably King's philosophical spokesman in the novel, he is reprimanding his dog, Kojak, availing him with instruction on behavior that is notable for its relevance to both the canine and human worlds: "Always remember, Kojak, that control is what separates the higher orders from the lower. Control!" (327). Bateman's seemingly innocuous remark turns out to be one of *The Stand*'s guiding principles. Throughout the novel, the degree to which an individual is capable of adhering to Bateman's principle of self-control signifies which side of the Rockies that character will call home. And this is especially true when this standard is applied to sexual choices and behavior. In the Free Zone, we see ample evidence of healthy sexual unions; most of Boulder's men and women do not use sex as a form of manipulation or degradation. Perhaps the best examples of such relationships are between Frannie and Stu and between Larry and Lucy. When Nadine Cross tempts Larry with the offer of her virginity, it is not an offer inspired by love or genuine affection; she comes to him out of selfishness: she wishes to use him to erect a barrier against Flagg's design to make her his dark bride. And it is thus significant that her seduction is interpreted by Larry as a kind of rape, since, like a rapist, Nadine is far more interested in power than she is in sex: "Let me finish. I want to stay here, can't you understand that? And if we're with each other, I'll be able to. You're my last chance. Make love to me and that will be the end of it. I'll be safe. Safe. I'll be safe" (758–759).

In his refusal to succumb to her demands, Larry shows a level of self-control and loyalty (to Lucy) that has long been missing from his personality. The scene highlights a moral "crossroad" for both Cross and Underwood. From the point of his rejection to the end of the novel, Larry's personal ethics are never again in doubt. It is important to note that his passage through the dark night of the soul is associated with refusing sexuality because the act would take place for the wrong reasons. His self-denial provides him with the opportunity to lay claim to Lucy—who is pregnant with his child—as a reward. Nadine, on the other hand, views her rebuff as destiny; unlike Larry, who finally discovers the capacity for exerting his moral will, she surrenders hers to the dark man. As she walks away from Larry, her corruption is symbolically ordained in King's description of the landscape with which she merges: "She was a black shape distinguishable from other black shapes only when she crossed the street. Then she disappeared altogether against the black background of the mountains" (759). Women such as Nadine Cross or Nona, in the early dark dominatrix tale named after her, employ sex to seduce and to manipulate rather than rape in King's universe. In both cases, however, King is unequivocal in the association he makes between violent or manipulative sex and the corruption of selfhood.

At the opposite extreme of the self-control extolled by Bateman and illustrated in Larry Underwood's final rejection of Nadine, King provides a group of immoral men who have used the collapse of civilization to indulge their hostility toward women. The four men who maintain "the zoo" have kidnapped eight women and hold them as sexual slaves. The sole purpose of this enterprise is the carnal gratification of the men involved; their captives are stripped of their humanity, reduced to orifices which are filled or tortured according to the daily whims of the men in charge: "'I'd get up in the morning, be raped two or three times, and then wait for Doc to hand out the pills,' said Susan matter-of-factly" (549).

In light of the close affiliation between sexuality and personal morality maintained throughout *The Stand,* it is interesting that when the women in "the zoo" are liberated by Frannie, Harold, Glen, and Stu, their response toward the men who have mistreated them is to return violence for violence. Dayna Jurgens, Susan Stern, and Patty Kroger, in particular, behave in a manner that is decidedly "unfeminine," shattering one captor's head with the stock of a shotgun, violently squeezing another's crotch, and releasing "a long primeval scream of triumph that haunted Fran Goldsmith for the rest of her life" (544). Rape has forced "the zoo" women to break with traditional feminine behavior; to survive these vicious sexual circumstances, they emulate the worst behavior of men. Their experience as sexual victims goes on to affect each of these women for the remainder of the novel. None of them fully recovers, suicide and self-immolation haunt them, and all are left incapable of divorcing sexuality from violence and deception. Dayna's choice of suicide, rather than aiding Flagg with information about the Free Zone once her identity as a spy is revealed in Vegas, is the first indication that Flagg's indomitable will, particularly over women, is not so indomitable. Dayna's suicide must be seen as an act of defiance against Flagg, and it points the way to Nadine's own death.

In Flagg's city-state and in the parallel microcosm of "the zoo," women exist to satisfy the dark and salacious sexual urges of the men in control. Nadine's artificially imposed virginity—insisted upon by Flagg and imposed at the expense of her natural and spontaneous emotions—is a condition analogous to that of the women who are held in sexual bondage in "the zoo." The language used to describe Flagg's "seduction" of Cross is always suggestive of rape. Interestingly, he "enters" her for the first time in a kind of psychological rape—sustaining the novel's affiliation between rape and a conscious choice to perform evil—that occurs the moment after she elects to ignore the voice of her conscience in order to plant the bomb that will destroy members of the Free Zone committee. The cold numbness and eventual catatonia Nadine experiences during and after Flagg's defilement is reminiscent of the chemically induced impassivity and sexual stupefaction experienced by the women held against their will in "the zoo": "Nadine was blind, she was deaf, she was without a sense of touch. . . . And she felt him creep into her. A shriek built up within her, but she had no mouth with which to scream. *Penetration: entropy*. She didn't know what those words meant, put together like that; she only knew they were right" (860). Nadine Cross sells her soul to the devil, serving as a dark parody of the Madonna herself. Her job is to provide the Dark Man with a Dark Child, and she does so first in the corruption of the boy-man Harold Lauder. In fact, Harold and Nadine are cast as parallel figures in their mutual loneliness, psychological susceptibility, and their view of sexual choices as a determination of selfhood. Not only does Nadine prey upon Harold's virginity, tempting him with promises of sensations never known, she likewise encourages his penchant for sexual perversion: "'We can do anything—everything—but that one little thing. And that one little thing really isn't so important, is it?' Images whirled giddily in his mind. Silk scarves . . . boots . . . leather . . . rubber. Oh Jesus" (793).

It is important that Nadine's "one little thing" is forever denied to Harold. The fact that Lauder technically dies a virgin, never having actually participated in intercourse, serves to highlight his failure to view sex as anything more than a self-enclosed masturbatory act—its sole purpose, his own orgasm. Nadine is willing to manipulate him via his own sexual fantasies, and she accomplishes this primarily through oral sex, becoming nothing more than an extension of Harold's chronic urge to masturbate (as he does on even the most inappropriate occasions—e.g., after stealing and reading the negative commentary in Frannie's journal). Harold and Nadine's sexuality thus mirrors their isolation in life; seduced by the urge to control the other rather than motivated by the selfless action of love, both characters end up committing suicide.

Most of the major events that occur in the novel—the choices that are made, the consequences that result from actions initiated are sexually motivated. Those characters in *The Stand* unable to resist sexual entrapment sever their connection to humanity and forge a link to evil. Flagg, Harold Lauder, The Kid, the "zookeepers," and others like them are modern versions of Adam after the Fall, who instead of only losing the Garden of Eden, have also relinquished their self-respect, the love of Eve, and the hope of any reconciliation with God. Other characters—Stu Redman, Larry Underwood, Glen Bateman, and Frannie Goldsmith—demonstrate control over their sexual selves and behave in a manner that is both altruistic and morally responsible. In this latter group, the truest model of human survival, we find the greatest hope for the future precisely because it has maintained contact with the greatest virtues from the past. Frannie and Stu begin to revivify their empty lives through the act of sexual intercourse: "Fran cried out her pleasure at the end of it, as her good orgasm burst through her" (559). In contrast, as Harold watches this healthy exchange from deep within the shadows, the seed of corruption is planted within him: "Neither of them saw Harold, as shadowy and as silent as the dark man himself, standing in the bushes and looking at them" (559). His next choice, to steal a look at her diary without permission, is another, metaphorical extension of the novel's rape imagery, as Harold violates both Frannie's trust and her personal privacy.

As T. S. Eliot lamented the death of civilization through sexual encounters and inferences devoid of love in *The Waste Land*, King likewise suggests that humankind forsakes its connection to both God and man in the degradation of sexuality. Ultimately, over the course of his writing career King has established a rigidly didactic continuum, especially in light of the consistency with which the subject is treated in his fiction and films. Only the most conservative form of heterosexual expression—missionary position intercourse between a man and a woman who love each other—is deemed "normal"; homosexuality is overwhelmingly viewed as deviant and corrupt; heterosexual sex that occurs outside the perimeters of love or as part of an adulterous relationship usually evolves into coercion; while bondage, cross-dressing, fetish indulgence, and even oral sex between consenting partners (recall the disastrous consequences of car sex in *Thinner*) verge into the abject. As King opines in the *Playboy* interview: "I'm not into the sadomasochistic trip, either, on which your competitor *Penthouse* has built an entire empire . . . despite all the artistic gloss and the gauzy lens and the pastel colors, it's still sleaze; it still reeks corruptingly of concentration-camp porn" (Underwood and Miller 45).

The collapse of civilization and civilized values in both *The Stand* and within the city of Lud in *The Dark Tower III: The Waste Lands* is signaled by many disruptive elements: the abatement of law, the physical degradation of the social infrastructure, the omnipresent threat of violence. But once again it is in his treatment of sexuality—specifically homosexuality—that King highlights most dramatically societal unraveling into perversity. The superflu in *The Stand* and post–nuclear war environment in *The Waste Lands* has not only depopulated the respective landscapes; it has also placed those few remaining survivors into an ethical vacuum: in the absence of official law, institutions, and traditions, the very concept of "civilization" is deconstructed and then reconstructed as deviant. Without an existing system to enforce restraint, individuals uprooted and wandering the waste land feel free to indulge in behavior that would have been socially objectionable in pre-apocalyptic America. Survival becomes an essential goal, decency and restraint are no longer operative values, and suicide is sometimes a preferable alternative in these landscapes without pity. As Gasher cautions Jake in *The Waste Lands*, "Beg if you want, dear heart. Just don't expect no good to come of it, for mercy stops on this side of the bridge" (462).

In both these texts, sexual deviance is the unnatural outgrowth of unrestrained impulse and expressions of fear and paranoia; and frequently, whenever King wishes to illustrate the large-scale breakdown in both societal and personal ethics, he does so through either the threat or the actualization of a violent homosexuality. This level of intimate deviance appears in the form of homosexual rape, and for those characters who embody its permutations most fully, The Kid (*The Stand*) and Gasher and Tick Tock Man (*The Waste Lands*), reliance on such an intrusive violence is an extension of their degraded personalities. For these adult males, boys and men are reconfigured as feminine, leading to warped expressions of homoerotic frenzy. Without the blessing bond of love, sex in King's world is always lascivious and malefic, as we find in the sadomasochistic intercourse that takes place between Trashcan Man and The Kid in *The Stand*: "Whining, Trashcan began to stroke him again. His whines became little gasps of pain as the barrel of the .45 worked its way into him, rotating, gouging, tearing. And could it be that this was exciting him? It was . . . 'Like it, dontcha?' The Kid panted. 'I knew you would, you bag of pus. You like having it up your ass, dontcha? Say yes, or right to hell you go'" (587–588).

Sex without love, be it homosexual or heterosexual, in King's moral universe is always a manipulative force that belies fundamental character flaws in an individual. Although he is confronted with heavily armed strangers at the gate of his dystrophic city in *The Waste Lands*, Gasher is focused only on capturing young Jake; his warped sexuality, in other words, has reached the point at which he is willing to risk even his own life and to allow the gunslingers to pass freely in order to possess the boy child. Gasher's sexual fascination with Jake, to whom he constantly refers as a "sweet little boycunt" and "sweet cheeks" (430) is an extension of his venereal illness, so advanced that Roland recognizes Gasher's imminent mortality and is sobered by it: "The oozing sores on his face had nothing to do with radiation; unless Roland was badly deceived, this man was in the late stages of what the doctors called mandrus and everyone else called whore's blossoms" (419).

The city of Lud in *The Waste Lands* has as much in common with Dante's city of Dis as it does with a post-apocalyptic portrait of New York. Along with its decaying bridges and populace on the verge of extinction, the city's value system is similarly fetid. Controlled by roving gangs of violent thugs who have separated into two warring groups—the Pubes and the

Grays, bent on mutual annihilation—the city's corruption is highlighted in the dark subplot of an adult masculine obsession with young boys. After crossing over the bridge into Lud, it is as if the Gunslinger and his posse have entered into a place that "reeks corruptingly of concentration-camp porn" with its corresponding social Darwinism and inversion of any notion of an acceptable sexuality. Indeed, normative heterosexuality and homosexuality defined between consenting adults is displaced by a rape culture that appears to prize young boys as the ultimate sexual prize. Gasher's violence toward Jake as they make their way through the forsaken cityscape on their way to the Tick Tock Man barely masks his sexual arousal; in fact, the two obscene impulses feed each other. In King's universe, this perversion of both healthy homosexual and heterosexual response is a metaphor for the loss of spiritual and social codes of ethics in a post-apocalyptic world. Homosexual pedophilia is thus coded by King to signal the final degeneration of an entire world gone insane.

In his article discussing homosexuality in King's novel *IT*, Douglas Keesey, attempting to rescue the narrative from the charge of homophobia, argues something different: "[I]f society is disturbed by the homophobic violence in [King's] fiction, it should recognize and criticize its own homophobia rather than blaming the writer for it. In such accusations, the writer becomes the scapegoat for homophobic attitudes that society can continue to hold" (189). While argued reasonably, this position completely lets King off the hook. He is, after all, the man in control of his art, and we should demand that art do more—by way of confronting instead of simply mirroring—existing social injustices. Indeed, over the years in nearly every other possible cultural context—the public school system, religious zealotry, governmental authority, gender relationships, and race and class delineations—King's fiction has relentlessly challenged the status quo. But whenever the writer confronts the issue of personal sexuality, particularly nontraditional forms of sexual expression, his staunchly progressive politics take a sharp turn right.

THE LIMITS OF LIBERALISM: HOMOEROTICISM

King's treatment of homosexuality throughout his literary career has been particularly less than enlightened. I can think of no evidence of gay or lesbian relationships that King portrays as mature, morally responsible, or loving, but there exist plenty of examples to assert that he employs homosexuality as a metaphor for oppression, and this is especially true in the context of adult male homoeroticism. In *The Shawshank Redemption*, for instance, Bogs and The Sisters are "bull queers" who assault Andy Dufresne, making his first few years at Shawshank prison nearly unbearable. While their intrusive violence leads Red to acknowledge that they "have to be human first" to qualify as homosexuals, the fact that both the novel and film define The Sisters solely in terms of their sexuality works as an implicit indictment of their homosexuality. The director of the film adaptation, Frank Darabont, has tried to distance himself from charges of homophobia by insisting that The Sisters are not gay but rapists who substitute men when women are unavailable ("The Buzz" 70). But as Edward Madden counters more convincingly, "The rapists, however, are still labeled 'queens' or queers: they are still marked as homosexual" (192).

Apt Pupil, like many other King narratives, features an old male–young boy relationship that protects a shared secret. Although this secret concerns Nazi criminal activity during World War II, the malefic bond that Dussander and Todd develop also possesses strong homosexual overtones, to the point where Todd has difficulties with impotence when his girlfriend Becky tries to perform fellatio on him; she later mocks him in the assertion that "maybe you just don't like girls." In the novel, Todd's homosexual impulses are more explicitly formulated; he fantasizes himself in front of a half-naked Dussander and a young Jewish female, the latter bound to the four corners of an examination table. The Nazi directs the boy to secure a hollow dildo over his erect penis, which he then uses to penetrate the girl. In this sadomasochistic threesome, Todd becomes a literal sexual "appendage" of the older man; the boy rapes the defenseless woman while Dussander is raping Todd scientifically, recording "pulse, blood pressure, respiration, alpha waves, beta waves, stroke count" (189). In the film version of *Apt Pupil*, the Nazi acknowledges that he and his pupil are "fucking each other," even though he means this metaphorically rather than literally. The homeless man that Todd and Dussander murder, however, interprets their relationship on a physical plane, initially offering himself sexually to the former Nazi under the not-so-mistaken belief that Todd and Dussander are engaged in a sexual liaison.

The physical connection that the teenager and Dussander do maintain includes a scene of quasi-erotic dress-up, where Todd insists that the old man wear a Nazi war uniform and parade in front of him. While Dussander prepares himself upstairs, Todd eagerly awaits his return in the kitchen; the sequence is highly suggestive of a lover anticipating the emergence of his beloved adorned in fetish clothing recently purchased for their mutual sexual arousal. Indeed, in this film homosexuality becomes yet another secret linked to the various historical secrets shared between the apt pupil and his teacher; as such, homosexuality is demonized by virtue of its association with Nazism. At the end of the film, Todd resorts to homosexual accusations as a means to intimidate Mr. French, the school guidance counselor; the boy's level of aptitude in manipulating the negative implications of homosexuality is meant to signify his graduation to a higher grade of evil. Though the novel details explicit homoerotic dream sequences to underscore the corruption of the Dussander-Bowden relationship, the film covers a broader range of implications—all of them negative. The murder of the homeless man, by self-admission homosexually inclined, is treated as nothing more than a final test of Todd's Nazi education, a rite of passage into the sensation of murdering ("How did it feel?"), while Todd's threat to blackmail Mr. French with a false sexual assault allegation carries the dual weights of pedophilia and homosexuality.

These examples underscore a plethora of similar homosexual and homoerotic couplings that appear throughout King's work. Without qualification these bonds are used to illustrate only psychological maladjustment and sexual depravity, as well as the degree to which the individuals involved have been morally tainted. Yet, ironically, some of the strongest and most life-affirming unions that take place in this writer's world occur in same-sex relationships. Andy and Red in *The Shawshank Redemption*; Edgecomb and Coffey in *The Green Mile*; Vera and Dolores in *Dolores Claiborne*; Roland, Cuthbert, and Alain in *The Dark Tower: Wizard and Glass*; and the numerous male-bonding permutations found in *Stand by Me*, *Hearts in Atlantis*, and *Dreamcatcher* are intensely intimate, but never sexual. King appreciates the value of same-sex bonds; they are, in fact, some of his most compelling portraits, but he steers clear of investing them with any kind of homoerotic charge—at least overtly.

In her essay "White Soul: The 'Magical Negro' in the Films of Stephen King," Sarah Nilsen argues that homoerotic interracial bonds exist throughout the cinematic universe inspired by King's narratives; covert same-sex sexual desire is located in a symbolic realm that is diffused through heterosexual coupling. Thus, the "homoerotic implications of the relationship between Red and Andy are neutralized through the cinematic fantasy of Rita Hayworth" (137). Similarly, in *The Green Mile*, when Coffey cures Edgecomb's urinary infection by squeezing his crotch, any homosexual rape inference is deflected when Paul later employs his newfound sexual potency to please his wife "several times" in one night. "The homosocial bond between Coffey and Edgecomb," Nilsen writes, "is a friendship dependent on the necessary sacrifice of the magical Negro so that white masculinity can be sustained, while simultaneously negating homosexual desire" (138). However, in a parallel scene that occurs later in the film and novel, Wild Bill expresses his sexuality without similar obfuscations, when he strokes Percy Wetmore's crotch while whispering in his ear that he is soft like a girl and that he wants to fuck his asshole, and later invites him to "suck my dick." Although his real crimes are murder and pedophilia, Wild Bill is a compendium of psychosexual perversions, and King makes it clear that overt homosexuality is among them. Thus, unlike the bond that exists between Red and Andy or Coffey and Edgecomb, where homoerotic impulses are kept in check by the presence of sexualized cinematic starlets and an erotically responsive wife, respectively, Wild Bill becomes another example of the nexus King forges between out-of-control (homo)sexuality and malefic intent. As with Wild Bill, The Kid (who rapes Trashcan Man) in *The Stand,* and Sunlight Gardner in *The Talisman*, many of King's most perverted adult male figures underscore their mental instability and social pathology through an out-of-control homosexual compulsion to rape boys and sexually naïve heterosexual males. Although these figures try hard to disguise their ardent homoeroticism through macho displays of masculine toughness and bravado, eventually their dictatorial violence expresses itself most essentially through their homosexuality. This compulsion, finally, should be viewed not just as an extension of their need to dominate others sexually; it is also a means for King to distance these characters from any degree of reader/viewer sympathy.

DOMESTIC HETEROSEXUALITY

Just as tightly controlled as his efforts to portray homosocial unions that negate or defray erotic desire in order to legitimize de-sexualized same-sex relationships, King shows no inclination to provide a counterbalancing force—examples of homosexuality as a potential alternative to the marital violence and sexual tyranny that the writer frequently associates with heterosexuality. Interestingly, the examples of homosexual rape and heterosexual marital sex in King's world are often disturbingly similar. King's gay men typically prey on the weak and vulnerable, take what they need without consent, and are concerned with only their own sexual satisfaction. Many of King's husbands share a similar bedroom agenda, particularly those males who populate the writer's "domestic fiction" beginning with *Cujo* in 1982 and culminating with the 1990s trilogy of patriarchal abuse: *Dolores Claiborne, Gerald's Game*, and *Rose Madder*. In all these texts, feminine bondage, as both literal erotic sexual foreplay and as feminist metaphor, is aligned with father-daughter incest, sexual and psychological violence against women, and the financial and cultural domination of women. Susie Bright recognizes and objects to the limits imposed by these gendered constructions when she posits that "King is an architect of female protectionism playing hard and fast under feminist rhetoric. Men, exemplified by Daddy and Husband, are pretentious brutes who are impossible to identify with" (54). Although King's intention is to create strong female protagonists who discover their own selfhood by eventually standing up to brutish fathers and husbands, he does so at the expense of men—who emerge as violent caricatures—but also at the expense of all sexual expression.

The important solar eclipse in *Dolores Claiborne* and *Gerald's Game* should be read as a metaphor for the condition of being female in a patriarchal culture: cut off, blocked, obscured. The symbolic eclipsing of a woman's life, these two texts suggest, occurs in that period when a man is sexually prominent in it. A female is free only when she acts on Vera's recognition that "sometimes being a bitch is all a woman has to hold on to" and escapes from beneath the sexual shadow cast by a man—be that man her father or her husband. Thus, it is no accident that each of these texts ends with women estranged from any kind of sexual activity, and they certainly want nothing more to do with men, especially in the bedroom. In some fashion, Vera and Dolores marry one another as a natural consequence of two "widowed" women who have "remarried," this time into a relationship based on respect and friendship instead of sex. Though Jessie Burlingame appears attracted to yet another disturbingly familiar lawyer-type, Brandon Milheron, at the end of *Gerald's Game*, it is also clear that her drawn-out foursome with husband Gerald, Raymond Joubert, and her father Tom Mahout has so scarred Jessie sexually that her libido may be stunted forever. As she concludes in a confessional memoir to her friend Ruth: "[I]f I never go to bed with another man, I will be absolutely delighted" (298). In *Gerald's Game* and *Dolores Claiborne*, all of King's female protagonists grow so disillusioned by abusive male sexuality that they retreat into asexual, exclusively female relationships.

Violent sexual predators roam the landscapes of King's universe, and they are invariably male. The figure of the heterosexual serial rapist is a recurring male figure throughout King's film and fictional canons; the prototype is Billy Nolan from *Carrie*, and his line of primitive descendants includes Steve Kemp and Joe Camber from *Cujo*, Frank Dodd in *The Dead Zone*, Buddy Repperton in *Christine*, the "zookeepers" in *The Stand*, Henry Bowers in *IT*, George Stark in *The Dark Half*, Joe St. George in *Dolores Claiborne*, Norman Daniels in *Rose Madder*, Ace Merrill in *Stand by Me*, The Sisters in *The Shawshank Redemption*, Wild Bill in *The Green Mile*, Jim "Zack McCool" Dooley in *Lisey's Story*, and Jim Pickering in "The Gingerbread Girl." So pervasive are these sexual deviants that one or more of his brethren haunts the perimeters of nearly every King film and fiction; he occupies a central narrative presence in at least half the examples cited above, and he is the violent antagonist against whom King's heroines must struggle.

All of these males bear easily recognizable familiarities: short of temper and intelligence, they cannot separate sexuality from sadism, and they view sexuality solely as a vehicle for controlling and punishing, particularly women and children. In the short story "The Gingerbread Girl," Jim Pickering, who is "not a very nice man" (94), has assembled a home in Florida that is used for the singular purpose of torturing and sexually abusing women, the "nieces" he brings in for his forays into perverted pleasure. When the murder of one these girlfriends is noted by Emily, the protagonist of the story, Pickering provides her with a dose of his charming hospitality: first duct-taping her to a chair, promising to rape her before he kills her, and then assaulting her with a variety of kitchen implements. He has no problem putting this perfect stranger into the role of one of his "nieces," picking up with Emily where he left off after bludgeoning Nicole. In fact, Emily recognizes her bond with his other women victims when she acknowledges herself as "The last niece . . . the one who had survived" (110). Like the archetypical Gothic heroine trapped in the Gothic villain's dungeon, Emily quickly recognizes that Pickering's house structurally serves his homicidal purposes: "The whole house was, including the room from which she had escaped—the room that looked like a kitchen but was actually an operating theater, complete with easy-clean counters and floors" (103). All of King's villains are reminiscent of classic Hollywood monsters in both their relentless pursuit and the capacity for both receiving and inflicting pain. In his quest to subdue Emily, it is clear that Pickering is motivated by more than just the fear of being caught and punished by the law; like the serial killer who cannot control his compulsion toward mayhem, he has developed an obvious mania for violence against women.

Devoid of tenderness and the capacity to love, these savage boy-men spend their days devising methods of spreading torture and destruction. They are always products of abusive and frequently broken families, and the levels of anger and hostility with which they greet the world reflect the parental legacy of neglect they have inherited. Over the decades, King has written about many unsavory male characters, but this group represents the "bottom feeders" among them. Alcohol and the incessant urge for vengeance inflame psychopathologies that point the way to rape and sexual perversion; in fact, most of these males, if they function at all sexually, require a strong element of violence as erotic foreplay. Consensual sex holds no real attraction for them. More preferable by far are the variant acts outside of procreative intercourse: sodomy, oral, hand jobs, and, in the case of Jim "Zack McCool" Dooley in *Lisey's Story*, meticulous attention to pain: " . . . it was the sound of her screams when Jim Dooley attached her can opener to her left breast like a mechanical leech. She had screamed, and then she had fainted, and then he had slapped her awake to tell her one more thing" (253). Most indicting—unlike King's flawed fathers, those men whose good intentions are always thwarted by the need to feed some personal narcissism, such as Jack Torrance in *The Shining*, Louis Creed in *Pet Sematary*, Andy McGee in *Firestarter*, and Larry McFarland in *The Girl Who Loved Tom Gordon*—the sexual predators in his work are without redeeming values; motivated almost entirely by self-interest and sadomasochistic pleasure, they lack the conflicted natures that inspire reader sympathy and identification with King's equally doomed fathers and husbands.

King "balances" his sexually maladjusted fathers and husbands with idealized figures of perfect husbandry. The moralistic boyfriends and husbands in his narratives—Stu Redman in *The Stand*, Scott Landon in *Lisey's Story*, Bill Denbrough in *IT*, Bill Steiner in *Rose Madder*, Mike Noonan in *Bag of Bones*, and Edgar Freemantle in *Duma Key*—are more than just good; they are chivalric counterpoints to the sexually depraved males who terrify women and children elsewhere in King. Wholly pure in mind and body, these mates prove, however, to be just as unimaginative as King's sexual predators. The latter repulse readers in the wake of their constant brutality, while the New Age perfectionism of their predictable counterparts bore us with their cloying sensitivity. Not coincidentally, perhaps, many of King's New Age males are also famous novelists, and they are married to women who worship their husbands' genius, both in and out of bed.

Those few successful marriages that do exist in King's world are so traditional that they are reminiscent of the 1950s, King's own childhood reference point. Although King himself grew up the child of a single parent, the domestic idyll of the American nuclear family is clearly what the writer has found in his own marriage and continues to employ as a model for several of his own fictional alter egos. When sexual intimacy occurs in these idealized relationships, however, it is of a highly sentimentalized variety: contact shared between appreciative men and women who neither resent one another nor harbor secret agendas in the bedroom. Consider, for example, this rarified moment from *Rose Madder*: "He began kissing her. Five minutes later she *did* feel close to fainting, half in a dream and half out, excited in a way she had never conceived of, excited in a way that made sense of all the books and stories and movies she hadn't really understood before but had taken on faith, the way a blind person will take on faith a sighted person's statement that the sunset is beautiful" (272). This response resembles less adult sexuality than the puerile headiness of adolescence, less the sharpened instincts one would expect in a woman emerging from an abusive marriage than the cultivation of childlike innocence.

Even after one of these spouses dies, as in *Bag of Bones* and *Lisey's Story*, the memory of his or her presence is so strong as to preclude a viable life outside the marriage years after its end. Although the surviving spouse is left young and vital, the loss of an idyllic marriage—and especially the lingering recollection of its sexual aura—makes the remaining spouse reluctant to pursue new, inferior partners. In *Lisey's Story*, Lisey views herself as the caretaker of her husband's literary and cultural legacy; this becomes her life's work. The novel begins with a sentence that essentially defines her place in the one-sided union: "To the public eye, the spouses of well-known writers are all but invisible, and no one knew it better than Lisey Landon" (3). Never once, however, in the course of this long novel does Lisey resent or struggle against the fact that her life—which continues long after Scott's death—has remained subordinate to her husband's success and fame. "With the curiosity of an archaeologist and the ache of a lover" (210), she immolates herself at the altar of his memory, even as the reader is left questioning the rationale behind such unconditional love. In the end, although Lisey proves far more interesting than the husband she idolizes, she adds to the romantic cliché of their marriage in perpetuating the role of the grieving widow. Moreover, while Scott's voice channeling through Lisey permits him a kind of spectral presence throughout this narrative, that voice never once chastises his wife's decision to sacrifice her life in the present in favor of paying homage to his dead past. Beneath the veneer of Scott's vigilant husbandry, then, lurks the need to maintain his superstar entitlement, even postmortem.

As a chronicler of postmodern Americana—particularly those elements in American culture that tend to provoke controversy and challenge norms and assumptions—King's attitude toward sexuality is remarkably staid. While highly attuned to the negative abuses that often characterize heterosexual marriages and the worst homoerotic compulsions, the writer is, on the other hand, closed to portraying liberated constructions of either homosexual or heterosexual unions. In fact, despite his occasional romanticized marriage, and that typically between a grieving widow or widower and a dead spouse, King tends most to envision sexuality in Victorian terms: as a vehicle for expressing darker visions of lust, the wellspring of a more thoroughgoing iniquity, with women and young males as the usual targets for such temptation.

King's body of work acknowledges that in spite of its various concessions to sexual liberation since the 1960s, American culture still remains deeply conflicted in its attitude toward the subject. Although sexuality is a ubiquitous presence in American life—in advertising, on the streets of our cities, and in an array of video formats that promote its ease of consumption and levels of promiscuity—we are still remarkably terrified of its deviant potency, no closer than were our parents and perhaps even our grandparents to viewing sex as an inclusive, less-than-monumental normative activity. As Bright ponders: "Why is semen—more than blood, pus, and sewage put together—the most grotesque bodily fluid in American literature? The King James Bible seems to be our companion reader to every Stephen King novel" (54). As is the case for many Americans, sex in Stephen King is either cloyingly romanticized—locked in the domain of rarified white, bourgeois marriages, such as those found in *Bag of Bones* and *Lisey's Story*—or it sinks to the level of vulgar appetite, in the form of brutal male rape assaults, both heterosexual and especially homosexual, and femme fatale duplicity, the latter best exemplified in *Christine*, Nadine Cross, and Nona. In either case, the subject remains imprisoned in the domain of juvenilia, outside the realm of a mature middle ground. As representation of a Victorian marital ideal or as a specific manifestation of gendered evil, King's attitude toward sexuality is typically to render it functional; sex in his work is never just harmless erotic play or a satisfying extension of adult need and expression. In fact, sex in Stephen King never just *is*, but instead exists metaphorically, in constant service to the author's larger narrative and moralistic designs.

Chapter 5

Why *The Shining* Still Matters: Revisiting and Reinterpreting the Novel and Films

Published in 1977, *The Shining* was Stephen King's first best seller. Nearly everything Stephen King has published since then—from short story collections and other novels to manuals on writing and books about baseball—have found their way to the best-seller list. They have all helped to make Stephen King America's Storyteller, one of the most recognizable living authors in the American canon. But ask any King fan, or any literary critic who takes this writer seriously, or any film aficionado with an appreciation for either the horror genre or Stanley Kubrick's cinematic canon, and it's likely that he or she will tell you there is something special about *The Shining*. If my various academic colleagues who teach King in high schools and universities around the world are an accurate barometer, this novel remains the King text most likely to find its way into the contemporary classroom. I believe it will be the representative Stephen King book that will endure as the writer's legacy one hundred years from now. One of the questions this chapter seeks to explore is, Why have this novel and Stanley Kubrick's 1980 film adaptation continued to occupy positions of such importance, resonating so many years beyond the shelf life of most best sellers and the movies that are based on them?

More than three decades after its publication, the novel remains arguably the most terrifying work in King's prodigious collection of ghosts, ghouls, and spectral phenomena. Kubrick's film typically appears near the top of every best horror film list, and this in spite of the fact that his movie is rather tame—at least by the terms usually used to evaluate horror films. The 1997 televised miniseries gets fewer accolades from critics and fans alike, but Rebecca De Mornay's strong and sexy Wendy emerges as the saving grace of an otherwise tedious teleplay. This chapter could conceivably focus on why the novel and film have become popular culture icons, referenced in contexts as different as an episode of *Friends* and shopping mall tee-shirts with the menacing face of Jack Nicholson from the "Here's Johnny" moment in the film. But for the fact that Jack Nicholson had won his first Academy Award for *One Flew over the Cuckoo's Nest* a year earlier, he might have been singled out for his dramatic performance in the role of Jack Torrance, another archetypical Nicholson character on the fringe of madness. Although different in their respective takes on the same narrative plot, King and Kubrick each produced classic psychological thrillers in the great and long haunted house tradition; their truest influences are Edgar Allan Poe's "Fall of the House of Usher," Shirley Jackson's *The Haunting of Hill House*, and Hitchcock's *Psycho*. And yet *The Shining* somehow manages to take the haunted house archetype to another level. As in his teleplay for *Rose Red*, King's novel recognizes the subtle play of psychological malady animating the inanimate in *Hill House* and then pushes these correspondences to their wildest extremes, while Kubrick's film, a tour de force in its use of music, color, spatial symmetry, and camera angles, manages to overwhelm us with its telescopic visions both of the awesome and haunting grandeur of nature and of the fragility of a single family's isolated doom. This chapter might also easily speak to the profound influence of King's and Kubrick's respective texts, for the overpowering image of the Overlook Hotel has irrevocably shaped all subsequent films and novels of haunted houses as well as most ghost stories. In the end, the story of the Overlook Hotel is the ultimate ghost story set in the ultimate haunted house.

These are certainly worthwhile pursuits that would help to explain the potency and longevity of both novel and film. But my intentions here are of a different nature; though they have made profound contributions as popular culture texts, *The Shining*(s) also possess profound cultural-historical resonance as specifically *American* works of art. It is on this level that I believe King and Kubrick created masterworks that are as deep a reflection of American culture as the paintings of Norman Rockwell or the music of Aaron Copland, although truth be told, the America represented in *The Shining* is certainly a discordant variance from anything we typically associate with Rockwell and Copland.

The actual plot of the book and film is so deceptively reductive and agonizingly repetitive that *The Simpsons* managed to distill Kubrick's two-and-a-half-hour production into a scorchingly effective ten-minute parody: alcoholic father and husband is seduced by a coven of ghosts who are permanent residents in a Colorado hotel. In order to join them, he is instructed to sacrifice his family but ends up killing only himself (and Hallorann, in Kubrick's surprise cinematic alteration). So perhaps many of us are drawn to this story because we have actually lived it: or if not lived it ourselves, we all know people with drug and alcohol problems who have sacrificed their familial bonds as a consequence of the addiction. We all know men like Jack Torrance who carry the vicious Mr. Hyde beneath the veneer of their cultured and educated Dr. Jekyll, separated only by several martinis that serve to blur the line between beast and civilized man. Like most of us, Jack carries tremendous internal scars. And through his understanding of where these scars originated, King creates a deep emotional connection with his audience. Alcoholism and drug abuse suggest all the symptoms of social decay and all the modes of self-destruction that currently flourish, largely tolerated, in contemporary America. King's treatment of these topics in *The Shining* differs from tabloid television, however, because it is not exploitative. When we watch Jack Torrance struggle with his alcoholism, we experience firsthand the ambivalence that comes with choosing to stay sober. There is none of the cloying complacency or spiritual transcendence that often attends this subject when it is discussed in celebrity magazines or on talk shows.

Midway through the novel, Torrance reveals the anguish of his struggle to remain sober; he understands that his family needs him to stay in recovery, but he also recognizes that sobriety is not very much fun. Initially, there is the righteous enthusiasm of getting your life back under control, but soon, as Torrance acknowledges to Lloyd the spectral bartender, "You start to see things . . . like how the floor of the Wagon is nothing but straight pine boards. Like how all the people sitting in the pews on the Wagon are these flatchested el birdos in long dresses with a little lace around the collar and their hair pulled back into buns so tight you can almost hear it screaming. And that's when you realize what the Wagon really is, Lloyd. It's a church with bars on the windows, a church for women and a prison for you" (242–243). Here is the brilliance of Stephen King's talent. Like Robert Louis Stevenson a century before, he gives us a character whose commitment to self-repression is so stringent that the compulsion to re-indulge his addiction literally consumes him. But unlike Stevenson, who stayed clear of linking either women or sexuality to either the unleashing of Mr. Hyde or the repression of Dr. Jekyll, King complicates Jack's response by contextualizing it into very specifically gendered terms. In Jack's mind, the "Wagon" is transformed into a world of puritanical women, a prison orchestrated by "this reekin bitch with blond hair playing the organ and tellin em to sing louder, sing louder" (243). Women are associated with sobriety and punishment; they put "those guys who used to be your friends, the winos passed out in the gutter" (242), into a prison that, at least as Jack describes it, proves to be even less tolerable than the prison of addiction.

What resonates here is not merely Jack's effort to rationalize his compulsion to drink. It is that Jack's drinking was and is a deliberate effort to undermine the authority of his blond wife, Wendy, who must be viewed as not far removed from the "reekin bitch" Torrance pictures as the jailor riding on board the Wagon. Once again we encounter the image of a prison associated with an American institution—marriage—and another of King's wayward male protagonists struggling with his commitment to it. What we have here is a very complicated offering. Jack Torrance drinks for reasons that he himself doesn't fully understand. But Stephen King does, and he presents enough evidence for his reader to make a judgment. For Torrance, despite his education and experience as a writer, women are uncomplicated stereotypes—they exist either for sexual enticement or punitive denial. Cast into this novel of alcoholism, Jack blames his recidivism on Wendy, whom he views at various moments as sexual enticement at war with overprotective motherhood. No need to mention which misogynistic extreme ultimately wins out; as a generation of horror films from *Psycho* to *Friday the 13th* posit, when in doubt, blame the mother. Like so many people mired in the cycle of addiction, Jack refuses to accept responsibility for his behavior, while he also romanticizes the joys of intoxication. In that part of his mind—the Peter Pan man-child rebel who associates drunkenness with personal expressions of freedom—his family is responsible for his irresponsibility; they keep trying to drag him into the dullness of an adult world where there is all work and no play. Jack Torrance conforms perfectly to the narrowness of American male escapism as described by Leslie Fiedler in *Love and Death in the American Novel*, where men are in constant flight from women who are either oppressive mothers or cloying wives. American literature is also replete with stories and novels that explore the world of substance abuse, but there are few examples that deal with this subject as compellingly as *The Shining*. Some day I would like to teach this book or film with a few members of Alcoholics Anonymous in the audience, as I am certain they would have much to say about Torrance's choices.

"WORK IN A CAR WASH": *THE SHINING* AS AMERICAN ARTIFACT

The Shining continues to intrigue us for many reasons. I keep coming back to those teachers of American literature who choose to pair King's novel with the classics of American literature, such as the stories of Edgar Allan

Poe, who was certainly no stranger to the world of substance abuse. *The Shining*'s emphasis on materialism, class differences, and the hegemonic structures of capitalism likewise finds immediate correspondences in other core American texts, such as Fitzgerald's *The Great Gatsby*, Wolfe's *The Bonfire of the Vanities*, and Ellis's *American Psycho*; and the text's importance as a narrative about the American frontier—its relationship to the West, to Native Americans, and to discussions of civilization and wilderness—aligns it with texts as diverse as Crevecoeur's *Letters to an American Farmer*, Hawthorne's tales, and Twain's *Huckleberry Finn*. There has always been much that is archetypically *American* about King's writing—its size, its tendency toward sentimentality and the endurance of hope in the face of the worst possible situations, its reliance on recognizable regional character types, the epic scope of his road narratives, the monumental battles between good and evil, and those tales detailing the corruption of innocence such as *Apt Pupil* and *The Body*. I'm certainly not the first to recognize this. Critics such as Jeanne Campbell Reesman have found in *The Shining* a "Young Goodman Brown" for our day, "in which the naturalist hero is destroyed by his refusal, or inability, to admit the awful power of that 'other' world of the unconscious" (106). Reesman also finds in the King text disturbing undercurrents that question our nationalistic drive for success with "deep doubts about such designs of power and wealth; [King] proposes a competing reality with his phantoms and demons" (107).

In *The Shining*, at least, I'm not sure how much this text's implicit examination of capitalism serves as a "competing reality" with the spectral figures that animate the Overlook Hotel. It is more accurate to say that the two forces—capitalism and supernatural evil—create a complementary nexus where the ghosts on board still represent the design and power of wealth and privilege. How else to explain the haunting conversation that transpires between Lloyd and Jack in the Gold Ballroom, where Jack discovers his "money is no good here. Orders from the manager" (346). When Jack inquires about the hotel's management, what it wants with his son and why Jack is not permitted to meet the manager, Lloyd's response is echoed by the other ghostly patrons in the bar: "Drink your drink, Mr. Torrance. It isn't a matter that concerns you. Not at this point" (347). Believing with a desperate zeal that the hotel wishes to make him part of its upper-crust infrastructure, Torrance is then condescendingly dismissed by a bartender, a reminder that at no point in his interaction with the spirits at the Overlook is Jack ever told the truth or allowed to see it undistorted.

This brings us to a consideration of the novel and the film that adds a level of cultural significance deeper than any discussion of substance abuse or marital discord. For *The Shining*, as much as any Stephen King text, is a critique of capitalism and its corrupting powers of seduction. In dealing exclusively with Kubrick's film adaptation, Fredric Jameson has much to say about the "working out of the class fantasies of contemporary American society," even though the film emphasizes the twenties as the historic moment that interfaces with Torrance's present. The twenties were "the last moment in which a genuine American leisure class led an aggressive and ostentatious public existence, in which an American ruling class projected a class-conscious and unapologetic image of itself and enjoyed its privileges without guilt, on the social stage in full view of the other classes" (Jameson 95). While King's novel locates the hotel's spectral epicenter in the forties, where it "forms an index of the whole post-World War II American character" (189), it is clear that King and Kubrick find agreement in their differing choice of historical epochs: the twenties and forties were both moments of triumph as America assumed its place on the world's stage.

Throughout both film and novel, Jack is trapped between classes; not quite working class, like Delbert Grady, Watson, or Lloyd, neither is Jack a member of the "managerial" ruling class, capable of identifying with its principal owner, Horace Derwent. He is, after all, a highly educated man, a teacher and a freelance fiction writer. Though this may overqualify him for the winter caretaker position, he finds himself, nonetheless, desperate enough financially to need the job. Moreover, in his former occupations as a writer and English teacher at a Vermont prep school, Jack made very little money; in the novel, he shows writing promise with an early publication in *Esquire* magazine, but these are hardly sufficient career credentials for admission into the elite patrician class associated with the hotel guests and Jack's sinister and well-connected benefactor, Al Shockley. In both novel and film, the gap that exists between Torrance's class status and his desire to rise above it is as much an omnipresent subtext as Jack's drinking problem. Although the hotel's ghosts covet Danny's supernatural gifts, they know the way to get him is through the boy's socially insecure father: "'And the manager puts no strings on his largess,' Grady went on. 'Not at all. Look at me, a tenth-grade dropout. Think how much further you yourself could go in the Overlook's organizational structure'" (356). The hotel seduces him with all the fantasy constructions that attend power, fame, and money in America: a bevy of masked and gloved women in "evening gowns and gleaming high-heeled pumps" (157), erotically charged and freshly bathed from Kubrick's room 237 (in marked contrast to Jack's bedraggled wife, Wendy, who wears no makeup, dresses down, and whose greasy hair is always in need of a shampoo). The ghost women in both film and novel are the prizes that await Jack's compliance with the hotel's design. They represent the promise of deathless parties and free booze, and for Jack Torrance the fledgling writer, instant literary stardom as the chronicler of the Overlook's history, of which I will have more to say later.

At the same time, the hotel also mocks Torrance's every effort to partake in the fruits that attend social privilege. The beautiful woman in room 237 transforms into a derisively laughing old hag, while Stuart Ullman echoes the rejoinders of Lloyd, Grady, and the ghostly management by deflating Torrance's class aspirations in the sobering acknowledgment that Jack is merely "an employee of the hotel, no different from a busboy or a kitchen pot scrubber" (182). Indeed, Kubrick's use of the "All work and no play makes Jack a dull boy" manuscript is the quintessential expression of the hotel's patronizing voice: Jack didn't author this third-person narrative mantra; he just had to write it a thousand times in an effort to inculcate it into his psyche. Just as Grady employs emasculating language in the red bathroom scene and again prior to releasing Jack from the locked food pantry, the hotel once more seeks to goad Torrance into violent action by referring to him derisively as a *boy* and further condemning him to the worst possible status in the lexicon of spoiled, rich party brats: that he is *dull*. The only way to escape his currently unfavorable social standing is for Jack to entertain his decadent hosts by following their carnival regime of misrule in subverting all conventional notions of work and play. After all, one of the benefits that attends upper-class license is a life of constant play devoid of any real work. So, while *The Shining* echoes an unmistakably *American* ideology in dangling the dream of social advancement and upward mobility in front of its bewildered protagonist, the reigning hegemony in place at the Overlook is more representative of rigid aristocratic European class demarcations—or, perhaps just as accurately, the ethos of corporate America management during the late 1970s and 80s, when the novel and film were produced: a callous social hierarchy where, if a man were only willing to sacrifice his family, he might open himself to advancement up the corporate ladder.

About midway through Kubrick's film, just after Danny has been attacked by the ghost woman in room 237 and Jack has lied to his wife about his own experiences with her, the two parents retreat to their "cozy" sleeping quarters within the Overlook and try to reason out what is happening to their son. Indeed, the quarters where the Torrances are housed within the Overlook is a further indication of their status as underlings at the hotel. Unlike the other sumptuous rooms within the hotel, Jack and Wendy's accommodations are cramped and threadbare: a small black-and-white television, a refrigerator, and a bed so large that there is not much room to even walk around them. Compare, for example, the lavishly decadent wallpaper and carpet (the latter bearing a woven design that is both phallic and vaginal, anticipating Jack's interaction with the wet bathtub ghost) that decorate room 237 with those found in the apartment where Jack and Wendy reside, or the tiny white bathroom to the right of the apartment with its single window so small that Wendy cannot fit through it to the spaciousness of the bathroom in 237 or the red lavatory in Colorado Lounge. Generally speaking, *The Shining* is not a claustrophobic film—at least not to the degree found in classic haunted house texts such as *The Haunting* or *The Amityville Horror*—but inside the Torrances' living quarters we are profoundly aware of the finite dimensions of space. And this awareness is important as an analog to understanding the level of class confinement that undermines Jack's psyche throughout the movie.

In this scene, Wendy is emotionally distraught, while Jack appears calm and rational for the last time in the film. Perhaps because he knows he is lying to his wife, Jack posits gently that since there was no woman in room 237, Danny must have hurt himself. Wendy doesn't buy into it very far and demands that the family leave the hotel to seek immediate medical treatment for their son. It is at this moment that Jack Torrance reveals the depth of his commitment to the spirits at the hotel in his fear that if he follows Wendy's suggestion to flee the Overlook, he will forfeit the social status he is trying to accumulate within the hierarchy of the hotel. His sudden fury indicates his own self-awareness of the precariousness of his place not only within the structure of the hotel, but also within capitalist America. He intuits that to abandon his job as the hotel's caretaker would jeopardize his getting hired in any future occupation: "I could really write my own ticket," he mocks, "work in a car wash, shoveling driveways. Would that appeal to you?" The obvious and tragically humorous irony here is in Jack's misapprehension of his own importance: as if his career as the winter caretaker of an empty hotel ("the owners have put their trust in me . . . I have signed a contract") is that much more prestigious than working in a car wash. Indeed, the degree to which the hotel manages to corrupt his thinking is often measurable in Torrance's inflated notions of himself as a potentially famous author and, even more absurd, future hotel executive.

Jack's inability to put his son's welfare in front of his own job prospects highlights the degree to which the values of the Overlook have displaced his commitment to his family and distorted his sense of reality. In fact, in his rant during this scene, Jack explicitly names Wendy—"I've let you fuck up my life so far"—as the source for his career, financial, and personal failings. But the Overlook is always a contrary mistress insofar as it mocks

Jack at the same time as it lures him to become part of its ruling hierarchy. In his position as an adult male who is a recovering alcoholic, out of work, and desperately seeking validation as a writer, Jack is terribly vulnerable to the hotel's criticism of his masculinity and social status.

After Wendy locks him in the food pantry, Delbert Grady releases Jack, but only after taunting him with an admission that he has "hardly taken care of the business we discussed," that the hotel hierarchy may have "underestimated [Wendy's] resourcefulness," and a growing trepidation on the part of the spectral management that Jack may not "have the belly" for murdering his family. After Grady presents Jack with his shortcomings, the camera cuts to a side diagonal shot of Jack's upper body focused on his face looking toward the pantry door, presumably at Grady on the other side of the door. Although Grady is not visible in this conversation, to a very real degree Jack is talking to himself (as he is during many of those moments throughout the film when a mirror is present behind one of the ghosts from the hotel), or at least an extension of himself, his dark alter ego. This other part of Jack, which is also a manifestation created by the hotel, is patronizing him throughout the conversation, and exhibiting who is actually in charge while also goading Jack into action.

Grady is not only a physical ambassador for the hotel, but also a resurrection of Jack's inner demons and desires coming to the forefront, with one big difference: while he was the caretaker, Grady got the job done. As his alter ego, Grady is underscoring all the things that Jack already knows about himself. From Nicholson's downcast eyes and his dejected "No need to rub it in" response to Grady's criticism, to the maniacal smile that slowly emerges on Torrance's face when he hears the pantry door open, the reaction from Jack during this conversation shows a mind wrestling with itself for the last time, giving way to the collective madness of the hotel that follows his emergence from the pantry. In response, Jack assumes the role of a bumbling employee disciplined by a condescending superior, begging Grady to "Just give me one more chance to prove it, Mr. Grady." This represents an ironic reversal in their roles, as Jack loses the social status Grady awarded him when they first met in the red bathroom. There, Grady the valet labors to clean the drink he has spilled on Jack's jacket while assuring him that Torrance is "the important one." Jack responds instantly to such affirmation, referring to Grady as "Jeeves, old boy." But as is always the case when Torrance interacts with the hotel's ghosts, Jack's social positioning erodes when he recognizes Grady as the caretaker who murdered his family. From this point on in the red bathroom, Grady usurps Jack's power and begins to instruct him on how to behave toward Wendy and Danny. Such a radical and abrupt shift in class status positioning merely underscores what we've seen in scenes prior to this one: the hotel seduces Jack with obsequious attention one moment, only to reduce him to white trash the next. All this serves to underscore Jack's class insecurity, trapped as he is between social classes and uncomfortable with viewing himself either as working-class laborer or hotel management.

It is no accident that the hotel sides with Jack against Wendy, Danny, and Hallorann. The hegemony empowered at the hotel represents an upper-crust, white male social dynamic; the Overlook's patriarchal management aligns itself, as it always has, with its own kind. Consequently, Jack is beset continually—one moment mocked by and the next invited to join—the hotel's constructions of masculinity and its subliminal connection to the remembered voice of Jack's dead father in King's novel. *The Shining* is as much about the sins of fathers as it is anything else; and in both film and novel extreme versions of masculinity and fatherhood are called into question because they legitimize the potential abuse of privilege and power that comes with these roles. Throughout Kubrick's films, father figures are monstrous and shocking, from Humbert Humbert in *Lolita* to Victor Ziegler in *Eyes Wide Shut*. The obscene paternity in Kubrick's *Shining* is a more spectral, less explicit presence than the role accorded it in King's novel, but fathers are nevertheless present in the form of Grady setting stern examples in the blood-red bathroom about the necessity of "correcting" wayward wives and children. Further, an oppressive fatherhood is also present in the patriarchal management of the hotel itself, dictating its wishes to Jack and demanding his obedience. In King's novel, the voice of Jack's father is conveniently aligned with the masculine ethos that animates the spirits in the hotel. Although Jack's father is pictured in King's narrative as strictly working class, the patrician ghosts at the hotel share behavior traits with him that cut across class lines. Fathers in this novel are pictured as selfish, misogynistic, alcoholic, and most important, prone to punitive acts of violence. There is a recognizable line that connects Jack's memory of his father's caning of his mother at the dinner table, to Delbert Grady's "correction" of his wayward wife and daughters, to Jack's own attacks against Wendy and Danny. This is why at the end of King's novel Hallorann remains concerned about Danny someday possibly evolving into a version of Jack. The black man warns the boy in explicit terms to "grieve for your daddy" because expressions of emotional loss are necessary to the healing process and likewise break from traditional forms of masculine repression and the repudiation of the feminine: "[W]hen you feel you have to cry over what happened to him, you go into a closet or under your covers and cry." But Hallorann also recognizes that too much time spent grieving over the unfairness of personal tragedy can turn even a sweet boy into a bitter man who might eventually come to identify with a father who tended to blame everyone but himself for his life's shortcomings. That's why he reminds Danny to "See that you get on. That's your job in this hard world, to keep your love alive and see that you get on, no matter what" (449).

Although not King's most feminist novel, *The Shining* is nevertheless a scathing critique of patriarchal abuses. In the male-centered universe of the Overlook, women, children, and ethnic minorities are subsequently disenfranchised and marginalized. Jack is the only heir to the house, even if the hotel is ultimately interested in securing Danny's powers, not Jack's. This last point is of central importance in King's novel, but in Kubrick's film it is actually deemphasized, one of the many possible reasons for King's well-publicized dissatisfaction with Kubrick's adaptation (see Magistrale, *Hollywood's Stephen King*, 197–200). In a role similar to Dr. William Harford in *Eyes Wide Shut*, Jack Torrance is at the center of Kubrick's *The Shining*, and both men undergo jarring dislocations that shake the foundations that hold together the fragile existences they have created for themselves and their families. Throughout Kubrick's filmic canon, distraught white males seek to find themselves in a social matrix that perpetually confounds and undermines their sense of security and selfhood. The Fall of the House of the Overlook carries with it the destruction of the family, and particularly conventional notions of fatherhood and masculinity.

Viewers of *The Shining* are often bedeviled by the last image in the film: Jack Torrance centered in a framed black-and-white photograph of a party at the Overlook dated July 4, 1921. Aside from confirming Delbert Grady's assertion that Jack "has always been the caretaker," what might this moment of temporal surrealism represent? Though one might desire to confer with Stanley Kubrick to ascertain the answer to this issue, if only that were still possible, his placing of Torrance in the 1921 photograph may be a final affirmation of Jack's psychological positioning: he has always been the caretaker because his sympathies have always been aligned with those of the spirits that reside at the hotel. Critic Jason Sperb in his book *The Kubrick Façade* opines, "it could just be the only place, cognitive or otherwise, where Jack possesses a sense of place and time" (102). His death in the hedge maze, then, simply completes his passage home. For the final image of Jack hanging on the wall and pictured among other photographs depicting the history of the hotel contrasts sharply with his frozen, tortured visage left out in the maze; in the latter, he is akin to some abominable winter snow creature, disheveled and unshaven, desperately lost in a punishing snowstorm that is a metaphor for his own unraveled psyche, while the photograph, in stunning contrast, shows him younger, vital, clean-shaven, smiling with a maniacal grin, and very comfortably situated. Aside from finally being properly attired in a stylish tuxedo appropriate for "the fish and goose soiree" he apparently missed when Danny and Wendy were around—and because he is positioned without a female partner, front and center of the group photograph—Jack also appears eternally subsumed as a hotel employee, rather than emerging on the register of its elite guest party revelers. His body language, with arms extended in a warm welcome to the camera, most likely is designed to show him as the maître d'hôtel, occupying a slightly more upscale role than Delbert Grady's "Jeeves" valet, as the eternal caretaker who has evidently taken to heart the Overlook's dictum that all work and no play did indeed make Jack a dull boy.

If this is a photograph from Kubrick's version of hell, Jack seems right at home. But it is also important for us to remember, even as the film fades to black, that Jack Torrance, albeit tuxedoed and deathlessly frozen in time, still hasn't progressed much beyond the guy who was afraid of getting stuck in that Denver car-washing job: he is still cast as just another hotel employee taking "orders from the House." The photograph that ends Kubrick's film perhaps features the same Jack Torrance from early in King's novel who, after uncovering the hotel's scrapbook in the basement, couldn't wait to write his exposé of the Overlook in his imagined role as its biographical Boswell. Al Shockley squelches that idea quickly in a short telephone conversation, turning abruptly from Jack's drinking buddy to "the self-interested moral equivalent of a robber baron" (Bailey 104). When Jack threatens to reveal the past history of the Overlook, the class difference between the two men asserts itself, and readers share Torrance's humiliation in recognizing the gap that exists between a desperate writer and a Medici prince: "We'll always be friends, and the dog collar I have on you will always be ignored by mutual consent, and I'll take good and benevolent care of you" (191). Like the Torrance-Shockley relationship, America sustains the delusion of a democratic society, but the truth is that class anxieties are boiling just beneath the surface, just like the old boiler hidden in the Overlook's cavernous basement.

Jack Torrance is attracted to the dead white males that inhabit the Overlook for exactly the reasons that Wendy, Hallorann, and Danny are not: his core definition of masculinity is exclusively aligned with status, career, and access to the trappings of privileged success—prestige, money, women, alcohol, and a reckless—particularly American—sense of masculine independence. Thus, it may not be a coincidence that Kubrick configures Jack's Overlook photograph during a July Fourth fete, seeking to capitalize on the ironic significance of that date in American history. Although we know very little about Jack Torrance's politics, I would speculate that he's far more likely to be a closet Republican, replete with an earlier era's faith in venture capitalism, than any stereotyped version of the progressive writer-private school academy teacher. Jack merely lacks the financial wherewithal, class birthright, and marital independence to come out of the closet and join the deceased movie stars, heiresses, and junk-bond traders who live to play and party every night while mocking all the "dull boys" outside their elite circle who actually have to work for a living. The historical moment when King's novel and Kubrick's film appeared coincided with the rise of Reaganism and the latter's unleashing of a deregulated capitalism that ultimately increased the gap separating rich from poor in America. In the age of Reagan, it was not only permissible to be wealthy, but also to flaunt it whenever and wherever possible. Jack's self-awareness of his exclusion from the social class that both patronizes and operates the hotel simultaneously fuels the resentment and anger misdirected against his family at the same time as it turns his fascination with the Overlook into an obsessive desire. Frank Manchel argues convincingly in his essay "What about Jack?" that Torrance deserves greater sympathy than he usually gets because he is trapped in a situation that makes him "the scapegoat for the sins of a patriarchal society" (82). By providing Jack with illusions of a celebrity lifestyle that attracts him so fatally, but to which he is always conscious of being excluded, the hotel ghosts pull him into their collective grasp, even if he is only to serve as a pawn in the Overlook's larger design. It is a hegemonic design that has historically been employed to manipulate while also enticing the lower classes, even to the point of their psychic exhaustion and physical extermination—promising the democratic American Dream of instant happiness via tremendous material wealth to everyone—but in reality only the place of the ruling class, that 3 percent of the American populace that controls 90 percent of the nation's wealth, is secure, while everyone else is left with only their dreams.

The thought of shoveling snow or working in a car wash is anathema both to Jack and to the men who built the Overlook on land that once belonged to American Indians; indeed, the structure is perched atop an ancient Indian burial ground where workers had to repel Indian attacks during its very construction. In Kubrick's film, the fact that the Overlook's lobby is literally decorated from floor to ceiling in Navajo and Apache motifs—on its wall hangings and ceiling borders, floor carpets and designs, and sculpture art—is further evidence of the manner in which generations of white ownership of the place have appropriated the traditions and resources of an indigenous population vanquished in order to make way for the colonization of the West. Located near the center of America geographically, the Overlook is also a testament to the triumph of white Protestant male capitalism—and its ability to exploit the labor and land of others to strengthen its own position. I don't think it is much of an exaggeration to posit that in the creation of the Overlook Hotel we find in microcosm the doctrine of manifest destiny: the necessary taming of the western wilderness—and the corresponding willingness to "overlook" the genocide of primitive cultures—for the construction of an American city on the hill, a palace so elite that it is open for only half the year, and serves, as Stuart Ullman acknowledges with pride, as "a stopping place for the jet set—all the right people." Kubrick's film goes even further to suggest the full scope of American racism in its references to Torrance's cheerful acceptance of the "white man's burden," Grady's off-the-cuff description of Hallorann as a "nigger cook," and the array of Navajo and Apache artifacts appropriated for adornment inside the hotel's public spaces. Indeed, in the historical matrix of these various racist allusions and cultural appropriations it is significant that Hallorann's visceral murder, which occurs to the defenseless and unarmed black man near the end of Kubrick's *Shining*, results in his bloody collapse atop a Native American floor design. Thus, Kubrick visualizes explicitly what he implies throughout the film: a stratum of violence against African Americans that is layered on top of the history of genocide perpetrated against the Indians.

In *The Wolf at the Door: Stanley Kubrick, History, and the Holocaust*, Geoffrey Cocks musters a fascinating if ultimately unconvincing argument that images of the Holocaust are "at the heart of *The Shining*, and it is therefore the Nazi devil that dwells deepest in the details of the film" (218). He argues that Kubrick was deathlessly fascinated with the history of the Holocaust but never produced a film on the subject. *The Shining*, Cocks posits, "was about mass murder, including the genocide of the Jews that Kubrick could not directly represent, in great measure because the threat was not only ruthless but personal and familial" (201). The truest holocaust at work in Kubrick's film, however, has less to do with the Nazis and the various far-fetched references Cocks traces to wolves and the absurd multiples of the number seven, and more with the genocide of the American Indian; in such a context, the famous river of blood flowing from the elevator shafts into the corridor of the Overlook forms a connection to the historical brutalization of Indians at the hands of white men who desired their lands.

The Shining would not be the only occasion where Native American burial sites serve as an intricate part of the plot. King's 1983 novel *Pet*

Sematary also features white male violations of sacred Indian ground; as in the construction of the Overlook Hotel, the males of Ludlow, Maine, intrude on a Micmac burial site to reanimate their dead. In a conversation with Stephen King several years ago, the novelist informed me that in writing *Pet Sematary* he researched many sources tracing the legend of the Wendigo, a mythological Indian monster that wanders the woods in wintertime searching for human food. Once touched by this spirit, humans forsake their social bonds and transform into vampire-cannibals, desiring the flesh of other humans. But what also seems important to note is King's particular adaptation of the Indian folk legend: in both *The Shining* and *Pet Sematary*, it is always adult white males who seek to impose their will without respect for Indian tradition or the latter's sanctification of the afterlife. The women of Ludlow, like those few who are associated with the Overlook Hotel, are either kept apart from these violations or know better than to participate in them. For such intrusions inevitably fare badly for those who would manipulate sacred land for their own purposes. Ironically, the white men in both texts are transformed into versions of the Wendigo vampire: the desire to destroy and possess the Torrances by the ghosts who reside in the Overlook and the hunger for human flesh that animates the walking dead upon their return from the Micmac graveyard throughout *Pet Sematary*. In both cases, white men lose their humanity because of their willingness to violate Indian customs for selfish purposes. Thus, the awakening of malefic supernatural energies associated with Indian legend in both *The Shining* and *Pet Sematary* can be interpreted as a kind of cultural retribution, the land itself reacting against violations originally performed by white males who impose their collective and individual wills upon Native American territory and myth, usurping primitive power for their own selfish agendas.

At the end of King's novel, the Overlook Hotel is destroyed; all that it once was withers and burns. But in Kubrick's film, the hotel stubbornly endures. A symbol of paternalistic and consumerist culture, built on Indian burial grounds, seducing vulnerable males with the promise of fame and fortune, the hotel's powers of seduction lure another questing individual to his doom, but the structure and the dream it represents remain. The prone body of Dick Hallorann, slaughtered before he can do much by way of rescuing the besieged mother and child, is a sharp contrast to the Hallorann who survives in King's original text. Assuming the role of the unselfish "Magical Negro," left to fill the paternal void of the tragically lost "white ghost" bad father, Hallorann's survival in the novel underscores the effect of a vanquished imperialist structure, represented in the smoldering ashes of the Overlook, and the wrong-headedness of an unbridled capitalism, destructive to both itself and others. Thus, in King's novel we witness the demise of an overbearing patriarchal hegemony, and the consequent hope for better days to come with Hallorann and Wendy guiding young Danny into adolescence and beyond. The novel, after all, ends in spring. Never much of an optimist, Kubrick kills Hallorann and leaves both hotel and hedge maze intact in the midst of winter, a lethal reminder that the evil labyrinths remain, ominous and threatening, awaiting their next male victim with a propensity for alcohol and self-aggrandizement. There is no "victory" in this film, only a transient sense of relief—Wendy and Danny get into Hallorann's snowcat and drive away—to head down the mountainside in a raging blizzard, their safety still very much in doubt. One wrong turn off the side of the mountain, one flip of the snowcat that the emotionally unstable Wendy is driving for the first time, could send them both into the same wintry eternity inhabited by their frozen husband-father. Novel and film thus war with one another to the bitter end, producing oppositional effects: the happily resolved ending so characteristic of Stephen King's fiction, and the searing pessimism that haunts nearly every film Stanley Kubrick ever made.

"A RESPONSIBILITY TO HISTORY": THAT ELUSIVE SCRAPBOOK

In an interview conducted with King several years ago, I asked him to consider what some critics and readers have interpreted as a cultural subtext for reading *The Shining*. Specifically, I wondered what he thought of those who view the book as a parody of the American Dream, where Jack Torrance appears "as a negative portrait of the American success story, [who] wants to write himself into fame and fortune at any cost. The Overlook itself is symbolic of a corporate organization that asks Jack to sacrifice everything, including his family and soul, for advancement of his career" (Magistrale, *Second Decade*, 18).

King responded with an equivocal answer. At first, he felt compelled to place his novel's tragic consequences squarely on Jack—that Torrance had made some deliberately negative choices and was solely responsible for what ensued. Such a reading diminishes the influence of the Overlook as a powerful projection of capitalist desire and affect exerting persuasive power over a vulnerable American male. But as King continued to reason his way through, he complicated his initial thoughts, gradually shifting the discussion away from Jack's personal flaws and toward those forces over which he could exercise little, if any, control: "Whatever is going to happen to him, in a way, has already been decided. Therefore, when he moves he carries his doom with him. . . . You can rise in the hotel hierarchy; you just have to be willing to tread on enough dead bodies. The hotel's entire history is evidence of this" (Magistrale, *Second Decade*, 18–19).

Jack Torrance is both responsible for his own doom and a pawn under sway of forces that manipulate him to the point of mental and moral collapse. This tragic complication is never wholly resolved, one way or the other, throughout either the novel or the film, and perhaps this is a reason that King initially viewed the work as a play, rather than a novel: "given an exposition of the supporting matter, which is dramatized in the book, it could be a play, even now" (King, "On *The Shining*," 1415). Like so many of Shakespeare's tragic heroes, Torrance is both helpless to alter the course of his own destruction and endowed with enough free will that he participates directly through his bad choices in the catastrophe that befalls him. In the novel, the first instance where we see this tragic dialectic played out is in chapter 18, "The Scrapbook." The scrapbook plays a very important role especially in the first half of King's novel: it the first evidence of the hotel's direct ability to seduce Jack, and likewise, of Jack's susceptibly to being seduced.

In Kubrick's film, the scrapbook occupies a much more subdued position; in fact, it is never actually mentioned by anyone in the film, including Jack. But its presence is notable in scenes that feature Jack at his typewriter. The scrapbook is typically pictured off in a corner of the mise-en-scène, and in the montage where Jack verbally harangues Wendy about interrupting his writing and breaking his concentration, the book is open in front of him. Presumably, its lurid contents feed and provide collaborative authorship for the production of Torrance's *All work and no play makes Jack a dull boy* manuscript. Moreover, although the scrapbook is never referenced, it is certainly the source for Jack's ability to recognize Delbert Grady's face in the red bathroom scene. Most viewers of the film do not notice Kubrick's subtle references to the scrapbook, but its notable presence in more than one scene indicates that the auteur clearly meant for us to pay attention to it and to view it as an allusion back to King's novel. So central is the scrapbook to King's narrative that it appears at a critical junction in the book and is the exclusive subject of its own chapter (18); moreover, it is possible to say that its existence and Torrance's attitude toward it point the way to the unraveling of the Torrance marriage and Jack's becoming subsumed by the powers of the hotel. In 1989 I asked King about the importance of scrapbooks and the fact that they feature prominently in *Misery, It*, and most notably *The Shining*. His response was to remind me that they are "devices that probe history in a manner that allows me to disclose the past so that it can possess immediate importance for the present . . . in the scrapbooks are things that people find unpleasant; they are not good memories" (Magistrale, *The Second Decade*, 10).

Like so many of the protagonists throughout King's canon, from Louis Creed in *Pet Sematary* to Jessie Burlingame in *Gerald's Game* to Kurt Dussander in *Apt Pupil*, Jack Torrance is a man who harbors secrets. Moreover, he carries his secret past like a vampire carries its history, as a burden that continually shapes events in the present. Torrance has labored hard to conceal from family and associates a violent past, childhood abuse at the hands of his father, and a persistent craving for alcohol. Though honesty in all actions may be a central maxim in alcohol rehabilitation programs, Jack is most comfortable in the shadowy world of secrets and deceptive behavior. Hallorann recognizes this immediately when he employs his psychic energies to probe Torrance, only to learn that Jack "had something he was holding in so deeply submerged in himself that it was impossible to get to" (89). As a record of the Overlook's secret and public past—the "unpleasant memories" of its history—the scrapbook represents a critical component in establishing collusion between Jack and the hotel. Between its covers Torrance finds a mélange of newspapers, letters, photographs, diary entries, and seemingly random notations that chronicle events from the hotel's sordid past. It is as if the Overlook is revealing its most intimate relationships to Torrance, filling the darkest chambers of the writer's mind with details of its darkest moments in history while he sits alone in a dark corner of its basement. "He wondered consciously whose book this was, left atop the highest pile of records in the cellar" (162). Discovering the scrapbook is for Jack like discovering in an attic the private diary and papers of a famous writer. Jack, in turn, bonds with the hotel's history, dimly aware of some unconscious bond that he shares with the place—perhaps it is the hotel's failure to live up to its expectations as a business venture; perhaps it is the sad vulnerability revealed in its flaws; perhaps it is simply that Jack feels privileged in gaining private insight into the hotel's secreted moments of spectacular decadence. Whatever the reason, from this point on Jack never views the Overlook with any degree of objectivity; his destiny is somehow irrevocably aligned with that of the hotel.

But what to make of King's "device," the effect this introduction to the hotel's nefarious history produces on Jack? Why does the scrapbook initiate so deep a compulsion in him that he abandons work on his play to concentrate upon the scrapbook exclusively? And, most curious of all, why does Jack keep the scrapbook to himself, refraining from sharing its existence—much less its contents—with either Wendy or Danny?

Inside the scrapbook is a secret history—a kind of anonymous diary of the hotel—that would immediately engage the imagination of anyone, particularly a fiction writer. In chapter 18, we view Jack as both reader and writer, since both his creative and analytical skills are piqued by what he discovers. Indeed, the chapter itself is written in the third-person point of view; this helps to create a sensation in the reader of peering over Torrance's shoulder as he reads along, even pausing with him to consider the implications of what is revealed. We become co-conspirators with Jack, involved in a subtle collusion that is so compelling because it delves into a yet undisclosed record of evil. Perhaps at no other point in the novel does the reader feel (quite unwittingly) closer to Jack Torrance; we understand his growing excitement as he probes the polyphonic narrative that constitutes the book because we discover it first-hand along with Jack. Unlike Wendy, who never does get to look at the book—indeed, is never told of its existence—King allows Jack and the reader to share in a secret knowledge that creates a nefarious bond among the reader, Jack, and the hotel.

Unlike Kubrick's screenplay, the scrapbook joins boxes of Overlook memorabilia in King's teleplay for the ABC miniseries of *The Shining*, and because these documents do not remain secreted in the basement, they take on a wholly different role than in either the novel or Kubrick's film. In the TV miniseries, Wendy is very much aware of the dark treasure trove Jack has discovered about the hotel. At one point, Wendy even pits her sexuality against her husband's interest in these papers. His obvious lack of interest in her white satin lingerie and come-hither invitation—"I've got something for you you're not going to find in any of those boxes, if you want it"—is really the first scene in the miniseries that signals Jack's psychic deterioration—his preference for the hotel in place of his wife. The scrapbook and its accompanying documents indicate the level of Torrance's distraction at the same time as they illustrate Wendy's own utter lack of interest in the hotel and its history, for she never shares any of Jack's fascination with the material, never once looking into the boxes to see what her husband finds so engrossing. In fact, quite the opposite occurs: for Wendy, the Overlook's history and its influence over her husband are further reasons to hate the place.

Chapter 18 in King's novel begins innocuously enough: on the first of November—not the night before, Halloween, when one might expect the Overlook to unleash its unholy energies, but the day after, All Soul's Day, when the malefic spirits are supposed to be safely back in their crypts—while Danny and Wendy are off hiking in the woods, Jack finds himself alone in the basement of the hotel searching for "good places to set [rodent] traps, although he didn't plan to do that for another month—I want them all to be home from vacation, he had told Wendy" (154). It is highly ironic that Torrance plans such a strategy against the vermin living in the basement, for it is clear that it is actually the hotel itself that has set the trap, deliberately waiting until the onset of winter for Jack to discover the scrapbook, as it will soon be too late for the Torrances to escape.

The scrapbook forms a microcosm of the Overlook Hotel's history. Unlike either the King miniseries or Kubrick's film, what the novel supplies are many of the actual *details* of what truly sparks Torrance's imagination, the insidious parallels that unfold between the hotel's infamous past and America's concurrent history of violence and corruption. As Torrance comes to recognize, the Overlook "forms an index of the whole post-World War II American character" (189). At its heyday, the hotel is supposed to represent the shining future that was to be America. Yet what is conveyed to Jack in the scrapbook is a hodgepodge of extravagance and the worst aspects of America: mafia connections, prostitution, adultery, corrupt politicians, murders and suicides constitute the underside of the Overlook. The hotel has encompassed throughout its history both the glamorous and the subversive elements of the American past. Its clientele included celebrities such as Marilyn Monroe and Arthur Miller before their divorce (perhaps offering a parallel to the would-be playwright Jack Torrance and his blond wife Wendy, who are also preoccupied with the issue of divorce), but also gangsters with such lovely sobriquets as Vito the Chopper. Jack relates to the greatness and possibilities of the place, but he is also drawn to its dark plotline as well. An odd but cohesive alliance forms between the abused man-child and the neglected, contradictory hotel he is hired to take care of. A record of Mafia murders, sexual violations, and seedy financial transactions complements each reference to a masked ball or a jet-set guest in the hotel registry: "God what a story! Screwing expensive whores on the third floor, maybe. Drinking magnums of champagne. Making deals that would turn over millions of dollars, maybe in the very suite of rooms where Presidents had stayed" (165). Notice the temptations that Jack catalogues here: illicit sex with exotic women, alcohol, money, and power. These are not only the pitfalls that destroy marriages; they are also corrosive influences that tempt a highly vulnerable ex-alcoholic and recently fired high school English teacher who is in desperate search for self-reinvention.

Chapter 18 also introduces Jack to Horace Derwent, the most famous of the Overlook's many owners. Derwent is the archetypical American capitalist, blending diversified business interests—"aircraft, movies, munitions, and shipping" (158)—under a pretense of sophistication and elegance. He is a composite of myth and reality—one part Howard Hughes, one part Jay Gatsby—a larger-than-life being who could be conceived only in the arena of the American cultural imagination. But perhaps what is most important about his character is that he has attained his fame and success through "means that were less than savory" (159). Associated with Derwent's character is a culmination of the many dog references that are maintained throughout King's novel and are associated with various abuses of male power and sexuality. Jack repeats his father's brutal words—"Goddamn puppy. Whelp. Come on and take your medicine" (337)—when he imagines himself responsible for the discipline of his own wife and son. As a reflection of his cruelty and decadent tastes, Derwent has transformed one of his lovers, Roger, into a man-dog—forcing him to wear a dog suit and perform tricks for the amusement of the hotel's guests in the faint hope that Derwent may allow him back into his bed. Roger is gay and Derwent bisexual, and the former's infatuation with the dashing young millionaire is so deep that he submits to canine humiliation. Harry's abuses highlight the brutal use of power in the masculine world; he can treat other men, even men with whom he has established romantic relationships, like dogs for his own amusement and self-aggrandizement.

The reader shares Torrance's enthusiasm and prurient fascination with Derwent and his cronies. The scrapbook holds some of the same attraction that many of us find in reading tabloid journalism: we are forever avid for stories of misfortune and death, particularly when they occur to the rich and famous. But the careful reader of this novel also recognizes that Jack is not merely intrigued by these facts; they wholly and dangerously absorb him. He wants to research the narrative further, to write and publish his findings, and in so doing, to attain an intimate share of the hotel's (sur)reality. The more Jack enters into the simulacrum of the Overlook rendered through the scrapbook, the more his bond with the place deepens until he eschews critical objectivity. Their protective posturing notwithstanding, Al Shockley and Stuart Ullman have, ironically, nothing to fear from Torrance's interest in writing about their hotel. As a fallen man himself, Jack has as much in common with the Overlook as any of its ghosts or living allies; almost from the moment he begins reading about it, Jack sympathizes poignantly with its moments of decay, and likewise shares vicariously in its triumphs during periods of past grandeur. In short, his exposure to this document creates an affinity for the place. Leonard Mustazza has considered this evolving interface between hotel and caretaker when he concludes, "no matter how much we sympathize with Jack, we must part company with him when he begins to be drawn towards the colorful figures of the hotel's past. In other words, King deftly begins the process of distancing us from [Jack] merely by making him admire the people who once occupied this place" (115).

Correspondingly, the more involved Torrance becomes with the scrapbook, the less interested he is in the writing of his play. King tells us that "In addition to his sudden diversion of interest to the Overlook's history, something else had happened. He had developed opposing feelings about his characters" (259). Jack's play, *The Little School*, was to afford him the chance to reestablish his literary worth; it is purportedly the main reason he takes the caretaking job, so that he will have the time and solitude to write. The play offers Jack the opportunity to reassert control over his mind and to redirect his imagination in a positive manner. Kubrick's film is less specific about Jack's writing project, but the director clearly understood that Jack's writing is a central element of the plot. In the novel and film, the introduction of the scrapbook distracts Jack, knocks him off course and into another orbit, the way a voluptuous mistress might capture a wayward husband from his wife. Indeed, the deception is so persuasive that Jack becomes convinced the hotel is a subject worthy of inspiring his greatest composition, when in reality his authorial energies are being siphoned away. And so important is this connection that Jason Sperb links Torrance's writing to his mental stability: "We do not begin to experience Jack's loss of reality until we also begin to see him fail to write his novel" (101). In Kubrick's film adaptation, the scrapbook is always associated with Jack's occupation as a writer. Not only is the book pictured next to the typewriter in each scene where it appears, but the *All work and no play* manuscript that emerges from that typewriter is linked irrevocably to the scrapbook that takes over Jack's artistic focus. Instead of inspiring his writing, however, the scrapbook signals his capitulation to the Overlook, his loss of authorial objectivity and control.

This is of course the real reason why the hotel makes the scrapbook available to Jack: to involve him personally, to make him an intimate and integral part of the Overlook's ongoing history. As this takes place, Torrance's loyalties to his family and his identity as both a writer and a human being ("a dull boy"), paralleling his waning interest in his real writing project, weaken; the scrapbook helps him see himself slowly transforming into an active agent for the hotel, tied to an important place with "serious responsibilities" that stretch beyond the mundane realms of family and work. The Overlook inspires the same personal commitment from Jack that it has elicited from the men who have owned and managed the place since its opening. And, like these other men from the hotel's past, Jack grows ever more inclined to sacrifice everything in his own world for its welfare: "He promised himself he would take care of the place, very good care. It seemed that before today he had never really understood the breadth of his responsibility to the Overlook. It was almost like having a responsibility to history" (161).

As discussed earlier in this chapter, the Overlook's history, paralleling the larger scope of American history itself, has always operated from an exclusively patriarchal design. Men have owned and managed the Overlook; men created its notorious reputation; and men—traditional American males—set the example for behavior that Jack hopes to emulate. Women are referenced in the scrapbook (and elsewhere throughout the novel and film) only as glittering ghosts—whores and decadent dolls wearing "gleaming high-heeled pumps," perfumed and naked beneath tight evening gowns and cat-masks, whose primary purpose is to enflame the masculine libido. Interestingly, at no point does Jack consciously allude to the restrictive gender posturing implicit in the history he uncovers. Perhaps this is because Jack himself subscribes to a similar ideology of gender. But in light of this complicit categorizing, it is crucial to note that at the end of chapter 18 in the novel, when Wendy interrupts his reading, Jack feels a need to hide the scrapbook from her. The moment she calls his name from the top of the stairs, Jack "started, almost guiltily, as if he had been drinking secretly and she would smell the fumes on him" (167). That Torrance unconsciously associates getting caught reading the scrapbook with his alcoholism is an important nexus to keep in mind, for both acts are done in secret, both produce high levels of excitement and guilt in Jack, both chronicle habits of violent and destructive behavior, and both deliberately exclude Wendy.

King very wisely never speculates about why Jack refuses to share the scrapbook with Wendy and, moreover, why he comes to associate its history with his own alcoholism. Instead, readers are left to explore these rich associations on their own. On a conscious level, Jack views the Overlook's story as a possible writing project: his opportunity to produce "that book he had semi jokingly promised himself" (156). The reader, on the other hand, is aware that Jack is being seduced into a dark world that he not-so-secretly covets. As Douglas Winter notes in *The Art of Darkness*: "The 'unsavory history' of the Overlook mirrors the equally 'unsavory history' of Jack Torrance, revealing the true ghost of *The Shining*" (49). The Overlook's history of decadence and greed, of violence and intrigue, stimulate the imaginative fantasies of a man who is down on his luck and unhappy about the prospects of his future. Torrance is a man searching for something to believe in personally—his career as a writer and his small family are about all he has left. On the other hand, the hotel's penchant for depravity attracts him for the same reason: Torrance's subconscious recognizes his own history of self-destructive urges in the Overlook's most iniquitous moments: "Once, during the drinking phase, Wendy had accused him of desiring his own destruction but not possessing the necessary moral fiber to support a full-blown death wish. Could it be true?" (185). Jack essentially answers his own question in his subsequent actions—by losing his job at Stovington Prep, his descent back into alcoholism, his estrangement from his family, and his eventual identification with the haunted creeps who inhabit the Overlook.

Yet America has always been the land of second chances. And just as the scrapbook chronicles the historical nexus between the hotel's regeneration, the rags-to-riches story of its principal owner, Horace Derwent, and the emergence of the United States after World War II as "the colossus of the world" (157), Jack is seeking a rebirth of his own in the hopes of "becoming a major American writer" (270). As the scrapbook documents the Overlook's rebirth in each new management era, Jack is also a man who has been given another chance to salvage his writing career as well as his marriage.

But just as the secret history of the Overlook—and America itself—is one of violence and corruption under the veneer of civilized affluence, Jack is reluctant to acknowledge his own participation (as both a child victim and adult perpetuator) in a history of dysfunctional behavior. Late in chapter 18, when Wendy observes his bleeding lip, a symbol of his frustration and struggle against alcoholism, she extends sympathy, asking, "It's been hell for you, hasn't it?" (167). Jack's response, however, is neither to acknowledge Wendy's offer of support nor to share his effort against addiction with her. He chooses instead to keep it all inside. By rejecting Wendy's invitation to reveal his deepest vulnerability, Torrance also fails to lighten his psychological burden. He believes he must repress the shadow of his past rather than employ Wendy or, for that matter, anyone else, to help him grow beyond its negative influence. His refusal to admit Wendy into the darkest corner of his psyche is closely aligned to why he is unwilling to share the scrapbook with her: this is a man whose habit of secret-keeping has always been more important to him than his marriage. As King has speculated, "the tragedy of *The Shining* might have been averted if somewhere along the line Jack had taken Wendy by the hand and said, 'Dear, I think I need counseling'" (Magistrale, *Second Decade*, 19).

On nearly every occasion presented to him, Jack prefers the lie to the truth, repression to disclosure. At the end of the scrapbook chapter, Torrance's pattern of preserving secrets from his wife even allows him to feign sexual arousal in order to distract her from discovering the scrapbook: "He slipped a hand over her taut, jeans-clad bottom with counterfeit lechery. . . . He was relieved that he had gotten Wendy away. His lust became less acted, more natural as they approached the stairs" (168). Like the ghosts who have preceded him at the Overlook, Jack is an accomplished actor willing to play any role in order to protect his perceived self-interests or those of the hotel. And, like the hotel's misogynistic society of men, Torrance shows a capacity to disrespect his wife, exploiting their sexual intimacy out of duplicity and paranoia. The "counterfeit lechery" that he summons here to manipulate Wendy out of the basement masks his *real* arousal for the pornographic sexuality that he prefers to indulge alone in perusing the pages of the scrapbook.

Little wonder, then, that in the televised miniseries the alluring Rebecca De Mornay, clad only in a shiny white negligee that accents her many curves, barely interests her husband on a cold winter night. Like many men, Jack initially preferred the male bonding rituals he established with his drinking buddy Al Shockley to his wife and family life; once he is snowed in at the Overlook, Jack's libido remains distracted and the distance between wife and husband is measured by the absence of married sex. Kubrick's film likewise underscores this distance by featuring Danny and Wendy watching together on television *The Summer of '42* apart from the father figure (who is also metatextually absent in *The Summer of '42*), or playing in the hedge maze while Jack plays a lonely game of catch with the hotel. Jack's growing isolation from his wife and son is an omnipresent element in all the *Shining* texts; and it reinforces the Oedipal resolution that ultimately ends Kubrick's film: Jack Torrance, threatened by his son, sets out to murder his wife and child only to be thwarted by the cunning son, who then runs off with his wife and leaves father for dead.

King's appreciation for Robert Louis Stevenson's *The Strange Case of Dr. Jekyll and Mr. Hyde* is everywhere apparent, both in his fictional and nonfictional prose. In King's novels, we see this literary influence most often in those characters, such as Louis Creed, Kurt Dussander, and Jack Torrance, who maintain secrets between males and from women. Midway through *Pet Sematary*, the novel King authored during his tenure as a writer-in-residence at the University of Maine, where he taught a course on the nineteenth-century gothic novel that included Stevenson's short novel, Jud Crandall offers his own insight into the gender gap: "The things that are in a man's heart . . . are secret things. Women are supposed to be the ones good at keeping secrets, and I guess they do keep a few, but any woman who knows anything at all would tell you she has never really seen into any man's heart" (120–121). The malfeasance that pervades that novel, epitomized in the exclusively masculine domain of the Micmac burial site, is restated in similar terms throughout King's canon. The writer's most treacherous formulations of sin, and certainly the most pervasive designs, are male-generated and male-sustained. From the carefully guarded episodes of governmental and patriarchal abuse in *The Mist*, *Apt Pupil*, and *Pet Sematary* to the unsavory history of the Overlook, King's portrayal of evil most often appears to require an active, illicit bond established between two or more males who are initiated into maintaining some secret covenant.

In her 1992 essay "In Words Not Their Own: Dangerous Women in Stephen King," Karen A. Hohne posits that women in King's fiction "are never allowed to speak themselves, to make themselves with words" (328). In contrast, Hohne argues, the "language of power" belongs exclusively to his male characters, thereby marginalizing women. While Hohne's thesis seems right, at least until the onset of King's feminist-inspired work published subsequent to her argument, such as *Gerald's Game* and *Dolores Claiborne*, it is likewise true that his male protagonists use the silence of secrets—that is, the deliberate omission of language—to exclude women from narrative action and empowerment.

Perhaps it is this very preclusion of women that makes the keeping of secrets so dangerous and ultimately self-destructive for the men who elect to maintain them. For their adherence pushes King's males toward isolation and into a state that forfeits the familial bond so sacred in King's universe. Although it is true that these men derive a certain level of perverse power from the concealed knowledge they possess, secret knowledge in King is always forbidden knowledge. The secrets men keep in his fiction do not merely highlight the dark divisions that separate men and women, husbands and wives; their tragic consequences also strike a Faustian note of caution—serving as reminders that these secrets exist to protect places men have no business going, barriers that were not meant to be crossed. No secret in King's universe ever goes unpunished; invariably, the men in possession of them become possessed by them, and these men ultimately lose their families, their happiness, and their sanity. "Truth comes out," Jack Torrance muses to himself unselfconsciously as he ponders the writing of an exposé of the Overlook Hotel, "in the end it always comes out" (222). It is a maxim Jack should have taken to heart and applied directly to his own life.

1408: THE SHINING REVISITED . . . WITH MODIFICATIONS

The significance of *The Shining* extends beyond the effect on its immediate audience and those many filmmakers and fiction writers who have been influenced by Kubrick's film and King's book. This novel and film possess a deep-seated resonance, as it so obviously has with Stephen King himself, haunting his writing career with its recurring tropes and archetypes in narratives as different as *Rose Red* and "1408." The latter first appeared as a short story in the 2002 collection *Everything's Eventual*, and then in its more expansive and compelling cinematic adaptation in the 2006 film directed by Mikael Hafstrom. The most obvious parallel between *The Shining* and *1408* is the use of a haunted hotel as a repository for evil, and even a mocking facsimile of Delbert Grady reappears in the voice of the hotel's telephone operator. But *1408* condenses the haunted-house archetype into a single room, whereas the sheer size of the Overlook and especially Rose Red sometimes weakens their respective hauntings by spreading them out over the grounds of such large structures. Also, both *The Shining* and *Rose Red* feature large casts of characters creating a deathlessly moving center where spectral energies cannot help but be dispersed. As a result of its narrowed focus, *1408* allows the audience to appreciate a more intimate and specific relationship between the spirits that haunt the text's main character, Michael Enslin, and the inadequacy of this protagonist's response to the loss of his only child, Katie, who died a year earlier from cancer. The film is particularly adroit at revealing slowly the central importance of Katie's role to the plot. *1408* heightens and intensifies the psychological hauntings that represent the best parts of *The Shining* and *Rose Red*.

In *1408*, the psychic drama that spreads out over the vast locales at the Overlook and Rose Red is concentrated into a single hotel room and on a single figure forced to confront his past and the direction of his life. In Kubrick's *Shining*, the moment when Wendy is trapped in their bathroom and Jack is outside on the verge of smashing in the door with an ax remains one of the most riveting scenes in the film. The immediate proximity of the two characters, the inherent danger imminent in the collapse of the door, and Wendy's complete entrapment inside this small space (paralleled in the open gap of the window that remains too small to allow her escape) places the audience in a position of fear and dread. We want to scream along with Wendy. This is the effect we experience through most of Enslin's entrapment in *1408*. The most persuasive aspects of both *The Shining* and *1408* exist in watching the painful psychodrama of an unraveling psyche turned inward against itself; physical space comes to mirror psychic space. *1408* is as much a "torture film" as its horror genre contemporaries *Hostel* or *Saw*, but it is a more satisfying aesthetic experience than either of these because it emphasizes the psychological and the uncanny rather than the gruesome and gory. Jack Torrance's psychological breakdown is a complex matrix of unresolved personality flaws that he never really comes to understand completely, much less to address positively—for example, his temper, his abusive childhood, his alcoholism, his urge to indulge secrets, his desire to attain success as it is defined by the powers at the Overlook, and his unresolved ambivalence toward marriage and parenthood. As we have traced elsewhere in this chapter, these flaws are exaggerated and then manipulated by the ghosts at the Overlook to serve their nefarious design; they may ultimately exploit Jack in order to possess Danny's psychic abilities, but Jack is also the type of man whose dysfunctional personality is at home in the Overlook's tragic trajectory and its unsavory history. Enslin is likewise a flawed character. His life is reduced to writing a series of ghost-busting books that mock efforts of hotels to advertise their speciously haunted histories in order to attract paying guests. As the Dolphin Hotel's manager, Mr. Olin, sums up Mike's work: "Your books are full of cynicism written by a talented, intelligent man who doesn't believe in anything or anyone but himself." Although we get only the tiniest bits of information about his relationship with his father, there is enough to allow us to speculate that Mike may have treated him badly (leaving him alone in an assisted living facility/hospital) and that he harbors a measure of guilt over his death.

Mike Enslin's career as a ghost buster, however, is less about locating ghosts than in dismissing evidence of their existence; his books are less important as Michelin guides to the dead than what they reveal about Mike's psychological state. Mr. Olin possesses a particular fascination with Enslin's evolution, and in the midst of his ordeal the hotel manager taunts him: "You don't believe in anything; you like shattering people's hopes. Why do you think people believe in ghosts? It's the prospect of believing in something after death. How many spirits have you broken?" In dispelling evidence of otherworldly activity, Mike confirms the nonexistence of God. More specifically, it provides him with a belief in the nonexistence of his daughter, so that he does not have to be tortured by her memory. Her death is evidence of an empty and indifferent universe where each of us lives and dies alone, and afterward there is nothing. Enslin's existential position has hardened him into cynicism. He revels in Torrance's similar tendency toward self-pity and an anger that masks deep-seated depression. At the start of this film, Mike has simply enacted Torrance's wish-fulfillment fantasy to be free of all marital and parental responsibilities. Thus, we witness in Enslin a more embittered version (because of the tragic loss of his daughter) of what Torrance eventually becomes: both fathers forsake their own families as well as the family of man.

The differences between *The Shining* and *1408*, however, are instructive to note. The ghosts in both hotels ultimately seek the self-destruction of Torrance and Enslin, but Mike is also given the opportunity for self-understanding. Torrance is effectively seduced and tricked by the spectral agents at the Overlook; by the time he dies, his level of self-knowledge presents him with neither solace nor aid. Mike's spirits likewise torture him—he acknowledges at one point late in the film that he resides in the ninth level of hell replete with the ice and cold that Dante found in his journey down to that circle—but they also educate him. Just as Dante came to view himself as a pilgrim learning as much about himself as the cosmological relationships between good and evil, man and God, Mike's self-imposed journey through the hell of 1408 is an effort to reveal and acknowledge his own sins, to find a way out of perdition. This is why the Dolphin Hotel's manager keeps his focus on the quest by asking, "What do you want to find?" in the course of his journey. It is also why the hotel room constantly mirrors back self-reflexive images of Enslin himself—from his lonely double residing in the apartment across the street, to the videotaped sequences from the past featuring Mike interacting with his family, to the computer's manipulation of his face and voice to lure his estranged wife to the hotel, to the room's extensive efforts to juxtapose the suicides of former guests with Mike's own self-imposed decision to isolate himself from his wife and the memory of his daughter. Within the confines of this solipsistic closed circuit, Mike is forced to confront the past life he has repressed. The room undergoes radical changes in its structure, transforming itself into the ocean, a frozen waste land, and finally a charred shell; the altering physical shapes of 1408 alternately reflect Enslin's spiritual emptiness and, conversely, the transformational energies of an emerging new identity. In the end, the hotel room turns into a charred, hollowed-out shell—nothing less than an extension of his subconscious. Perhaps this is why the film keeps suggesting that Mike is experiencing a drug-induced hallucination (via the bottle of alcohol the hotel manager provides) or that he is trapped in a dream induced by a surfing accident from which he cannot awaken. It is no mere coincidence that the hotel is located in New York, the city he abandoned when Katie died and the place where his wife still resides. His choice to return here suggests an unconscious need to confront himself—that part of himself and his past that remains unresolved—and find atonement. Thus, for a man who could not cry for his dead daughter and chose to abandon his wife at the moment when she most needed him, an ocean of symbolic tears keeps threatening to drown him.

Like Louis Creed in *Pet Sematary*, whose failure to seek comfort in other humans after his son is killed pushes him into an inhuman association with a malign supernaturalism, Enslin is faced with the choice of self-destruction or self-renewal. Where Torrance and Creed align themselves with the suicidal impulses of the Overlook and the Micmac burial ground, respectively, Mike is "not easily rattled" and fights against the evil design at work in the room that keeps pushing him toward either the open window or the open noose. In driving Enslin toward despair, the powers of 1408 seek to destroy him, but instead Mike internalizes the room's judgment that he has "been a selfish man" and from it earns what psychotherapist Carl Jung called *maturation*. By turning his anger outward against the room rather than inward against himself, he earns Olin's admiration: "Well done, Mr. Enslin." Just as important as his refusal to capitulate to the hotel's self-destructive encouragement, he also reconciles with his estranged wife—the ending shows them living together again—and finally permits himself to grieve over his dead daughter. His visions of Katie and the presence of her voice on his tape recorder also affirm the existence of an afterlife—proof, as if any more were needed, that death is not the end and that Katie exists in some spectral world beyond our own.

All families have histories. The families at work in *The Shining*—Jack's family, Wendy's family, the Torrance family, even the family of revenants in the Overlook—are constantly at odds with one another. Jack's and Wendy's familial ghosts (in the novel, Jack's father and Wendy's mother) have immutably shaped the personalities of their children and warped their perceptions of parenting; their son, Danny, is caught in the middle of this battle, with both sets of grandparental ghosts leaving their mark on the boy through their corrosive influence on his parents. Jack Torrance, and to lesser extents Wendy and Danny, are doomed by their respective familial histories—alcoholism, violence, and psychological abuse are their inheritances. Throughout King's novel, whenever a familial ghost from the past appears to affect the present, a tear in the current family's fabric occurs. *The Shining* is thus a relentlessly negative history of parenting and families—haunted, torn apart, and threatened by the recollected ghosts of the past—and the destruction of the Overlook and the Torrance family occurs, at least in part, because of these dysfunctional family bonds. In summoning and appropriating the voice of Jack's father, the hotel enlarges the novel's definition of a negative patriarchy that we have considered elsewhere in this chapter. In *1408*, however, the role of family is more protean, less fixed by destiny or mother/father complexes. The character of Mike Enslin shows that families do not have to self-destruct because of the past, but, rather, also possess the potential to heal and learn from tragic experience—that the love bond uniting parents to one another and to their children is capable of transcending even death. From his experience among the dead inhabitants of room 1408, Mike rejoins the living, even as he must accept the fact that his daughter is irrevocably gone. On the tape recorder at the film's conclusion, his dead daughter asks him, "Don't you love me anymore?" Enslin learns that a father's love transcends even the death of his only daughter.

Close to the end of his ordeal, Mike confronts an imposing door suspended in the center of his surreal hotel room. Readers of *The Dark Tower* will recognize this door as another symbolic threshold of possibilities linking one plane of reality to another. Just as the surrealist painters, Rene Magritte in particular, understood that there are many doorways that extend through the imagination to places that exist beyond the rational world, Mike crosses this symbolic threshold to leave behind his old self (which appears to drown continually throughout the film) and to pursue a new life with his wife and an honest, reconciled memory of Katie. The ending of the film suggests that familial forgiveness is possible; the ghost of their lost daughter, effectively counter-pointing the malefic spirits who inhabit 1408, has returned in order to bring her parents back together. In his effort to explain to his wife why he had to leave her in the first place, Mike says, "every time I looked at your face I saw Katie's." The fact that he returns to his wife after his experience in 1408 signals Enslin's willingness to accept the loss of Katie, the love of his wife, and a measure of self-forgiveness. As he acknowledges with his last words in the movie: "Sometimes you can't get rid of bad memories; you just got to live with them."

In this way, *1408* provides a radically different take on the familial tragedies that drown the characters in both *The Shining* and *Pet Sematary*. It is the story of a man tested and restored, of a man who opens himself to tragic transcendence rather than shutting down in despair. As such, Mike is redeemed by his experience inside 1408, distinguishing himself from Jack Torrance, who is doomed by his exposure to the evil patriarchy at the Overlook. It is also no accident that their contrasting fates can be defined in their differing attitudes toward their respective families. At its best in King's work, family operates as a *ka-tet*, a small, self-enclosed community working together to survive the oppressive and destructive energies at work in the world. The spectral forces in *Pet Sematary*, *The Shining*, and *1408* are all malefic; they wish only the worst for the human beings whom they haunt. But in contrast to the malicious hotel management (including the officious Mr. Ullman) found in *The Shining*, the slippery character of the black manager, Mr. Olin, in *1408* is ultimately revealed as a supernatural agent of good, another of King's "Magical Negroes"—indeed, a more whimsically ambiguous version of Dante's Virgil that points the pilgrim-protagonist homeward toward self-redemption and reconciliation with his long-suffering family.

Chapter 6

Challenging Gender Stereotypes: King's Evolving Women

What about Wendy Torrance? Like Kubrick's film, which turned out to be a vehicle for Jack Nicholson that firmly cemented the on-the-edges-of-madness-and-society character studies that have subsequently defined his Hollywood persona, from The Joker to the neurotic writer in *As Good As It Gets*, the preceding chapter on *The Shining* shows its own gender bias: it focuses almost exclusively on Jack Torrance. Consequently, it reveals very little about Wendy's character. Just how important is Wendy to *The Shining*, and how do we explain the differences among her character portrayals in the novel and the two filmic adaptations? I have always felt that Kubrick selected Shelley Duvall (while coauthoring the movie's screenplay and in casting her for the part) as a deliberate foil for Nicholson; the director wanted a simpering dishrag of a wife so as not to distract viewers' attention from her husband's exuberant portrait of eroding sanity. Even Kubrick's acrimonious off-camera treatment of Duvall, difficult as it is to watch detailed in his daughter's documentary *Making "The Shining,"* suggests the auteur's attitude toward his actress came chillingly close to mirroring Jack Torrance's treatment of Wendy. Although her apparent cocaine use and constant complaints about her physical ailments provide a less-than-flattering portrait of Duvall's professionalism, Kubrick's haranguing and personal insults went beyond method acting or any effort to heighten Duvall's professional focus by keeping her in character; it bordered on misogyny, especially when contrasted in light of the obsequious respect Kubrick awarded Jack Nicholson. *Making "The Shining"* is worth a close look for many reasons.

Not the least is that, given the class and gender dynamics that are so central to *The Shining* itself, Kubrick's own attitude toward his actors supplies another layer to these issues, especially since the director appears to channel several of the movie's male characters—from Delbert Grady to Torrance himself.

Early in Kubrick's film, Wendy is pictured alone in the Overlook's white kitchen, taking the lid off a large can of fruit cocktail as she prepares a meal. She is listening to a female news reporter on local television talk about the case of a missing Aspen woman—Susan Robertson—who "disappeared while on a hunting trip with her husband" somewhere in the Rockies. This moment does not exist in King's novel; it is clear that Kubrick inserts this news report—and makes certain that it is a female voice delivering it—as a means for foreshadowing the imminent danger that Wendy will be facing at the hands of her own husband. In fact, this is just one example of the television continually "shining" in *The Shining*: what it broadcasts—from the missing woman on the newscast; to the abandoned housewife featured in *The Summer of '42,* the film Danny and Wendy are watching together in the Colorado Lounge; to the deathless pursuit with intent to kill in the Road Runner cartoons that Danny views on two separate occasions—always mirrors terrifying events that are interfacing in present time. Indeed, *The Simpsons*' stunningly accurate parody of Kubrick's film, "The Shinning," is a homage to the importance of cable television, recognizing that its loss (along with the absence of Duff beer) is a reason for Homer's murderous rage against his family, as well as his potential salvation: "sister, mother, secret lover." Thus, it is most appropriate that our last image of TV in Kubrick's film appears from inside the confines of the Torrance apartment, telecasting a blank stream of incoherent blue snow while a befuddled Wendy tries to figure out how to get out of the hotel, down the side of the snowy mountain, and away from her deranged husband.

One of my students, Dana Hard, after doing some research on the Internet, pointed out to me that the missing woman from Aspen featured in the *The Shining*'s fictional news report happens to share the same last name, perhaps not so coincidentally, with the infamous serial killer Ted Bundy's last murder victim, another Colorado woman, Shelly Robertson, who was abducted on July 1, 1975, just two years before filming began on Kubrick's set. Aspen was also the Colorado town where Bundy was finally apprehended, and Colorado, along with Utah and Washington State, remained one of Bundy's favorite hunting grounds, accounting for five of his twenty-five murders. Bundy's confession to multiple female murders, leading to his trial that began in

January 1980, riveted the attention of the world, which learned of his heinous acts via the television; his crimes catapulted him into celebrity status. Bundy's attitude toward serial killing—viewing his murdering as a macabre mixture of play, sport, craft, and intellectual challenge—is remarkably similar to the distorted matrix affiliated with "play" at the Overlook, as discussed in the preceding chapter. Thus, while *The Shining* shares much in common with multiple American archetypes, myths, and intertexual allusions to American literature and film, its last link to America may be through one of its most infamous serial killers, a man who, like Torrance himself, was a schizoid mix of educated, charming, and brutally bestial.

Bundy often received help from nature to conceal his crimes; because of bad weather, the body of Caryn Campbell, abducted by Bundy on January 12, 1975, was not found until over a month later underneath heavy Colorado snowfalls. Similarly, the television voice of a male meteorologist in Kubrick's film informs Wendy that the forecast of an imminent snowstorm, interrupting a spate of beautiful weather, "right here towards Colorado, right now as we talk," is likely to impede the rescue search for Robertson. If Kubrick's use of Robertson's surname was intentional, the director may have meant to provide viewers with two nexus points: a means for reinforcing the Colorado locale (as most of the film was actually shot in Kubrick's London studio) and, more intriguingly, another use of the television as a simulacrum for perceiving events going on inside the Overlook. If this is indeed a deliberate inclusion and not just a coincidence, the impending snowstorm and Bundy's reign of brutality against Colorado women are subtly aligned in a moment where reality and cinema blur, leaving Wendy, as much as the unfortunate Susan Robertson, at the center of the coming storms, environmental and human. In words that cast a frightening parallel to Jack Torrance's gender antagonism in *The Shining*, Ted Bundy believed that all males shared to some degree a fraternal antipathy toward females: "I'm just like the guy next door—I'm the stranger beside you. We serial killers are your sons, we are your *husbands*, we are everywhere [italics mine]" (http://www.pureintimacy.org/piArticles/A000000433.cfm). Wendy's look of obvious distress as she listens to the story of the missing female and the dire snowstorm forecast are open to interpretation: Does she simply fear for Robertson's fate from the typical position of compassion mixed with impotence we all feel while listening to televised news tragedies happening to someone else, or is Wendy's facial anguish more in line with a dawning, if still unconscious, *empathy*—that these two wives lost in the Rockies share a common destiny at the hands of their negligent hunter-husbands?

THE FEMINIST COMPLAINT: VICTIMIZED WIVES, GRUELING MOTHERS

Wendy's characterization in the novel and even more so in the teleplay (written by King), however, suggest a greater range of possibilities for her character than merely the helpless victim of a deranged male sociopath found in Kubrick's and Diane Johnson's coauthored screenplay. One of the few redeeming elements of the televised miniseries *Stephen King's The Shining* is Rebecca De Mornay's portrayal, which restores and expands the resiliency found in the female protagonist of the novel. De Mornay's Wendy sustains her resolute distinctiveness from Jack and the spectral powers at the hotel. Watching nervously as her husband grows increasingly angry with Danny, blaming the child for many of the torments inflicted on him by the ghosts at the Overlook (interestingly, whenever Jack gets mad in Kubrick's adaptation, it is always *at Wendy*, which suggests that the two Jacks have differing agendas and treat their respective wives and sons with uniquely different levels of respect), Wendy is the only member of the family to remain calm. Indeed, De Mornay's character does more than serve Jack breakfast in bed or wait patiently for him to finish writing before entering the room. Her Wendy is an artist in her own right—a painter who works in oil and charcoal media—and we watch her labors in front of canvas more than we actually see Jack write.

Moreover, De Mornay's performance demonstrates that while she begins to understand with great clarity that she is trapped in an abusive relationship, she always refuses to be intimidated by her husband, forcefully reminding him to "remember your temper—no matter what Danny has done." When the hotel ghosts begin to address her directly, she responds with a defiant, "You can play with me all you want, but you're never taking my son." This is a far cry from Duvall's nasal, hand-wringing concern about getting Danny to a doctor. At the ABC-TV press conference held before the premiere of the miniseries, De Mornay indicated that she was sharply cognizant of the "female physically locked in this relationship as an allegory" for domestic abuse, and that because of its frequency in American society—"it's happening all over the place"—she "thought it important to play [Wendy] and give her the integrity and the intelligence that she deserves" ("At *The Shining* Press Conference" 25). When Steven Weber's Jack Torrance begins to attack Wendy physically, delivering a series of brutal blows from his croquet mallet, De Mornay's Wendy still manages to keep her wits about her and escapes by throwing a croquet ball at his head and delivering a kick from her high-heeled boot to his groin. The viewer of both cinematic adaptations cannot help but compare De

Mornay's resiliency and confrontational assertiveness with Duvall's whiny effort to defend herself on the stairs of the Overlook by taking lame jabs at Jack with a baseball bat. Though both Wendys defend their young sons against the unfair accusations of their Oedipal-enraged husbands, De Mornay is a more proactive presence, putting her own body between Danny and Jack.

She also recognizes the collapse of Torrance's mental status sooner and is thus not distracted from her husband's threat, as is Duvall's character, by the presence of "someone else in the hotel." Duvall's Wendy waits for Jack to investigate and thereby remains susceptible to his lies about the ghostly revenant in room 237; Jack never deceives De Mornay's Wendy, as she sees things much more clearly than he does throughout the miniseries. She knows Jack is being unduly influenced by the hotel, but she also recognizes that he and the hotel form an alliance against her and Danny. Duvall's character doesn't get to this point until Jack finally threatens to bash in her brains on the stairs of the hotel. His condemnation of her powers of intuition seems dead-on when he tells her, "You've had your whole fucking life to think things over. What good is a few more minutes going to do you now?" Lastly, De Mornay's Wendy never loses her sex appeal or libido, which only deepens our sense of loss as we watch Jack sacrifice opportunities to share in them. Duvall's Wendy, in contrast, never does embody much sexuality, but to be fair, neither does Nicholson's Jack.

In many ways, these two dramatically differing versions of Wendy Torrance—the female who remains always a victim trapped in a psychotic cycle dictated by her husband, versus the assertive, independent woman who deliberately separates herself from the madness of masculinity—can be seen to embody the range of female characters in King's canon. In King's fiction we find a plethora of wives who suffer the agonies of marriages to serial misogynists who are out of control, their behavior the consequences of alcoholism or other drugs, a history of incest and child abuse, low self-esteem, sadistic impulses, economic pressures, self-pity and guilt over the loss of a job or a child, or any combination of the above. Kubrick's Wendy is the archetype for several of these King wives, ranging from Charity Camber in *Cujo*, to Rachel Creed in *Pet Sematary*, to Beverly Marsh Rogan in *IT*, to the pre-self-conscious Jessie Burlingame in *Gerald's Game* and Rosie Daniels in *Rose Madder*.

Each of these women is a long-suffering model of passive obedience. Their willingness to endure husbands who have clearly crossed the line from occasional bouts of marital anger and frustration into patterns of psychological, physical, and sexual abuse is less a reflection of their generosity of spirit or patience in the face of domestic turmoil and more an indication of their own masochistic self-loathing. These wives, like Wendy Torrance, are apologists for their husbands' deteriorating mental conditions; they refuse to leave these men because they don't believe they deserve better; and they tend to confuse the onset of psychosis with being "grouchy." Late in *The Shining*, Wendy is the last barrier standing between the hotel, its vamped ambassador in the form of her deranged husband, and her endangered son. King's novel highlights the desperateness of this situation in Wendy's daydream fantasy about being rescued by another man, "a soap opera Galahad who would sweep Danny and her onto the saddle of his snow-whiter charger and take them away" (367). But as she recognizes the unlikelihood of such an occurrence, she is forced into a moment of critical introspection that underscores her fear of impotence: "Would she stand frozen with terror, or was there enough of the primal mother in her to fight him for her son until one of them was dead? She was soft. When trouble came, she slept. Her past was unremarkable. She had never been tried in fire" (369). Instead of reading the situation accurately, and then taking themselves and their children away from seriously disturbed men, many of King's isolated wives tend to wait for a "soap opera Galahad" (who is by necessity another male) to show up with a convenient snow cat and rescue them, or they hang around until it is too late for any kind of rescue at all.

The monster in King's *IT*, is, like many of the other vampire figures that represent the various forms of malfeasance in King's universe, a shape changer. In fact, It arguably contains several monsters simultaneously, even if it is capable of physically manifesting only one creature at a time. But most of all, the evil locus of this book tends to change into monstrous incarnations that are particular to the child it puts under siege. For example, It appears to Mike Hanlon at the Ironworks as a bird resembling the movie monster, Rodan; for Bill Denbrough, It usually appears in the form of Pennywise, the clown who murdered his brother. For the single female in the Losers Club, Beverly Marsh Rogan, It is always an embodiment of her father, even when the monster takes the shape of the witch from the tale "Hansel and Gretel": "She turned, swirls of red hair floating around her face, to see her father staggering toward her down the hallway, wearing the witch's black dress and skull cameo; her father's face hung with doughy, running flesh" (572). Like the father in the "Hansel and Gretel" fairy tale, Bev's father, Alvin Marsh, has betrayed her. Her whole attitude toward men has been shaped by his abuse and neglect. And as a consequence, she comes to identify masculinity with monstrosity, but also inculcates the belief, handed down from father to husband, that she deserves the punishment that men keep claiming is her due. Whenever Alvin Marsh appears to his daughter, even as a ghost when she is a grown woman, sexual incest and violence inform his every gesture: "I beat you because I wanted to FUCK you, Bevvie, that's all I wanted to do . . . I wanted to put you in the cage . . . and get the oven hot . . . and feel your CUNT" (572). Alvin's constant refrain—"I worry about you, Bevvie, I worry a lot"—is meant to suggest the obsessive nature of the incestuous urge toward his daughter. Punctuated by blows from his fists, which indicate the level of his own sexually sublimated frustration, It finds in Alvin Marsh an avatar for the dark paternity found in "Hansel and Gretel" and extends it to include the masculine authority figure threatening her adult life—her husband, Tom Rogan.

It is probably true that in the novel version of *The Shining,* Wendy Torrance's failure to assert herself in the face of her husband's mistreatment has its roots in her childhood development: she is unable to overcome the loss of self-confidence that is the result of her mother's incessant, demeaning criticism. Bev Rogan's childhood also is responsible for her choices as an adult, preventing her from recognizing that Tom is merely another version of her authoritarian father. Just as victims of abuse often interpret abuse as an expression of love, and then perpetuate the abusive behavior themselves, Bev is unable to escape the pattern that her father established during her adolescence. So, when Tom Rogan beats her, we witness her regression to childlike helplessness, especially in her stilted linguistic constructions: "'*You can't . . . you aren't supposed to hit me. That's a bad basis for a . . . a . . . a lasting relationship.*' She was trying to find a tone, an adult rhythm of speech, and failing. He had regressed her. He was in this car with a child. Voluptuous and sexy as hell, but a child" (108). Bev's language collapse is impressive here because it is so underdeveloped; she may understand intellectually that domestic violence is "a bad basis for a lasting relationship," but emotionally she has learned to expect it. Even as her husband whips her across her breasts for getting a parking ticket, an act that brings her back into intimate contact with her father, King recognizes that childhood abuse is often the precursor to adult masochism: "He was good. He rarely bruised. It didn't even hurt that much. Except for the humiliation. *That* hurt. And what hurt worse was knowing that part of her craved the hurt. Craved the humiliation" (120).

To greater or lesser extents, all the adult members of the Losers Club are forced to regress back to their childhoods, and each of these childhoods is a personalized mixture of triumph and pain. But Bev is the only female in the group, and she is likewise the only member of the club whose childhood has continued to influence her adulthood to the point where she actually marries the monster. The surviving males have gladly repressed the memories of their childhood battle against It; this has been an apparent requirement for them to establish adult lives. While all the Losers become highly successful as adults, a ploy aided by It to keep them far away from Derry, and Bev is certainly as successful in the world as her male friends, she is also more like Mike Hanlon than any of the other characters in the novel. Because Mike remains behind in Derry in order to monitor the violent surges in the town and their potential correlation to the reemergence of It, his role is that of a sentinel: keeping an omnipresent vigil on It. As a result, he remains stuck in a hometown library job with very little money or prestige. Beverly may appear to be the highly affluent creator of Beverly Fashions, Inc. in Chicago, but, like Hanlon, and unlike the other Losers, she has not managed to escape the daily tyranny of It. The difference between Mike and Beverly, however, says much about gender possibilities in America; Mike *chooses* to remain behind. He willingly sacrifices his own career opportunities—as well as demonstrating his bravery—to help protect Derry's children. The adult Beverly remains trapped in a daily cycle of abuse in which she is unconscious of its dysfunctional link back to her childhood in Derry and her own impulse toward self-immolation. In her marriage to Rogan, the slightest infraction—a parking ticket, showing up late for dinner, wearing the wrong clothes or lipstick, smoking a cigarette—is enough for Beverly to reawaken the wrath of It, the father-monster-husband she grew up with and has now married: "There had been other lessons to learn since, a great many, and there had been hot days when she had worn long-sleeved blouses or even cardigan sweaters buttoned all the way to the neck. Gray days when she had worn sunglasses" (111–112). As Lant and Thompson point out, "In King's vision, the macabre is often brutally and violently sexual because, male or female, the most unspeakable monsters do not always lurk uninvited in our closets; they might, indeed, share our beds" (5).

Like Alvin Marsh and It, Tom is also a sadist who senses his wife's vulnerability and preys upon it. In his description of Beverly's adult life, King makes it clear that she comes to "crave the humiliation" associated with her past ("First the surprise. Then the pain. Then the [nostalgia] look of memory" [108]) and even finds sexual arousal from the worst acts of cruelty Tom foists upon her (110–111). Beverly is so trapped by her past and her present self-immolation that it requires multiple beatings and a monumental effort sparked by the call to return to Derry before she finally packs her bags and leaves her husband. And just as important to remember, Bev's ultimate bid for freedom is ensured only because she falls in love with Ben Hanscomb. He secures and validates her place among the other Galahads of the Losers Club. While she is certainly a maternal-sexual figure for the boy-men heroes in this club, Beverly also appears as another version of the embattled Wendy Torrance, searching for the protective security of a white knight to rescue her and ensure her selfhood. In their final battle against It, she lends encouragement and comfort to her male heroes, but she herself is apparently powerless to engage in actual hand-to-mind combat against the monster.

All the males use their own and collective imagination(s) to thwart the monster, but language fails Beverly once again; her contribution is strictly sexual: though she cannot hurt the monster herself, she is capable of unifying the male heroes in their first battle against It by taking their virginities. Although meant as a prophylactic against It's powers to isolate and alienate, Bev's willingness to engage in sexual intercourse with each of these young males strains the credibility of the narrative by revealing King's limited range of insight into an adolescent girl's true psychosexuality. Bev both initiates and, oddly, is the only one to find pleasure from sexual penetration. The boys are all terrified, rightly so, but Beverly encourages them to engage her physically from a position of confidence and control that we don't see from her anywhere else in the novel, especially as an adult woman. At any rate, the collective deflowering of the Losers Club is a highly awkward moment in this male-driven narrative that, in spite of its intended positive associations, comes to resemble a gang rape, and thereby may suggest as much about Beverly's future connection between pain and sexual arousal as it does about her inclination to provide a physical demonstration of love for her endangered mates.

SELF-RESCUE GENDERED FEMININE

During the first two decades of his career, several feminist scholars observed that the roles King traditionally allotted women in his fiction and specifically female sexuality itself were patronizingly restrictive and frequently negative. In 1982, critic Chelsea Quinn Yarbro was first to lament that "it is disheartening when a writer with so much talent and strength of vision is not able to develop a believable woman character between the ages of seventeen and sixty" (65). Mary Pharr, in a seminal essay that broadened and deepened Yarbro's position, noted, "Despite his best efforts, King's women are reflective of American stereotypes. . . . His most convincing female characters are precisely those who are least threatening to men" (21). In a critique devoted to language ideologies and empowerment in King's novels, Karen Hohne recognized the significance inherent in Beverly Marsh's self-imposed gag while attempting conversation with her husband, and opined that "King's universe is crowded with well-modulated Barbie dolls, each barely distinguishable from the next, all with lame or non-existent personalities. The most important female characters vary almost not at all from one work to the next, speaking in uncharacterized language, having no language ties that set them off from each other or even mentally disabled men like Tom Cullen in *The Stand*" (329). Burns and Kanner were even more specific when they examined King's treatment of female sexuality: "Menstruation, mothering, and female sexual desire function as bad omens, prescient clues that something will soon be badly awry" (171). In her discussion of *IT*, Karen Thoens reduced the monster in the text to an essentially female archetype: "It could be repulsive female sexuality. But mostly, it is actually She . . . It is your mother. It, nameless terror. It is bloody, filthy, horrible. The boy-men heroes have returned to Derry to face IT again, HER, the bitch" (137). King's maternal figures generally fare almost as poorly as his fathers. Linda Anderson's essay, "OH DEAR JESUS IT IS FEMALE: Monster as Mother/Mother as Monster in Stephen King's *It*," finds fault with all the mothers present in the novel, especially in their inability to protect their children. She concludes that the males in the novel "must kill the monster who stands for all of their monstrous mothers" (120).

Sharply aware of such criticism and generally concurring with it—when *Playboy* quoted Yarbro's charge to him in 1983, King called it "the most justifiable of all those leveled at me" (Underwood and Miller 47)—King has labored over the years to create more human and less stereotypical female characters. The nineties reflected King's efforts to redress the first half of a career filled with females who were either "barely distinguishable Barbie dolls" or seductive embodiments of evil. It is worth noting that the proactive version of Wendy Torrance played by Rebecca De Mornay does not appear until 1997, seventeen years after Shelly Duvall's portrayal, and twenty years after the original publication of the novel. This time frame significantly parallels the evolutionary development in female characters as they emerged in the career trajectory of Stephen King.

However, the critical world has been slow to recognize the extent of King's progress in gender discourse. In 1998, Kathleen Lant and Theresa Thompson published their regrettably named study, *Imagining the Worst: Stephen King and the Representation of Women*, a collection of eleven essays analyzing many of the most important females to emerge from King's canon, especially those who emerged from the writer's best efforts at creating authentic women characters. Even after novels such as *Dolores Claiborne, Gerald's Game*, and *Rose Madder*, whose female protagonists suggest a new understanding and direction for King, the editors could find only one essay, Carol Senf's treatment of *Dolores Claiborne* and *Gerald's Game*, that recognizes and applauds the direction of this new work. In their Introduction to the volume, Lant and Thompson conclude begrudgingly that "his representations of Everywoman often provoke hostility as well as admiration. When analyzing King's depiction of women, it is tempting to relegate him to the category of unregenerate misogynist or conversely to elevate him to the status of newly sensitive male" (4). Faint praise, at best, especially in unison with the other essays in the collection that likewise display a similar failure to intuit Senf's trenchant insights into King's "radical condemnation of both men and political institutions who use the power of the patriarchy against women and children. [His novels] celebrate women who manage to carve out positions for themselves" (95).

Misery holds a pivotal place in this discussion, as the novel signals a transition that begins to emphasize a new significance for women characters. Here we encounter one of King's first attempts to create a fiercely independent woman who is neither Madonna nor whore. Her psychopathology notwithstanding, Annie Wilkes is one of the few women in King's canon who wields real power, and for more than just a scene, even if she does fail to exercise it responsibly. Although *Misery* is not a feminist text, as it remains mired in the anarchic, potentially castrating nature of women, its female character is a prototype—at least in terms of her independence, intelligence, and angry resolve—for future King female protagonists who follow her. Linda Badley accurately assesses that "*Misery* blamed a sadistic and all-devouring matriarchy for the protagonist's victimization." The novels that immediately follow, however, "correct the misogyny implicit in *Misery*, transporting its situation and setting into Female Gothic and taking the woman's point of view" (66).

As discussed in chapter 1, King's landscape was populated almost exclusively with heroes rather than heroines until the 1990s. In *Gerald's Game, Dolores Claiborne, Rose Madder, Bag of Bones,* and *The Dark Tower* (in creating Susan Delgado and Susannah Dean), however, the writer expands his fictional microcosm to include women who "carve out positions for themselves." The females in these novels differ markedly from those who appear elsewhere in King's canon. All of these wives and mothers possess highly impressive levels of inner strength and independence. Like their male counterparts in earlier works, the heroines of these books are situated at crisis points where they must either rise above their oppression or capitulate to it entirely.

To return to Karen Hohne's persuasive essay on language and gender constructions in King's fiction, she suggests that women in his narratives "are never allowed to speak themselves, to make themselves with words. They get little dialogue, their speech is generally flat and undistinguished or stereotyped" (328). I think this judgment was accurate until the nineties, when King started crafting female characters whose language was not only distinctive and their own, but also occupied a pivotal position in the respective narrative. When King began focusing attention on women's issues, his fiction became more circumscribed, revolving around an individual and her domestic plight, and told from the perspective (or *points* of view, in the case of Jessie Burlingame in *Gerald's Game*) of the female protagonist. In *Dolores Claiborne*, for example, the author completely eschewed his traditional third-person point of view in order to provide Dolores with an autobiographical voice and consciousness. This departure from an omniscient authorial position to a first-person monologue signals the importance King invests in legitimizing Dolores's perspective and the domestic issues that constitute the telling of her story. Further, because of this text's narratology, Dolores incorporates her own distinctive linguistic idioms and cadences. Her language, frequently coarse but always honest, is not only personalized but regionalized as well: in her story we hear the authentic voice of a working-class Maine woman that Karen Hohne found missing elsewhere in the King canon. Colleen Dolan recognizes that Dolores "alienates the people, especially the men, of Little Tall Island with her snappish tongue and sarcastic wit," and that she is "one of those steely-headed, truth-telling old women who make the rest of us cringe. Her tact filter is missing. She says whatever comes to mind and it is usually the ugly, critical truth" (156).

King traditionally divides his novels into sections, and then subdivides these sections into chapters. *Dolores Claiborne* is a radical departure from this narrative structure, as there exist no divisions of any kind in the narrative text; instead, Dolores tells her story via a free association monologue, starting in the middle of what she has to say and working back and forth from past to present. This chronological structure sometimes appears as confusing to the reader as Faulkner's *The Sound and the Fury*, but the device serves a similar purpose: to help the reader see that events that occurred in the past are still impacting the present. If we view this strategy in gendered terms, the novel implies that the strong female voice guiding us through this narrative has earned its right to the language and personality being revealed on the page. In other words, the events of the past have made Dolores Claiborne into the independent, self-determined character we find narrating this text in present tense. The structure of the narrative suggests that the suffering endured and difficult choices enacted have not rendered her into a Faulknerian daze, exemplified in the incapacitations of Reverend Hightower in *Light in August* and Quentin Compson in *The Sound and the Fury* and *Absolom, Absolom!*, who are both left immobilized as a result of the tragedy they have witnessed; in contrast, Dolores's tragic experiences have forced her into becoming a person of action who is liberated by her actions. As Sharon A. Russell opines in discussing the fates of King's female characters, "the women's lives really begin when they awaken to the possibilities of adult action. They finally understand what it means to be an adult and make decisions and take action once they see possibilities which have been hidden by the stupor of their lives" (153). So, in *Dolores Claiborne*, narrative structure is a key to character development: Dolores emerges in control of both the events of her story and the manner in which these events are told.

A similar narrative structure informs *Gerald's Game*. Men in this novel disappear from the active, present-tense landscape after the first chapter. Although Jessie must wrestle with her father, his single act of quasi-incest during an eclipse, and a husband who essentially views his wife as a pornographic toy, the men in this book are summoned via memory. As such, they are enclosed in a world that Jessie must re-experience, but which she can also control. After her husband's untimely exit in the first chapter, the rest of the story takes place in Jessie's head. Thus, like Claiborne, she puts herself in a position to interpret events, long repressed and left unconnected, that have occurred; she learns to gather strength from her women friends—ranging from Ruth Neary, a radical lesbian feminist, to a younger version of herself (Punkin)—who appear as extensions of her own psychology; she learns the value of forgiving herself for the victimization she has undergone while placing the blame for her multiple personality disorder more accurately on masculine sexual manipulation. In short, although tied to the bed for nearly the entire novel as a consequence of a marital bondage game that goes horribly awry, Jessie is, finally, tied even tighter to the job of self-discovery, to an honest introspection that literally and symbolically keeps her bound to Gerald's bed. What she learns from the contending voices in her head eventually sets her free—for the first time in her life she is free to think and act for herself, without male interpretation or revision. The greatest disservice her father, Tom Mahout, does to his daughter after their unfortunate sexual tryst under the eclipse is to make her feel guilty about his sexual urge, cleverly blaming the impulse on the child rather than accepting blame as the adult parent. Although the "sexual accident was about as serious as a stubbed toe" (187), Tom sets his daughter on a lifelong path of repression, convincing her that female sexuality is illicit and dangerous and needs to be kept in check: "I never want boobs and curvy hips, she thought dully. If they make things like this happen, who would?" (164).

Consequently, the bondage game that husband Gerald plays with her becomes a metaphor for the control imposed initially by her father, and, by extension, the restraint imposed on all women by the patriarchy. It is worth noting that on all the earlier occasions when the Burlingames played their bondage games, Jessie was the one tied up, never Gerald, and he was always the one to initiate and escalate the level of bondage she underwent. Similarly, it is Tom Mahout's idea that he and his daughter should have a "date" without other members of the family present on the day of the eclipse, that she should wear her "pretty new sundress" because it "was also too small and too tight," along with her peppermint lipstick because "Daddy had said he thought it was pretty, and that had transformed it into the most valuable of her few cosmetic resources" (137). Like her father, then, Gerald dictates his will upon Jessie, transforming her in his kinky sexplay into "an actress. Or a call-girl. One of the really high-priced ones" (14). While Gerald interprets her verbal objections as part of a scripted sexual scenario—"She was *supposed* to protest; after all, that was the game" (3)—Jessie is actually beginning to confront the sexualized secrets and subtexts of her adolescence. From her father to her husband, Jessie's life has been tied to masculine projections of sexual images and needs. Both men assign personae onto Jessie—prepubescent girlfriend, call girl, actress—in a way that reflects their desperate need to transform her beyond the mundane roles of daughter and wife. Ironically, this does not speak to Jessie's inadequacies, although she believes this is the case, so much as it speaks to the insecurities and obsessive sexual imagination of most males. This is part of the psychosexual baggage that Jessie (like most women, for that matter) intuits from the most important men in her life: that she is never good enough as she is, but must always reinvent herself into a pornographic image in order to please them. Even her father justifies his behavior by confessing that the reason he pursued Jessie was that her mother "hasn't been very . . . well, very affectionate lately, and that was most of the problem today. A man has . . . certain needs" (181). As a result, her lethal kick to Gerald's crotch, viewed in this context, is less an accident than a displaced urge to castrate her father. Even before she undergoes her interior psychodrama, Jessie understands that "She had ceased to be here when the keys made their small, steely clicks in the locks of the handcuffs" (5). What replaces her is one of the most consistent indictments found throughout King's canon, from the vampires in *'Salem's Lot*, to the ghosts at the Overlook, to the societal groupthink that characterizes the dominions of Flagg and the Crimson King: the urge to take a human being and transform that person into a malleable thing: "She thought of those air-filled dollies now, their pink skins, lineless cartoon bodies, and featureless faces, with a kind of revelatory amazement. It wasn't horror—not quite—but an intense light flashed on inside her" (5).

Prior to the work King wrote in the nineties, her psychosexual burden would have remained Jessie's to carry, unabated, for the remainder of the novel. But the bondage—as metaphor and actual sexplay—in *Gerald's Game*, as the title of the book implies, belongs to Gerald's marital past, not to Jessie's imminent future. From the multiple voices that create a cacophony in her mind emerges a woman in possession of a single-minded will to survive, and to triumph over the adversity that the most important males in her life have placed in her way. In both *Dolores Claiborne* and *Gerald's Game*, women usurping control over the telling of the narrative—that is to say, finding their own inimitable voices to express themselves and their history via the narrative itself—undercuts traditional patriarchal dominion while affirming feminine empowerment supported by the storylines.

Gerald's Game and *Dolores Claiborne* are among the most effective illustrations of King's career-long fascination with creating interrelated subject matter and concurrent plotlines connecting separate texts. Both these books share not only the issue of father-daughter incest and moments when Dolores and Jessie either view or sense each other's presence in each respective novel, but they also employ the same 1963 eclipse as a defining moment. In *Gerald's Game*, the eclipse signals the start of Jessie's descent into the silent darkness of shame and loss, whereas in *Dolores Claiborne* it is the event that liberates both Dolores and her daughter from the oppressive shadow of their husband/father. King provides the same detailed map of the path of the eclipse as a frontispiece to both novels. The point at which the "path of totality" begins is Dark Score Lake, where Jessie is molested by her father. The point at which the solar path ends is located over Little Tall Island, where Dolores kills her husband because he has sexually abused their daughter, Selena. The movement of eclipse parallels the movement of evolving female empowerment in these two texts: from the shadow that begins Jessie's victimization while sitting on the lap of her father to its passing in Claiborne's bid for freedom against another oppressive male. Thus, it is important that the moment in *Gerald's Game* when Jessie "envisions" Dolores occurs immediately after Dolores "*made him fall down the well*" (167). Although Jessie recognizes that both women are "*in the path of the eclipse*" (167), Dolores has just completed the task that Jessie must now embark upon: she must follow the older woman in the act of self-liberation. Dolores Claiborne is, in other words, a "future version" of Jessie herself, finding in the darkness of the eclipse a means for facing the light of truth and acting accordingly. Though the actual eclipse in both narratives is important, its metaphorical significance is even more so. The path of the eclipse occurs in any woman's life, King suggests, when she is consumed within a man's penumbra: in these novels, this shadow extends all the way from Jessie's and Selena's adolescence to the end of Dolores's wifehood.

Taylor Hackford's film version of *Dolores Claiborne* illustrates the true effects of the eclipse as a gendered construction in its portrait of Selena, who does not have a major role in King's novel, but who in the film dramatizes the consequences of her father's sexual inappropriateness. Jennifer Jason Leigh plays her character as a contrast in black and white: her pale skin, devoid of makeup and appearing drained of blood as though she is the victim of a vampire, is set off especially against the black clothing and black leather gloves she wears as a kind of uniform throughout the film. But the dark void of the eclipse is most accurately symbolized through her secretive alcohol and pharmaceutical addictions. As a result of her need to repress the childhood memory of incest with her father, Selena has ironically followed him into a pattern of shadowy behavior—like him, she suffers from addiction (she drinks the same brand of "Black and White Scotch" that Joe consumes the day Dolores murders him) and because of him, her sexual relationships with other men are now dysfunctional. Turning her back on the problem, as Selena has tried to do throughout her young adulthood and does so literally in the bathroom of the ferry after her revelatory flashback, only complicates the situation and compounds the guilt felt by the victim. Selena confesses to her mother that "There's been a whole lot of nobodies" in her life. If her romantic-work association with her boss at the magazine is any indication of the other male relationships she has encountered, Selena appears incapable of forming intimate bonds with men because of her inability to trust them. The addiction and the problem with trusting men are evidence of the ways in which her life has been eclipsed as a result of inappropriate contact with her father.

In addition to providing women who act rather than merely being acted upon, these texts also argue that the courage required for acting is provided via contact with other women. There are plenty of authentic male friendships in King's universe—the four boys in *The Body*, Andy and Red in *Shawshank Redemption*, Roland and Eddie in *The Dark Tower*, Stu Redman and Glen Bateman in *The Stand*—that lend depth and enrichment to the male characterizations in each respective text. Contrastingly, there exist no similar female friendships with other females in King's canon prior to the nineties; this absence mirrors and at least partially explains the scarcity of strong and believable female characters. Just as Dolores walks a parallel path that Jessie will likewise follow, Vera (Latin for "truth") supplies Dolores with a harsh but effective alternative to female victimization. After murdering their husbands, both women become outcasts in Little Tall Island society, and must turn to each other for support and friendship. In *Dolores Claiborne*, Vera and Selena shape Dolores's action as much as Ruth and Punkin influence Jessie. Although Jessie's "voices" are primarily extensions of herself, they serve in a role that is similar to Vera's relationship with Dolores: forming an often harsh, but always honest and sympathetic, support group. In contrast to the singular actions that characterize male behavior in *Gerald's Game, Dolores Claiborne*, and *Rose Madder*, women are eventually defined in each of these texts by virtue of their relationships with other women. As Dolan notes, "Vera and Dolores have traded in cruel relationships with men for nonsexual love between female friends. In King's stories, sexual relationships are fraught with danger and male domination. Dolores's and Vera's nonsexual friendship was safe" (160).

The bonds that women form through their common experience is so important that King acknowledges it in the dedication to *Gerald's Game* by recognizing various female relatives who have borne his wife's maiden name—Spruce. Presumably, these are the women who have influenced her most profoundly, and at the same time, all the women whom Stephen King understands Tabitha to be. The novel's dedication may also reflect the influence the Spruce women have exerted on King himself—as a writer and as a male. It's a simple acknowledgement of domestic evolution: after enough years a husband comes to understand that his own life owes a debt to his wife—and to the other females around him—with whom he has chosen to live. In his fight against the various demons in his personal life—alcohol and drugs, for sure, but also the hazards that come with attaining fame in America—Stephen King understands this particular debt better than most men. Indeed, in a conversation he once told me that it is likely he wouldn't be alive today without Tabby's presence in his life.

As we have seen, the feminist-inspired fictions that King produced during the nineties did much to redress the charge that he was as restricted in his ability to create real female characters as is the genre for which King is best known. The number of self-empowered female characters who populate the horror genre has dramatically improved in recent decades, due largely to the proliferation of Final Girls such as Ripley in the *Alien* series and Clarice Starling in *Silence of the Lambs*, but the majority of the films and novels in the field are still trapped in the cycle of busty coeds who are kidnapped, stripped, and tortured for the titillation of an adolescent audience, as witnessed in the so-called torture-porn industry, which features films such as *Saw* and *Hostel*. This makes King's efforts all the more laudable, as his reputation and the impact of his work have helped to challenge and expand the range of possibilities for women characters in the genre. For as much as it might be argued that *Misery, Dolores Claiborne, Rose Madder*, and *Gerald's Game* are not horror tales per se, they all nevertheless contain the prime requisite element found in horror: the presence of an out-of-control monster. That the monster in each of these narratives derives its energies from a decidedly human source instead of the supernatural does not diminish the horror potential; in fact, for some readers and film viewers, the husbands and fathers in these texts are all the more terrifying because they are humanly real, rather than paranormal.

Yet, as strong and independent as the women featured in the aforementioned books are, perhaps the one major flaw in each of these narratives is the monster. The men in King's feminist fictions are severely drawn, as caricatured as the women characters for which he was so justly criticized in his earliest writings. They are vicious, one-dimensional miscreants that sacrifice everything—families, marriages, children, and their own sanities—in their will to dominate and, even more objectionably, sexually violate daughters and wives. We all know men capable of such behavior, but I would also hope that most of us view them as the animals that they are, as anomalies that need to be caged rather than as accurate portrayals of typical husbands and fathers.

Jack Torrance is certainly transformed into a domestic monster in the course of *The Shining*, but what makes him so engaging as a character is his ability to complicate that very judgment, to solicit sympathy from us right to the end. We know his potential, appreciate his extensive effort at wrestling with his personal demons and family history, remain cognizant of the supernatural powers that overwhelm him at the Overlook, and recognize, finally, that under different environmental circumstances, and with a greater measure of assistance from friends, family, and perhaps the right kind of psychiatric counseling services, Jack might have turned his life around to become the kind of man that at least Rebecca De Mornay's Wendy and Danny deserve. We never get the same kind of opportunity to respect the men in *Dolores Claiborne, Gerald's Game*, and especially *Rose Madder* because they are never that ambivalent; they remain too preoccupied with getting drunk, sexually abusing their daughters, and humiliating their wives when they are not tying them up in bed. Perhaps the problem here centers again on the ideology that attends narrative emphasis. Just as we began this chapter discussing Kubrick's Wendy Torrance as a whimpering foil serving as a platform for Nicholson's over-the-top Jack, the men in these books exist to perform a single purpose rather than assume complicated lives of their own. In his effort to present sympathetic women who are given control over both the telling of their narratives and the future direction of their lives, King reduces the males they must confront to base appetites. They are thus tools serving the narratives' larger feminist design, less flesh and blood creations than creatures without redeeming values—finally, detestable, male-bashing stereotypes—whose evil presence is primarily to showcase the noble women they thwart. I won't go so far as to say that their stereotyping diminishes the plotlines in which they appear, because that would take something important away from the dignity of the individual struggles and choices that the women in these books earn. But readers looking for strong, independent women characters who have also found a way to interact with men on even the most cursory level will need to look elsewhere in the King canon.

THE QUEST SHARPENS: THE WOMEN OF *THE DARK TOWER*

Out of King's feminist decade in the nineties emerge two of the most impressive women in his entire canon: *The Dark Tower* brings us Susan Delgado from *Book IV: Wizard and Glass* and Susannah Dean, a major player from *Book II: The Drawing of the Three* until the end of the series. *Wizard and Glass* is published in 1997, just two years after the writer completed his domestic cycle featuring empowered women; Susannah's character is the only constant female presence throughout the course of the epic fantasy. What is perhaps most impressive about both these Susans is this: although they remain characters in fantasy novels, they come to revel in the same independence of spirit that defines the wives who emerge from King's domestic cycle of fiction, and they do so while maintaining an active, functioning sexuality via fundamentally healthy relationships with men.

Although trapped by economics and her manipulative aunt into entertaining the idea of becoming Mayor Thorin's mistress, Susan Delgado is never comfortable in this role and undermines it at every opportunity. She allows Thorin to relieve himself by rubbing against her from behind, but permits this only so she can avoid the even more odious act of having to sleep with him. She is smart enough to understand that her extraordinary beauty makes men act like fools and beasts in her presence, but true enough to herself that she manipulates them only to the extent that she must in order to survive. When we are first introduced to her on the road outside Hambry, she is on the verge of undergoing a humiliating virginity exam at the hands of the old witch, Rhea of the Coos. Everyone in Hambry intimately connected with Susan seeks to impose his or her design over her body: Rhea is interested in her sexuality as a means to extend her own influence in the town and as a long-distance opportunity to punish Thorin; the mayor has no real love for Susan, and seeks only to buy her as his "cully" to obtain an heir and exploit her beauty for his own sexual urge; and although prissy and moralistic, her aunt Cordelia functions as a pimp, interested only in her share of the monetary rewards that attend selling her niece into sexual servitude. Until Roland arrives on the scene, Susan's naiveté and lack of standing in the community leave her open for such abuse. She has no friends to advise her, and in the void created by her recently deceased father, she is vulnerable. She understands that her sexuality is the only leverage a young woman possesses when she is alone in the world, and she thus unwillingly participates in her own exploitation because poverty and isolation limit her options.

For all these reasons, then, Delgado inhabits a domestic trap similar to those that often imprison other King females. Although they represent differing social classes and occupations—Dolores Claiborne is uneducated, working class; Rose Daniels is the unassuming wife of fourteen years married to an abusive cop; while Jessie Burlingame is college educated, the trophy wife of a highly successful lawyer, and a stay-at-home housewife—all these women are in positions to empathize with Susan's economic and sexual disempowerment. And in each of their respective narratives, the horror they are made to experience is, to greater or lesser degrees, linked to male sexuality. The problem of how to survive in a world controlled by men, especially economically, is directly relevant to why these single females feel trapped into staying with males who exploit and abuse them sexually. In finding their way out of these domestic situations, Dolores finds guidance and encouragement from Vera, Jessie finds similar strength from Ruth Neary's voice, and Susan is similarly aided by the arrival of Roland Deschain.

Roland's presence is that of lover–surrogate father, providing her with a greater measure of self-worth and an alternative to self-degradation. But note the unambiguous difference between Roland and the other male "protectors" from King's domestic cycle: Susan's sexuality blossoms when she mates with the young gunslinger, and it is through the power of this discovery that she summons the self-respect to reject the selfish manipulations of her aunt, Thorin's contractual sex, and Hambry's larger (male-centered and male-controlled) corruption. Their erotic love story is the core tale-within-the-tale of *Wizard and Glass* and, in the end, it is Susan, even more than Roland, who emerges as the more complete human being from this relationship. But Roland is also indelibly transformed by his union with her; the memory of their tragic love affair is never very far from his thoughts. Even years later it is responsible for the quiet melancholia that shadows his personality (he has sex with other women in *The Dark Tower*, but never mates or marries), and revenging Delgado's murder becomes one of the great motivators that

Roland uses when fighting the collective energies in Mid-World responsible for her death. In the course of her story, Susan transforms herself from victim to rebel, confident enough in herself and her choice of Roland as her lover to meet him for sex and counsel despite the approbation that she knows would attend their discovery. She helps him and his two friends continually throughout the narrative to subvert the corrupt power structure threatening Hambry; she sacrifices her own life so that the gunslingers may succeed in springing their trap against John Farson's men and the Big Coffin Hunters. When she is betrayed by her cruel aunt and burned at the stake by the townspeople, King links Susan to Joan of Arc, another pre-feminist rebel who was punished for her transgressions against traditional social codes of feminine conduct.

Susannah Dean never shares the same stage with Delgado in *The Dark Tower*, but the former, even more than Susan, emerges as one of King's most fully developed females, invested with multiple personalities that reflect a broad swath of characters from erudite and affluent modern woman (Odetta Holmes), to vulgar and uneducated street fighter (Detta Walker), to feral Gollum-like mother for the demonic embryo she carries within her uterus (Mia). All these personalities are aspects subsumed within the composite, but in the main, Susannah is Eddie Dean's wife, companion, and the only female member of the *ka-tet*. She is a gunslinger whose general sweetness of feminine spirit is counterbalanced with fierce insight and the ability to kill without remorse. In short, Susannah embodies the softer side of Roland's nature most of the time—his knight-errant commitment to the suffering of the weak and dispossessed—while at the same time sharing his uncanny ability to recognize deception in others, to punish them with impunity, to attain gunslinger-level skill and instincts in the use of multiple weapons, and to keep her focus on the value of the *ka-tet* and its quest to find the Tower.

In contrast to the limited role Bev plays as the only female member of the Losers Club when they confront It the second time, essentially relegated to sidelined cheerleader, Susannah holds her own verbally and militarily alongside the male members of the *ka-tet* on nearly every important occasion. Verbally, she chastises anyone who disrespects her as a Negro, disabled, or female. In *The Wolves of Calla*, Eben Took pays when he makes the mistake of feeling too comfortable in his own store and calls Susannah the racist slur, "Brownie." In response, she "seized the man's thumb and bent it back. It was dexterously done. 'Call me brownie again, fatso, and I'll pull your tongue out of your head and wipe your ass with it'" (524). In consultation with the males in her *ka-tet*, Susannah provides her opinion on nearly every issue, and her voice is genuinely respected. But it is as a warrior that she emerges as an unequivocal equal to the males of *The Dark Tower*. Her ability to shoot Roland's pistol is almost as skillful as Roland's himself, and probably better than her husband's.

While Eddie and Roland are always associated with their phallic pistols, Susannah also masters the feminine plates. The riza-plates of Calla Bryn Sturgis, titanium disks with razor-sharp edges except for the spot to be grasped by the thrower, are linked exclusively with the women of the Calla. Susannah learns the art of killing with these plates within a very short period of time. She leads several of the Calla women—the Sisters of Oriza—in heaving these lethal objects against the wolves who enter the town in search of children. It is no mistake that King wishes us to form a parallel between the Calla mothers and a pregnant Susannah defending the town's children against their would-be kidnappers with domestic objects adapted for warfare. The riza-plates maintain several feminine associations: the center of the plates are often decorated fancily with scenes that celebrate rice, the staple crop of the Calla; and throwing these plates is an exclusively feminine activity, a skill that only the town's women-mothers appear to have mastered. So, while the dishes produce a level of violence just as lethal as Roland's guns, they remain exclusively feminized objects in their beauty (they fly elegantly for fifty yards or more), efficiency (they cut cleanly with scalpel-like precision), origins (they are domestic utensils adapted for violence), and subtlety (unlike the guns they produce instant death with stunning silence). Before releasing their dishes, the Sisters of Oriza scream the word Riza once, in honor of Lady Riza, patroness of the plates, a sound that is powerful and athletic while also filled with respect. Susannah opines that "There's an elemental satisfaction to giving that scream and then throwing. . . . I *felt* like a hawk. Riza! O-*Riza*! Just saying the word puts me in a throwing mood" (640). It is safe to assume that the Lady Riza dishes wielded by Susannah and the sisterhood of the Calla prove to be the margin of surprise and lethality needed for the gunslingers to defeat the wolves and save the town. As Roland concludes, "it's safe to come up now. Lady Oriza has stood friend to the Calla this day. And to the line of Eld, as well" (895). In the heat of the climactic battle that ends the *Wolves of Calla*, it is important to remember that it is the women of the Calla, losing a female dish thrower in the process, rather than the men, who join the outside hired guns, stand up to the outlaws, and defend the town. This striking inversion of gender roles links Susannah and the Sisters of Oriza with the Sharon Stone character in the film *The Quick and the Dead*, insofar as they are not typical women characters found in the Western genre; instead, they adapt and transcend gendered behavior to meet the requirements of the situation.

Although both Susannah's legs are amputated from the knees down, and she is forced to ride long distances in a wheelchair or strapped into a saddle behind Eddie or Roland, and her developing team pregnancy brings her physical and emotional pain, she never complains or requires special handling. Indeed, throughout *The Wolves of Calla* she is well aware that she carries an abomination in her uterus that is not the progeny of her husband, yet she maintains a Spartan-like control over her anxieties and never blames the other men in the *ka-tet* for her sacrifice (she is forced to copulate with a hideous male demon to enable Jake to cross into their world). In fact, Roland and Eddie express their worry over her pregnancy more than Susannah does.

When Mia takes control over Susannah's volition and the complicated pregnancy they share in *The Dark Tower*, essentially kidnapping Susannah and forcing her to participate in the birth, Susannah does not panic and actually tries to warn Mia that she has been duped by Richard Sayre and the other minions of the Crimson King seeking to bring the evil child, Mordred, into the world. Although exhausted by her ordeal in the birthing process, Susannah still manages to kill Sayre and wound Mordred as she escapes her captors. In the final volume of the saga, Susan is again placed in a position of helplessness when she must watch her husband die a slow death. And once more, instead of turning inward to self-pity as a result of her tragedy, Susannah models her disciplined reaction after the tradition of the gunslinger legend, turning her sadness into wrath at the battle of Devar-Toi, eventually exiting the narrative alone and harboring the hope that she may be reunited with Eddie in another reality.

Her relationship with Eddie is best viewed in light of the changes that affect him while she is his lover and wife; he evolves from a slack-jawed drug addict in *The Waste Lands* into a gunslinger-warrior whose self-discipline nearly measures up to that of Roland himself. Susannah rounds out and softens the hard edges that often threaten to impede the moral development of Roland and Eddie. Her presence and smart counsel sometimes keeps them both from sliding into masculine displays of ultra-violence that might jeopardize the lives of innocents, the *ka-tet* itself, or the quest they share together. Roland finally recognizes the depth of her influence on his life late in the last volume of *The Dark Tower*, as she is the last of the *ka-tet* to take her leave of the gunslinger before he reaches the Tower itself: "She had brought grace to his life. It wasn't a word that had occurred to him until she was gone" (942). Yet as we have seen above, when necessary and appropriate, Susannah feels none of "the sickness, the feeling of uselessness" that typically plagues Roland after his "five minutes of violence" is over each time they must employ bloodshed (*Song of Susannah* 894–895).

Arguably more kin to Zena the Woman Warrior than she is to the existentially burdened Roland, Susannah Dean combines masculine and feminine gender traits into a unique character. On the last leg of the journey, Susannah proves her real worth. She willfully travels with Roland through the wintry cold to the base of the Dark Tower. Without her help, Roland would be killed by Dandelo, a trickster out to kill the gunslinger; she befriends Patrick and nurses him back to human status; and when she has finally had enough of the quest, she takes her leave of Roland and makes her way back to America, hopeful that she may be reunited with Eddie. This is not a woman who merely serves her men; it is the men who serve this woman. In the end, Susannah may best be viewed as an amalgamation of Jessie Burlingame (bravery and self-knowledge born from her multiple personalities) and Dolores Claiborne (her unsentimental willingness to do whatever the situation requires, including murder).

We began this chapter talking about the various representations of Wendy Torrance that evolved in three very different interpretations of *The Shining*. In the end, all these Wendy(s) come down to the issue of survival—her own, of course, but even more important, the survival of her child. Dolores Claiborne shares the same point of view; mothers, especially those dealing with imperiled children, have always represented the strongest and most resourceful women in King's fiction. At the same time, however, the females who follow Wendy in the canon—Rose Daniels, Jessie Burlingame, Susan Delgado, and Susannah Dean, all childless women—have emerged as examples of individuals who are evolving as people, not just in their roles as protective mothers, and, perhaps most telling, their stories are every bit as interesting as work King has written about boys and men. The most important thing this writer has done in terms of rectifying the weaknesses unwittingly drawn in earlier women characters—including Wendy Torrance and Bev Rogan—has been his willingness in the past two decades or so to allow females to become primary protagonists in his novels, rather than continuing to relegate them to secondary, supportive positions as beautiful muses in male-driven plots.

Perhaps the truism that middle-aged males begin to explore their "feminine" side is one explanation for King's desire to develop more viable women characters, and, equally as important, plots that revolve around issues immediately relevant to women's lives. It certainly would have been easier for a man of Stephen King's popularity and reputation to go on writing the same kind of genre fiction that he produced during his first two decades of publishing, and that has justifiably been responsible for bringing him this popularity and reputation. But King has always tried to avoid the creative trap that ensnared John Grisham, Dean Koontz, Anne

Rice, Dan Brown, and others like them—all highly successful authors—but also authors who have carved out flourishing careers by essentially recreating the same storyline book after book. The energy King has expended on creating more viable female characters, specifically since 1987, and exploring contemporary women's issues is unmatched by any other male novelist writing in America today. His laudable efforts to include fiction that addresses issues especially relevant to half the population is yet another reason for King's emergence as America's Storyteller.

Chapter 7

Gothic Western Epic Fantasy: Encompassing *The Dark Tower*

Near the end of *Book VI: Song of Susannah*, Stephen King, the author of the 3,872-page *The Dark Tower* opus, the longest published novel ever written in English, invents a literary character named Stephen King. Anyone who is a fan of the Hollywood films adapted from King's fiction will recognize here an extension of his cinematic homage to Alfred Hitchcock, as the writer often makes personal appearances in movies adapted from his screen and teleplays: a pizza delivery man in *Rose Red;* the preacher at Gage Creed's funeral in *Pet Sematary;* the band conductor directing a spectral orchestra in the television miniseries adapted from *The Shining;* one of the frontier guards and a loyal citizen of the Free Zone who appears late in *The Stand.* King even introduces the technological meltdown at work in *Maximum Overdrive* when he tries unsuccessfully to operate an ATM in the film that he also directed. But *Song of Susannah* is the first time that Stephen King has ever featured himself as a functioning character in one of his own books. In doing so, he has literally tried to answer the metafictive question E. M. Forster initially raised in the 1920s when considering the role of novelist to his own novel: "Instead of standing above his work and controlling it, cannot the novelist throw himself into it and be carried along to some goal he did not foresee?" (145).

Writing this tome in the first decade of the twenty-first century, the fictionalized King who appears in it is a throwback to a portrait of the artist as a young man: Roland and Eddie, two of the principal characters in *The Dark Tower*, go back in time to meet their creator, the young father and fledgling novelist in 1977; this Stephen King would shortly publish *'Salem's Lot*, the book that first introduced readers to Father Callahan, but more of that later. The Stephen King that Roland and Eddie encounter in the kitchen of a summer home somewhere in central Maine has not yet become America's Storyteller; he is an unassuming guy who is not just a little afraid of the gunslinger character he has invented and who, at this moment, absurdly, confronts him in the flesh seeking answers to questions King hasn't thought of yet. Ironically, King's Roland, because he possesses the benefit of future time, knows more than the writer who created him. King began to write about Roland as early as 1970, but in this time-warped conversation set in 1977 he is forced to acknowledge that the gunslinger "started to scare me, so I stopped writing about you. Boxed you up and put you in a drawer" (286).

This metafictive autobiographical–virtual reality scenario is certainly bizarre, as confusingly surreal as it is uniquely original, but it also underscores one of the major elements from the science fiction–fantasy genre that informs *The Dark Tower*: time travel and multiple planes of temporal reality coexisting and interacting simultaneously. Furthermore, by writing himself and "real world" Maine into the fictional narrative, he is linking autobiography and the real with genre fiction and the imagined, as if there really are portals to other worlds beyond our own; this, too, is in keeping with the concept of parallel universes, all of which are interconnected via the Dark Tower. It is also not the first time that King has allowed a literary character to come off the page and face his author. In *The Dark Half*, George Stark, a vicious literary thug invented by mild-mannered Thad Beaumont, comes to life and confronts his creator with the desire to kill the author and take over his life. Something similar occurs in the novella *Secret Window, Secret Garden*, where author Mort Rainey interacts with one of his literary characters, John Shooter, who accuses the writer of plagiarism. In the end, Shooter is revealed to be an alter ego created by Rainey as a psychological reaction to his guilt associated with an earlier act of plagiarism. These same levels of author-character ambivalence animate the interaction between Roland and Stephen King, as the writer informs his protagonist that "Things changed for me after I put you away, my friend, and for the better. I started to sell my stuff" (286). Indeed. But as it turned out, King never relinquished his compulsion to revisit the gunslinger and to make him the central figure in the quest to find the Dark Tower. Over the years the tale evolved into more than just the occasional storyline he whimsically pulled out of the drawer and resuscitated.

The Dark Tower can be appreciated as a means for unpacking the King canon, an umbrella text encompassing the whole of the writer's fictional oeuvre; by this I mean that it encapsulates and interfaces with many of the core plots, characters, and subject matter of King's work. *The Dark Tower* is therefore a kind of Unified Field Theory for King—that is, he has constructed a grand narrative that not only provides the keystone to all his other works, but also unifies the realms of fiction with those of nonfiction (e.g., the autobiographical element). *The Dark Tower* is a multi-layered universe in which multiple worlds coexist. This, too, is in keeping with science-fiction elements of time travel, wormholes (portals to other worlds), and multiverses, all of which many physicists seriously posit are real possibilities as scientists themselves similarly struggle to create a United Field Theory designed to reconcile the Theory of Relativity and Quantum Mechanics. And like Roland, consumed with the need to find the Tower in order to restore its stability, King's enormous fan base continually motivated the writer to return to the tale with a compulsion that often seems to have bordered on obsession. King the Word Slinger and Roland the Gun Slinger share something in common, despite their occupational differences; it is as if they are alter egos, or Twinners. Both would appear to maintain deeply held convictions and commitments that often leave them socially alienated and misunderstood. In his occupation as a writer, King is about as alien to mainstream America as a gunslinger in New York City. Moreover, it is the storyteller's job to make sense out of chaos, to find forgotten truths hidden under heaps of broken images. Roland would seem an integral part of this enterprise in his effort to find and sustain the Beams that hold up the Dark Tower, and this in spite of the fact that he often appears as a man out of place and out of time. Both King and Roland believe that there are codes of heroism that transcend and interconnect with the codes of prior eras; it is the job of each to rediscover these codes and put them into play.

KING'S PLACE IN *THE DARK TOWER* . . . AND VICE VERSA

Chronologically, the saga took thirty-four years to complete; it embraces King's career as a writer, as he began the first volume several years before publishing *Carrie* and finally completed the saga with the release of the last two volumes in 2004. During the time in between, King would revisit the story periodically, publishing volumes that tended to reflect the writing he was doing in other books at the same time. For example, the alternate worlds that coexist simultaneously and are permeable through literal doorways in *The Talisman* and *Hearts in Atlantis* resemble closely the dual worlds from which the "walk-in" characters emerge and exit through various doors available in *The Dark Tower*. The construction of parallel universes, one firmly established in the Real, or postmodern America, the other set either in a fanciful medieval past (e.g., the Territories in *The Talisman*) or in an equally unworldly dystopian future where a discarded technology is inoperative on an agrarian frontier (e.g., the Mid-World of *The Dark Tower*) has fascinated King throughout his career. *The Dark Tower* saga also reflects King's career-long fascination with culling together diverse genres—in this case, the epic, the Western, gothic romance, science fiction, and fantasy—into a hybrid text where various elements of literary and cinematic traditions and mythologies interface, coalescing into something completely unexpected.

The essential plotline of *The Stand*—wherein the world must reinvent itself as a consequence of a technological meltdown—bears particular relevance to *The Dark Tower;* it is likely that the collapse of several of the Beams that support the Tower itself and the multiple worlds that are dependent on it bear some kind of connection to the technological disruptions that have polluted the universe of Mid-World. The Beams themselves appear to exist in King's America as well as in Mid-World, although both their potency (e.g., clouds that align themselves along the arc of a Beam and the Breakers at work destroying the two remaining Beams) and their imperilment are a more pronounced presence in Mid-World. The city of Lud and the frontier towns that are featured in *The Dark Tower* are all places that show evidence of post-apocalyptic suffering from some kind of technological disaster, clearly radioactive in nature, with abnormal and hideous incidents of birth defects, computer malfunctions, and a general inability of those remaining in Mid-World to operate the sophisticated machinery from the past. As in *The Stand*, the littered detritus of gasoline pumps, highways, computers, robotics, and railway lines attests not only to civilization's passing in *The Dark Tower* but also to the dwindling of technological influence in the face of magic, the latter rising as the former wanes.

Mental fusion as an exotic collective tool employed for destructive purposes is a central theme in the novel *The Tommyknockers;* a similar misuse of telepathy is at work among the Breakers at the Dear-Toi prison camp in the last volume of *The Dark Tower*. The Tommyknockers, an advanced alien species, vamp the brain energies from the citizens of Haven, Maine, just as the children of Calla Bryn Sturgis are kidnapped to provide brain food to increase the Breakers' efforts to erode the Beams supporting the Dark Tower. But one can also trace the existence of unique kinds of "Breakers" throughout King's universe—they are characters such as Carrie White, Danny Torrance, Jack Sawyer, and Ted Brautigan—individuals who are in possession of extraordinary abilities that permit them to engage in mental telepathy and travel between worlds.

Many of the same personalities that haunt *The Dark Tower* are likewise present in other King narratives: the low men and Ted Brautigan, the unfortunate man they pursue relentlessly in *The Regulators* and *Hearts in Atlantis*; the figure of the Turtle in *IT* as a representation of "the white" or the power of good that grows in importance in the last two volumes of the *Dark Tower*; the same evil dark man variously called Walter, Marten, or Richard Fannin is also named Randall Flagg in *The Stand* and *The Eyes of the Dragon*; a shape-changer and the focus of evil in the novel *Insomnia*, the Crimson King, returns as Roland's nemesis who seeks to thwart the gunslinger's quest by destroying the Dark Tower; and, most notably, Father Donald Callahan is summoned for an encore from the pages of *'Salem's Lot*. Of all these recurring figures, Callahan's return—beginning in *The Wolves of the Calla* and continuing through the final two volumes—is the most developed and the most engaging. One of the complaints that many readers share after completing *The Dark Tower* is dissatisfaction with King's portrayal of evil. The various incarnations of the Dark Man in this series—whether he appears as Flagg, or Fannin, or the Crimson King—lack coherency and depth. Tolkien never permitted the reader access to a physical embodiment of Sauron beyond the image of his omniscient eye, but his presence is nevertheless keenly felt, especially the closer the hobbits get to Mordor. Moreover, the fact that we never actually see Sauron connected to a body makes him all the more terrifying and sinister. Not so with King's evil representatives. Their lack of physical presence and amorphous intellectual design—what, for instance, do they ultimately hope to gain out of the destruction of the Tower?—weakens the seriousness of Roland's quest. Further, these various men in black don't seem to communicate very well with one another or their author, as they appear in one volume, only to disappear in the next without much explanation or actual effectiveness. Of all the various ambassadors of evil in *The Dark Tower*, only Mordred seems to understand his malefic purpose and to maintain his focus on Roland's demise.

When readers leave Callahan, the Catholic priest at the end of *'Salem's Lot*, he has just been humiliated by Kurt Barlow, the Type One vampire in the novel. When Barlow submits him to a test of faith in God, Callahan proves unworthy, and as punishment for his weakness he is allowed to live but only after being forced to drink Barlow's tainted blood. He thereafter commences wandering the earth in thirsty search of both alcohol and absolution. Over the years, his self-pity and alcoholism are gradually channeled positively into decades of aiding the poor, first in a soup kitchen in New York City, where he is pursued relentlessly by the low men. Then, later, he is reborn as a clergyman in Calla Bryn Sturgis, where he comforts and guides his fellow Mid-World citizens while also serving as a sentinel keeping watch over Black Thirteen, the evil energy in a ball that slumbers restively under the floorboards of Callahan's church. Clearly, King means to give the prodigal priest a second chance in sending him off to Mid-World, and Callahan makes the most of this redemptive opportunity.

Facing Barlow in *'Salem's Lot*, he exposed his cowardice; his failure to stand up to the vampire's evil revealed not only the priest's lack of faith, but also resulted in the murders of Mark Petrie's parents. From *The Wolves of Calla* and through the next two volumes of *The Dark Tower*, however, we meet a more resolute Callahan whose self-fortitude has been hardened by years of intense critical introspection; emerging from his descent into alcoholism and negation, the priest turns himself into a vampire slayer, killing the undead wherever he finds them, in New York as well as in Mid-World. So, when Roland's *ka-tet* encounters him in the Calla, Callahan no longer cowers; he fights alongside the gunslingers against the robotized Wolves.

In *Song of Susannah* and *The Dark Tower*, the priest is again prepared to die following Jake's lead in their attempt to rescue the pregnant Susannah at the Dixie Pig. To help highlight the contrast between the two Callahans, let's consider his crucifix in *'Salem's Lot* and the scrimshaw turtle in his later incarnation. When confronted with Barlow's challenge, the priest is unwilling to face the vampire without relying on his crucifix; this icon, however, proves to be without power because the priest cannot cast it aside and fight the vampire with his faith alone. Two decades later, just before Jake and Callahan enter the Dixie Pig to do battle against the vampires holding Susannah, Callahan finds the scrimshaw turtle she has left behind for her rescuers to find. In contrast to the earlier crucifix, the turtle reinvigorates the power of his faith—and Callahan's spiritual renewal is highlighted in his understanding of what it symbolizes: "Callahan was surprised by its weight, and then struck almost breathless by its beauty. He felt the same dawning of hope. It was probably stupid, but it was there all right" (*Susannah* 343). Unlike the priest's crucifix, which loses its glow when confronted with the depths of Barlow's darkness, the turtle, which King reminds us in both *IT* and throughout the final two volumes of *The Dark Tower*, "bears us all on his shell, and serves Gan, the creative overforce" (*Susannah* 394), reflects back the priest's spiritual renewal, his personal courage forged from suffering and an escalating confrontation with evil's minions. When challenged by Barlow in *'Salem's Lot*, Callahan worried about getting out alive; in *Song of Susannah* and *The Dark Tower*, when given another chance to face vampires, Callahan's focus is no longer on himself and his own survival. Instead, he administers last rites to Jake, understands that "it might be a bad idea for us to be taken alive" (*Susannah* 337), and willingly sacrifices himself to save Susannah, a member of the *ka-tet*. In *Lot*, the priest cowers in his own fear and disgrace. This time, his faith does not fail him because he has earned it. As a result, Callahan exits the King universe linked to the great warriors in the writer's canon—the quartet that confronts Flagg in *The Stand*; the small band of resisters in *The Mist*; the Losers who face the monster in *IT*; Dolores Claiborne, Vera, and Selena, who share a commitment to each other that allows them all to triumph over levels of patriarchal abuse in *Dolores Claiborne*; Dick Hallorann in *The Shining* and *IT*; Andy Dufresne in *Shawshank*. All these characters share with Father Callahan the same willingness to exchange self-sacrifice for the survival of friends and ideals: "Callahan strode briskly toward the others. His fear was gone. The shadow of shame that had hung over him ever since Barlow had taken his cross and broken it was also gone" (*The Dark Tower* 14–15). In *Lot*, as Sharon Russell points out, the male *ka-tet* fails in their battle against the town vampires "because they do not work together. When they separate Barlow can successfully attack and destroy them" (Russell 38). This time, however, Callahan appears to have learned from his earlier failing: he now identifies himself as an integral part of a larger whole. This identification provides the priest with more than just courage; it gives him a whole new identity. Just before their battle with the vampires inside the Dixie Pig, Callahan asks, "After we bring her out of there, Jake, am I a gunslinger?" (341). It is actually the very question he has been successfully answering for the past twenty-five years since leaving *'Salem's Lot* in disgrace.

THE EVOLUTION OF A GUNSLINGER: ROLAND'S WESTERN MOLD

Let us return to Stephen King's nervous admission in *Song of Susannah* that he abandoned work on *The Dark Tower* early in his career because Roland started to scare him. How could a mere literary invention, Roland Deschain of Gilead, provoke such an overreaction, especially in a writer who would soon specialize in creating monstrous vampires and vicious psychopaths such as George Stark? Perhaps it wasn't just Roland's aggressive personality that was responsible for King's professed reluctance; the envisioned length and scope of Roland's story might have also constituted a large part of the author's fear. When we consider the size and amount of time involved in producing this opus, especially when viewed from the perspective of a young, nascent writer uncertain about the details of the story beginning to unfold, the intimidation potential grows exponentially.

Why then, if this is an honest admission by the metafictive author, did King feel compelled to continue revisiting this figure over the next thirty years in six long subsequent volumes, making Roland Deschain the single most important character to emerge from his fictional canon? After all, once Thad Beaumont managed to destroy George Stark, readers of *The Dark Half* came to understand completely Beaumont's reluctance to re-conjure this dangerous alter ego for use in another novel. The explanation King supplies in the last volume of *The Dark Tower* is that Roland and Jake, the latter sacrificing his own life in order to rescue King from the real-life car accident that involved the writer back in 1999, were ultimately responsible for bringing him back to writing about the Beams and the Tower. Without their miraculous metafictive intercession, the novel would have us believe, Stephen King would have never finished his magnum opus: "'I lost the Beam,' King said. . . . 'You didn't lose it, you turned your coward's eye away [Roland counters]. My friend had to save you for you to see it again'" (*The Dark Tower* 564–565). Although this speculation becomes an integral part of Roland's quest as well as fueling his amusing antipathy toward his author-creator, there may also be other, less specious reasons that King felt compelled to return to his long saga of the gunslinger.

In chapter 5, dealing with *The Shining*, I discussed the many ways in which that novel reflected King's fascination with, and understanding of, American capitalism's secreted past, forming a dark matrix that is embedded in Jack Torrance's personal-historical relationship with the spirits that animate the Overlook Hotel. His link to Childe Roland and the heroic epic tradition notwithstanding, King's gunslinger is also representative of a primal American archetype. For while the saga conjoins primarily the worlds of medieval fantasy and postmodern America, it is also very much shaped by the classic American Western, informed as it is by the masculine code of ethics that informs the genre. We've seen some version of this Western before, rooted as it is in the work of John Wayne and Clint Eastwood, but *The Dark Tower* doesn't quite fit comfortably in the twentieth century, as King finished it in the twenty-first, remaking the image of the Western hero for one more and perhaps the last time.

The American Western hero is ideally suited to a frontier environment and mentality. By its very definition, the frontier exists on the threshold between civilization and wilderness, law and anarchy. From the early colonialists, such as Crevecoeur and Jefferson, to the *Terminator* series, Americans have always been fascinated with formulations of the frontier and its corresponding contribution to the symbology of place. All of America was frontier at one point, from the dark woods beyond the Puritan's city on a hill, to the great expanse of uncivilized plains and mountains that extended beyond the Mississippi. Now a figurative frontier has emerged, as we struggle on with the same pioneer spirit of Daniel Boone to explore reality in outer space, under the ocean, and into the realm of spirituality. I would even suggest that our ever-increasing involvement in Iraq and Afghanistan is a continuation of frontier exploration and colonization and the concept of Manifest Destiny. Instead of Indian fighting, we now fight terrorists. Roland's emergence in yet another King frontier saga carries with it the trappings of the American Western myth—the gunslinger is as unique to the American landscape as the wide-open prairies and forests in which his journey unfolds both in Mid-World and in "real" Kansas.

In the end, Roland emerges as another figure in King's gallery of American males, joining flawed but nevertheless heroic characters such as Ben Mears in *'Salem's Lot*, Johnny Smith in *The Dead Zone*, Ted Brautigan in *Hearts in Atlantis*, Paul Sheldon in *Misery*, Stu Redman in *The Stand*, and Andy Dufresne in *Shawshank*. Although certainly much more violent than these others, Roland is as much a portrait of the American hero as any to be found in King's canon. Standing against odds that are not in their favor and clearly demarcated in terms of good embattled against evil almost to the point of allegory, the narratives in which these men appear nonetheless hinge on the choices they make. They are not only at the centers of their respective plotlines; they are also the moral centers of King's universe, as much a part of whatever forces are holding up the Tower as the Beams themselves. Just as important, these King males stand apart from the crowd by virtue of their intelligence and self-reliance—of them all, only Stu Redman remains married—and their isolation is a big part of what makes them so archetypically American. Even though he is descended from the Line of Eld, Roland shares much in common with the common-man heroes found throughout King's canon, but invested with something special. Above all else, he is an individualist, and he lives according to a set of ethical principles that the majority would not understand, much less be capable of emulating. It is finally the distinct American-ness of the myths informing Roland's quest that propels *The Dark Tower* beyond its tedious obsession with locating the Tower itself. As in *The Talisman*, *The Stand*, and *IT*, it is the journey and those characters who must undertake it that possess more meaning and vitality for the reader than the long-anticipated (and sadly anti-climactic) destination waiting at the journey's end. King himself appears to anticipate this situation when he reminds the reader in an "Author's Note" at the end of *The Dark Tower* that "It was all about reaching the Tower, you see—mine as well as Roland's—and that has finally been accomplished. You may not like what Roland found at the top . . . I wasn't exactly crazy about the ending, either, if you want to know the truth" (1048). Perhaps this last admission is the final connection that *The Dark Tower* shares with the rest of King's canon: it is also a work featuring parts that are more impressive than the whole.

The Dark Tower thus poses yet another window on King's career-long exploration of the American character, as the gunslinger embodies the spirit of the American wanderer. Like the *Huck Finn* prototype that has influenced so many of King's texts, from the Danny-Hallorann relationship in *The Shining* to Jack Sawyer's character in *The Talisman*, *The Dark Tower* features again a social outsider–outlaw whose restive quest for adventure takes him to places that are often as dangerous as they are lonely. Americans remain inordinately fond of personalities that drift in and out of settled society, testing its mores and levels of tolerance before lighting out again for the territory ahead of the rest. Even today, two in ten American households move every fifteen months to two years, to say nothing of the frequency of movement aligned with individual Americans devoid of familial ties. Although a majority of Americans are not loners, there is something about the myth of the archetypical loner figure that Americans seem to identify with. And the most forbidding of these personality types are those drifters that emerge from western dust: Billy the Kid, the Dalton Brothers, Ted Bundy, Charles Manson, Bonnie and Clyde. An anomalous combination of Western myth and alienated American reality, all these Americans, those from fiction as well as those real enough to gain mythological status, must be seen as kin to Roland Deschain: nihilistic and unanchored; and when they venture into society, they often end up killing, or dead, or both.

Roland is, finally, a figure who blends both the medieval romance of Mid-World with traditional definitions of American masculinity. Perhaps this explains his choice of a *ka-tet* composed exclusively of Americans and his fascination (he remains in awe of aspirin's miraculous ability to heal) to learn as much as he can about the culture from which they came. For Roland is unconsciously linked with those American males, both real and imaginary, who are associated with a fiercely independent spirit and will and an *otherness* distinct to American culture; in other words, you would be far less likely to find a Roland Deschain emerge from Europe or Japan. In literature and film, Huck Finn, Henry Thoreau, and the rootless outsiders of Steinbeck are his brothers, but so are Ishmael, the lone survivor in *Moby-Dick*; the nonconformist wanderers celebrated by the Beats such as Allen Ginsberg, William Burroughs, and especially Jack Kerouac; Marvel Comics' existentialist superhero, Ironman, who may be tortured by his corporate identity but never by his commitment to violence as a solution; Marlon Brando in *The Wild One;* and, most defiantly, the alienated antiheroes of Westerns from *The Magnificent Seven* and *Unforgiven* to Cormac McCarthy's *No Country for Old Men* and *The Road.* On the other hand, Roland is also kin to America's most infamous serial killers, a figure whose penchant for violence and mayhem, for acts against established order and authority, is barely counterpointed by his commitment to noble quests.

Though always aligned with those fighting against forces that serve the Crimson King, Roland is not much of a negotiator; words ultimately matter less to him than action. In fact, he is most comfortable in active opposition to authority—providing orders to his allies about how to conduct themselves in combat or planning an effectively gruesome battle strategy. As King informs us early in the journey, the gunslinger "had never been a man who understood himself deeply or cared to; the concept of self-consciousness (let alone self-analysis) was alien to him. His way was to act—to quickly consult his own interior, utterly mysterious workings, and then act" (*The Waste Lands* 29). Roland reveals his humanity sparingly, and most notably as a young man, when he falls in love with Susan Delgado in *Wizard and Glass.* But this adolescent version of the gunslinger—dreamily preoccupied with sexual liaisons and romance—is so foreign to his temperament elsewhere in *The Dark Tower* that Cuthbert and Alain, his warrior sidekicks, are baffled and disturbed by his atypical behavior.

In Roland we see the essence of the American cowboy-mercenary-politician—an ambivalent figure who is as fearful as he is fascinating, as likely to destroy a village as he is to save it. For right alongside his restlessness exists a reliance on and a propensity toward aggression; indeed, violence is his instinctual response to all conflicts. Roland conducts himself by modeling an ideology nearly identical to the one that has framed American foreign policy since World War II: anytime verbal negotiations threaten to break down, he pulls out his gun and initiates a bloodbath. Moreover, as we journey further along into the series, Roland's tendency is to abandon negotiating altogether. (But it should be noted that the closer the *ka-tet* gets to the Tower, the less human are its enemies. The Wolves of Calla, for example, are actually cyborgs wearing wolf masks, and the guards at Algul Siento are a bizarre mix of spiritless low men, humanoid-bird-rodent hybrids called *taheens*, and rejects from the American penal system, such as Pimli Prentiss.) Nevertheless, Ted Brautigan, who has spent enough time in Connecticut to understand the gunslinger in distinctly American terms, recognizes Roland's propensity for aggression within a very short time after meeting him, noting, as the two plan their attack on the prison at Algul Siento, "You mean to spill an almighty lot of blood." And Roland's reply is just as emphatic: "Indeed I do. As much as I can" (*The Dark Tower* 421).

King understands well enough that his readers will recognize in Roland a version of Dirty Harry, Shane, the Man With No Name, Walt Kowalski, and all the other convoluted versions of outlaws and avenging American iconoclastic antiheroes that have roamed across our collective cultural consciousness for the past half-century. All these are embodied in Roland's ideology and physical gestures, from his clear attraction to mortal combat even when he is massively outnumbered, to his moral righteousness in his dogmatic belief that he is fighting the good cause, to his silent grimaces of pain each time he must overexert his arthritic hips and hands. In *Gran Torino*, Clint Eastwood's Walt Kowalski overcomes his deep-seated racism, old-man cynicism, and even lung cancer to emerge as a Christ-like figure willing to sacrifice himself in order to rescue his besieged Asian next-door neighbors. Like Roland and the other aforementioned American heroes, Kowalski asks nothing in return for doing the right thing; when he sees injustice, he simply takes violent action to counter it. Roland behaves in a similar manner throughout his interactions with the suffering mortals he encounters on his life journey, most of whom neither fully appreciate his example nor measure up themselves to his courage and higher sense of purpose. All these spectral cultural figures, totems of masculinity, and avatars from a distinctly American sense of a heroic tradition are what give substance to Roland's personality; his regal ancestry rooted in Mid-World as the son of the last Lord of Gilead, descendant of Arthur Eld, pales in importance to his mythic inheritance as a son of Sergio Leone, Sam Peckinpah, and Clint Eastwood.

David Davis, in writing about the codes of Western behavior, includes violence as an elemental rite of passage: "Of course, most cowboy books and movies bristle with violence. . . . These bloody escapades are necessary and are simply explained. They provide the stage for the hero to show his heroism, and since the cowboy is the hero of the preadolescent, he must prove himself by [preadolescent] standards" (28–29). In Tull, when the townspeople attack the gunslinger at the urging of the dark man, it is clear that Roland has no compunction about his use of force. It is probably true that violent force remains Roland's hallmark throughout the saga, but in the early books he lacks any sensitivity to the moral complexity and responsibility that attend its usage. King tells us, for example, that after completely eliminating the town of its human inhabitants, Roland "ate hamburgers and drank three beers. . . . That night he slept in the bed where he and Alice had lain. He had no dreams" (*Gunslinger* 64). The Slow Mutants lose whatever humanity they may still retain when the gunslinger shoots indiscriminately into their midst "without allowing himself to think" (179). The gunslinger may hunt the man in black for a reason that is semi-comprehensible to himself alone, but it is apparent from the first four stories of *The Gunslinger* volume that Roland has much in common with the amoral dark man he pursues.

In the "Afterword" to *The Gunslinger* volume, King alludes to Robert Browning's poem "Childe Roland to the Dark Tower Came" as the primary influence in the construction of his own epic saga: "I played with the idea of trying a long romantic novel embodying the feel, if not the exact sense of the Browning poem" (221). Browning's Childe Roland has spent "a life training for the sight" (Browning 1043), and his journey to the Dark Tower is heroic if for no other reason than the knight's perseverance. In many ways, King's narrative is characteristic of the same epic tendencies found in Browning's poem, given the difference in genre, as an epic is traditionally a poem, rather than a novel(s). Roland is the central heroic figure, and though he is not literally superhuman, he does possess skills and talents that seem to stretch the limits of human potential (e.g., his ability to shoot unerringly despite missing fingers on his right hand, his telekinetic gifts). Like the Browning poem, *The Dark Tower* is filled with perilous journeys and adventures full of physical and mental dangers that fail to deter the progress of the main character. As is also the case with King's last gunslinger, Childe Roland seeks a vision he neither understands nor precisely knows where or how to pursue. But the very pursuit of an idea, a person, or a thing to its most profound level of meaning or being is a quasi-religious occupation Browning praises in many of his poems; such tests of perseverance strengthen the individual's spiritual resolve: "When, in the very nick/Of giving up, one time more, came a click" (Browning 1043). Childe Roland shares with fellow Browning subjects Rabbi Ben Ezra and Fra Lippo Lippi an understanding that the sufferings of this life are a vehicle for the soul's education.

King's Roland Deschain comes to parallel Browning's protagonists in each of the aforementioned aspects, but his spiritual evolution is as slow and tentative as the quest to find the Dark Tower. In the first two volumes at least, it is clear why the Stephen King character in *Song of Susannah* acknowledged some anxiousness in writing about Roland: the early gunslinger is a man without attachments; he is loved by no one, and there is no one for him to love. He lacks a sense of community or purpose beyond the incessant hunt for the man in black and, by extension, the Tower itself. Indeed, in his rootlessness, his belief in violence as a solution to most problems, and his studied amorality, he most resembles the man in black himself. Throughout most of the epic's first volume, *The Gunslinger*,

Roland is at the nadir of his spiritual development; he must learn why "the man in black travels with [Roland's] soul in his pocket" (90) and how best to extricate it so that it may belong to Roland once more and serve the greater good affiliated with the Tower's Beam. Roland's early spiritual malaise is perhaps best illustrated in his failure to save the young boy, Jake. Forced to choose between capturing the man in black and letting Jake fall to his death, Roland lets the young boy die. This choice parallels Roland's obsession with the Tower: he is willing, at least early on, to sacrifice everything and everyone in his life in pursuit of this amorphous goal. The Roland who enters the second book, *The Drawing of the Three*, is best summed up by Eddie Dean, who pronounces an accurate condemnation of the gunslinger: "There are people who need people to need them. The reason you don't understand is because you are not one of those people. You'd use me and then toss me away like a paper bag if that's what it came down to" (170).

There is, however, a discernible difference between this Roland and the man who evolves in subsequent volumes of *The Dark Tower*. Just as Father Callahan undergoes a metamorphosis during his years in exile, Roland's personality likewise modifies as a result of his commitment to the members of his *ka-tet* and the gradual understanding of his role as the last gunslinger, a force of rough justice in the world bound by the code of his kind to help those in distress. One might argue that Roland's metamorphosis begins as early as the second volume in the series, *The Drawing of the Three*. Here, Roland's propensity toward violence is definitely tempered—more appropriate to the situation and to the behavior of a heroic personage. Moreover, in serving as the distraction that saves Jake from being murdered by Jack Mort, Roland displays the fullest extent of his development as a moral agent. Unwilling to allow the boy to die a second time as a result of his own selfishness and negligence, Roland relinquishes his hold on Mort long enough to permit Jake's escape. It is the first time in *The Dark Tower* that the gunslinger demonstrates a determined willingness to sacrifice the successful completion of his journey-quest because of its cost in human life. The gunslinger's choice of self-sacrifice, risking the quest for the Tower itself, is repeated elsewhere in the series, such as his willingness to comb the booby-trapped city of Lud in his search to rescue Jake when he is kidnapped by Gasher and Tick-Tock Man in volume three, *The Waste Lands*.

Roland's development as an epic hero—and also as a moral agent—seems to hinge on how well he manages to protect Jake. The Roland who appears in the first volume of the saga has no commitment to the boy. But by the last volume, Roland's pain over Jake's "second" death is palpable.

Perhaps it is because Jake is always a child as well as a gunslinger, or perhaps it is the father-son bond that the two establish. Either way, Jake's welfare steadily grows in importance for Roland. He loses both Eddie Dean and Jake in the final volume, and while he grieves deeply for Eddie—a definite sign of the gunslinger's maturation—losing Jake seems to saddle Roland with a profound sadness that only a parent who has lost a child is capable of feeling: "the boy who he loved more than all the others—more than he'd loved anyone ever in his life, even Susan Delgado—had passed beyond him for the second time" (*The Dark Tower* 573). When Jake departs the narrative, Roland's focus blurs and he loses a step; his compelling search for the Tower and the importance of containing Mordred don't appear to resonate with the same urgency once Jake is irretrievably taken from him.

EPIC VERSUS GOTHIC: THE PRICE OF ANSWERING THE *TOWER*'S CALL

The Dark Tower is built on a series of back-stories—every member of the *ka-tet* has a history—and it is through the interweaving of these stories that the group shares in one another's past and achieves community. As they persevere toward the Tower, each member of the *ka-tet* grapples with his or her own destiny as well as working to uphold the unity and power of the group dynamic. Thus, each member develops his or her sense of selfhood as both independent beings and as a part of a larger gestalt. The individual coexists within the group's identity, but the two never completely merge.

Roland's ambiguous love for Eddie and Susannah grows in depth and intensity as the story progresses. From Roland, Eddie and Susannah learn the combat skills and mental discipline tied to the gunslinger lineage. Eddie, in particular, evolves from a pathetic junkie desperate for a fix to a "man who behaves with all the dignity of a born gunslinger despite his addiction" (*Drawing of the Three* 156). In fact, one could argue that Eddie ultimately transcends his mentor, as Roland's nature tends to blind and contain him; Eddie, on the other hand, possesses the power to open himself to new worlds, new possibilities. From Eddie and Susannah, Roland is properly educated in virtues that are sorely underdeveloped: friendship and love, certainly, but also the knowledge that the *quest* to find the Tower turns out to be just as important as the Tower itself. The people he has loved in the course of his long journey—the *ka-tet* most of all, but also Susan Delgado, Ted Brautigan, Sheemie, Cuthbert and Alain, and even Oy the billy-bumbler—teach Roland that his life's goal is less physical than it is spiritual, and in this way the gunslinger comes most to emulate the heroic tenets of Browning's Childe Roland. As Joseph Campbell argues throughout his monumental study *The Hero with a Thousand Faces*, the epic journey is always an instrument for the hero's moral education.

In *The Theory of the Novel*, however, Georg Lukács limits Campbell's faith in the epic as a tool for education by placing chronological restrictions on its effectiveness. Lukács posits that the epic form loses its significance once it tries to cross over into modern literary narratives, and that the explanation for this is that society has moved beyond the "age of the epic," never to return again, because "we have invented the productivity of the spirit. . . . We have invented the creation of forms: and that is why everything that falls from our weary and despairing hands must always be incomplete" (33–34). The epic can no longer accurately represent our fractured world because the belief system of the epic—synonymous with the equipoise inherent in a medieval cosmology—is no longer possible to sustain in a fragmented, unsettled world. Instead of maintaining its faith in tradition and a viable past worth fighting to preserve, the epic tendencies available in *The Dark Tower* are undercut by the presence of more modern Gothic sensibilities, and this holds true in explaining both the general erosion of the form's potency as well as its specific employment in King's seven-volume text. The romance tradition that embodied the epic structure is undermined by the intrusion of modernity's chaos—the latter's violence and corresponding loss of meaning, its palpable sense of alienation and corruption. Even Mid-World, King's own projection of a medieval universe, cannot remain insulated from the intrusions of modernity and its overriding sentiment of doubt.

So, while we might acknowledge *The Dark Tower* as a unique blend of Gothic horror and epic fantasy, as is the case in *The Stand* and *The Talisman* as well, this admixture is a restive one. The *Dark Tower*'s Gothic sensibilities, after all, clash most blatantly with the noble intentions that define its epic quest. The endangered quaintness of Mid-World and the justifications for why the Beams supporting it need to be restored and fortified are continually challenged by the Gothic waste lands that permeate places such as Calla Bryn Sturgis and Lud in Mid-World, and Kansas and New York City in King's parallel universe. Outside the immediate members of the *ka-tet*, there are also precious few human beings worth saving in *The Dark Tower*, and many of those who are, such as Susan Delgado or Father Callahan, are destroyed by the very forces that Roland seeks to thwart. In fact, as Roland slouches toward his Tower, he comes more and more to resemble the Gothic antihero than the traditional epic hero; by the end of his long saga, there is not much more left for Roland to learn, and as he looks back on his education, he cannot help but see it soaked in blood and grief. There is something of the Byronic figure in his melancholic sense of loss, especially following the deaths of Susan and Jake. Like many Gothic monsters and villains, Roland's suffering—physical, emotional, psychological—comes most accurately to define his character; he is the emotive center of this journey and his behavior sets the tone for everyone else, including the reader. Critic Frederick S. Frank believes that the Gothic tradition embodies an ancestry of anguish, manifesting itself in the actions of the Gothic antihero, which symbolize defiance and outrage as well as suffering. This cry of anguish can be heard from Manfred in Walpole's first Gothic, *The Castle of Otranto,* to characters including Lewis's Ambrosio, Shelley's Victor Frankenstein, Stevenson's Henry Jekyll, and many of the central protagonists in the fictions of Poe, Hawthorne, and Melville. In King's Roland, we see the brooding darkness of the handsome and psychologically distressed Gothic male. In spite of his long association with the *ka-tet* and the occasional female lover, such as Rosalita Munoz in *The Wolves of Calla*, Roland remains essentially a solitary figure, impossible to know, who only reluctantly shares the intimate details of his life. Like many Gothic protagonists throughout literature and film, Roland generally tends to maintain a lonely and sinister independence from social ties. His quest comes to resemble closely the prototypical Gothic obsession, as he, like Melville's Captain Ahab, willingly sacrifices a large piece of his own humanity in his relentless pursuit of the Tower.

The early Gothics, from the last decades of the eighteenth century, sought a return to the ambience of the Middle Ages: a renewed fascination with the mystical and the inexplicable as well as an intensified interest in the battle between good and evil. Politically, the genre embodied the awareness of social upheaval that characterized an age of revolution. Psychologically, the Gothic signaled a turn from the portrayal of manners in an integrated society to the analysis of lonely, guilt-ridden outsiders. Roland and his *ka-tet* grow increasingly estranged from the inhabitants of both Mid-World and New York, the two primary locales for this saga. In fact, the single bond that unites all the members of the *ka-tet,* including the late addition of Father Callahan, is that they are all alienated figures estranged from their native worlds. Jake is a single child of parents who do not understand him; Eddie is a heroin abuser lost in the shadow of his mean-spirited older brother; Susannah is a black woman struggling with multiple personalities; and Roland never does completely recover from the loss of Susan Delgado in *Wizard and Glass.* It could be argued that Roland's obsession with the Dark Tower is transformed into a surrogate replacement for the loss of Susan; he displaces his guilt and anger over losing her onto the quest to save the universe by righting the Tower. As a young man, he may have failed to rescue his besieged maiden, but he'll make up for it as an old man in rescuing the besieged Tower.

The Gothic environment of crumbling castles, supernatural animation, and mysterious forests is revisited in *The Dark Tower* as King's *ka-tet* wanders along a blasted landscape where the divine order is under siege and the vacuum created by social upheaval typically leads to lawlessness and power oligarchies in the hands of the most ruthless. Despite the vastness of their journey, the *ka-tet* encounters very little beauty along the way—no descriptions of inspiring landscapes, few examples of kindness unselfishly bestowed among humans, or even much gratitude from the supernal Beams that are rescued at such a tremendous human cost. The dark road they travel, whether along the interstates of contemporary America or the dusty dirt paths of Mid-World, is more reminiscent of Cormac McCarthy's *The Road* than it is Walt Whitman's sunny journey of hopefulness. The sickness of radiation poisoning and long-term consequences of unattended petrochemicals permeates the landscape. The threatened status of the Tower requires a multidimensional explanation, but surely its endangerment is both reflected in and caused by the collapse of an ecosystem to which the Tower is intricately connected. In Mid-World in particular, genetic deformities and abnormalities abound. North Central Positronics, the computer corporation that produced Shardik the Bear, Blaine the Mono, Andy the Robot, and the Wolves of Calla, remains a faceless entity that symbolizes the disastrous consequences of unregulated corporate "progress" and an amoral reliance on computers and robotic life forms. This is also another way that *The Dark Tower* intersects with Gothic science; the abuse and misuse of cyborg robotics is an issue that ties King's saga to dystopic texts confronting the same issue, such as *Frankenstein, Blade Runner, Total Recall, Minority Report,* and *The Matrix.* Although King does not develop it sufficiently, there even appears to be an unholy collusion between the polluted physical environments of Lud, the Mejis, and Calla Bryn Sturgis and the computer technology that is discarded or left barely functioning on the outskirts of these cities and towns. Indeed, the cities and villages that the *ka-tet* visits in both worlds are fallen and corrupted. Thus, the Gothic's characteristic fascination with evil, fixation on rebellion against optimistic virtues and the righteousness of social convention, and its emphasis on disorder, chaos, and fear for the future resonate with some darkly sympathetic chord in King's construction of this narrative.

One of the most Gothic elements in *The Dark Tower* is the increasing sense of doom that grows ever more palpable as Roland nears his destination. Despite his deepening association with the other members of his *ka-tet* as the series evolves, there is an essential part of Roland that none of the others is capable of penetrating: the brooding Gothic man of sorrow who defines himself via his isolation from human society and his alacrity for aggressive action. Each of the last four books shares an identical narrative design structure that builds to a climactic crescendo of brutality in the final chapters. And although Roland never does relinquish his reliance on his old ways and past knowledge, especially by way of employing violence as a solution to all conflict, the grief he is made to experience as a result of this commitment complicates his personality by opening the gunslinger to the consequences that attend a life of aggression. Indeed, the Roland who exits this epic has, in the course of many years, lost most of the people he cared about to the violence he has dedicated himself to perpetuate: "*I only kill my family*, Roland thought, stroking the dead billy-bumbler" (*The Dark Tower* 960). He has dragged others into his quest and made them both kill and die in pursuit of a life's mission that Roland likewise imposes on his associates. As such, Roland must accept some measure of responsibility for what he has set in motion and forced others to participate in. The gunslinger acknowledges at least this much late in the last volume as he prepares to say good-bye to Susannah: "And he did owe this woman a debt, he reckoned, for had he not pretty much seized her by the scruff of the neck and hauled her into this world, where she'd learned the art of murder and fallen in love and been left bereaved? Had he not kidnapped her into this present sorrow?" (*The Dark Tower* 921). Although Roland's life's work has been of his own choosing, as no one has "seized [him] by the scruff of the neck" and forced him to accept the challenge of the Tower, this is nonetheless an apt description of the gunslinger as well.

By the time he actually reaches the end of his voyage, the young stud warrior whom readers followed in *The Gunslinger* and *Wizard and Glass* volumes with some of the same combination of fear and awe that the Stephen King character confessed to harboring back in 1977, has transformed into a world-weary old man arguably defined more by what he has lost on the road to the Tower than by the values that the Tower purportedly represents: "He felt quite sure that this was his last march. He didn't believe he would ever leave Can'-Ka No Rey, and that was all right. He was tired. And, despite the power of the rose, sad" (*The Dark Tower* 944). At the end of this long saga, the amorous suitor of Susan Delgado has transformed into Mordred's "Old White Daddy," a hobbled adult, full of adult aches and pains, adult darkness, corruption, remorse, and regret. In short, the idealistic epic adventurer slips into the brooding Gothic antihero, an elaborate illustration of the Shadow side of a decent man. The gunslinger in volume seven is still desirous, but also confused, alone, bereft. His tragic trajectory thus follows those life histories perhaps most readily identifiable with Gothic scientists from the nineteenth century, such as Victor Frankenstein and Henry Jekyll: what begins as a quest to enhance the world ends in a somber and sobering cautionary tale about the dangers of hubris and the indulging of personal obsession. We make the choices to bring out the good or evil in ourselves, and sometimes these choices create monsters that emerge in spite of the pursuit of righteous causes. Gothic literature abounds with characters that begin their tales with good intentions and confidence, only to be seduced by their own ambitions, tragic innocence, or thwarted by nature itself—in either case, leaving dispossessed men in the valley of sorrow. Self-knowledge may be one of the major identifiable traits of the epic narrative design, but in the Gothic such introspective insights tend to occur too late or not at all.

Roland relinquishes the crystalline focus, the defiant virtue that characterizes his early vision and motivation. Wracked by pain and exhaustion (both spiritual and physical), bereft of his *ka-tet*, and carrying the burden of his own history that casts a shadow as long as that of the Tower itself, the gunslinger that exits this narrative resembles closely the depleted Gothic antiheroes—Manfred, Don Juan, Henry Jekyll, Victor Frankenstein, the Ancient Mariner, even Roderick Usher—as well as certain epic heroes—Odysseus, Achilles, Don Quixote, Childe Roland, but most of all, Frodo at the end of *The Lord of the Rings*—weary survivors whose journeys have exacted a severe toll. Campbell tells us that the epic hero must lose himself to find himself; and at the end, when his duty is completed, he "brings back from his adventure the means for the regeneration of his society as a whole" (38). However, of all the aforementioned epic heroes, only Tolkien's Frodo seems to be as singularly empty as Roland at the end of *The Dark Tower*; that is, both stumble around in darkness more than the triumphant epic hero who returns to be welcomed back and claim his rightful place in the community. Critics, readers, and King himself may be most comfortable viewing *The Dark Tower* saga as an epic with Roland as its hero, but in truth, it ends with probably more in common with the Gothic tale of the psychically lost, guilt-ridden outsider. In their quests to uphold a semblance of goodness in a fallen world, Frodo and Roland, like their fellow Gothic brethren, have wandered a long way from any unequivocal definition of goodness as well as home, so far afield that home becomes just a vague, barely recognizable memory that is no longer accessible, and goodness merely a relative concept.

I have always believed that the most emotive part of Tolkien's wonderful trilogy centers on the displaced Frodo that we leave at the story's conclusion. He occupies a psychic space that is very close to where we leave Roland at the end of *The Dark Tower*. Although both are triumphant in their adventures, they end their respective tales more diminished than when they began. Sam returns home to marry and procreate, the Shire is cleansed of its postwar vagabonds and thieves, and Mordor collapses in on the weight of its own evil. But in helping to rescue Middle Earth from the destructive design of Sauron and his minions, Frodo has moved beyond his life's station as a humble hobbit. Like Roland, he has perhaps witnessed too much; his hobbit naiveté and rustic simplicity are compromised by the experiences of his long journey and the burden of carrying the ring. There is no eager bride awaiting his return; apparently, none of the pleasures in which Frodo once indulged still hold the same delight. Indeed, the adventurous young boy we grow to love from the first volume returns in the last as wizened as the old wizard Gandalf. The Shire is suddenly too small, too quaint, too provincial to bear the weight of his experience in the larger world. So Frodo vanishes, like Ishmael or Cain, off on his own to wander Middle Earth, and lands beyond. And he must depart the Shire the same way that Roland must enter the imperious Tower—alone, by himself—because there is no one who could possibly understand what he has been through, the tests he has passed, what they have exacted from his spirit, and, most of all, the incessant call of the ring. Although he is ultimately able to resist the siren song of Precious by destroying it in the fires of Mordor, Frodo has nevertheless bonded with the ring, felt the power of it, lost his innocence to its seductive corruption, and thus can never again return to his former self. By the conclusion of Tolkien's fantasy, Frodo is pulled into a connection to Gollum that both he and the reader would never have thought possible—a nexus of tragic sympathy at least, however unwitting—that is certainly stronger than whatever connections he still shares with his fellow hobbits back in the Shire.

The Shire that Frodo and his friends return to find—with its corrupt bureaucratic officials and weak-willed hobbits, the mills and factories that have replaced trees and hedgerows, the vile odors and polluted streams that have displaced the domain's sweetness, and the general air of civic degradation and indifference—resembles the Mid-World waste land that Roland and his *ka-tet* endeavor to fix. In the end, the battle to save Mid-World and Middle Earth is as much about saving the physical environment from the multifarious corruptive forces that would poison it as it is about defeating the more obvious avatars of evil—the Crimson King and Sauron. Thus, both sagas embody the theme of the destructive consequences inherent in change and the need to protect the Earth from those who would debase it in their bid for dominance. This general theme of debasement enlarges to include Roland's *ka-tet* and Frodo's fellowship of hobbits as well. Roland and Frodo pulled these individuals out of their former lives, as mundane and as self-destructive as many of them were, and took them on an amazing adventure. Each of the characters that embarked on these adventures was changed by it; in the process, they all became something better than their former selves. Perhaps Roland's and Frodo's personal journeys were self-paved paths to hell, yet these paths were nonetheless worthy of a grand story. King's and Tolkien's narrative mode of storytelling serve as aids to helping these characters master their trauma. Education through experience and suffering enlarges the spirit, gives it confidence and stature, especially for a naïve little hobbit and a monomaniacal gunslinger who were both transformed into world-wise (and world-weary) wordslingers. At the same time as all this is true, it is highly ironic that, while Frodo and Roland are capable of revivifying their respective worlds and their respective *ka-tets*, their own psyches were depleted as a direct consequence of their redemptive quests. They may be the transcendent heroes of their individual books, but they also exit them exhausted, in the absence of friends and devoid of purpose.

Works Cited

Anderson, Linda. "OH DEAR JESUS IT IS FEMALE: Monster as Mother/Mother as Monster in Stephen King's *It*." *Imagining the Worst: Stephen King and the Representation of Women.* Ed. Kathleen Margaret Lant and Teresa Thompson. Westport, CT: Greenwood Press, 1998. 111–126.

Apt Pupil. Dir. Bryan Singer. Screenplay by Brandon Boyce. Perf. Ian McKellen and Brad Renfro. Phoenix Pictures, Canal + DA, Bad Hat Harry, TriStar, 1997.

"At *The Shining* Press Conference." 9 Jan. 1997. ABC-TV. Rpt. *Phantasmagoria* 5 (1997): 24–32.

Badley, Linda. *Writing Horror and the Body: The Fiction of Stephen King, Clive Barker, and Anne Rice.* Westport, CT: Greenwood Press, 1996.

Bailey, Dale. *American Nightmares: The Haunted House Formula in American Popular Fiction.* Bowling Green, OH: The Popular Press, 1999.

Beahm, George. *Stephen King Country.* Philadelphia and London: Running Press, 1999.

———. *Stephen King from A to Z.* Kansas City: Andrew McMeel Publishing, 1998.

Bloom, Harold. "Introduction." *Bloom's Modern Critical Views: Stephen King.* Ed. Harold Bloom. Philadelphia: Chelsea House, 2007. 1–3.

Bright, Susie. *Sexwise.* Pittsburgh: Cleis Press, 1995.

Browning, Robert. "Childe Roland to the Dark Tower Came." Appendix to *The Dark Tower VII: The Dark Tower.* New York: Simon and Schuster, 2004. 1035–1045.

Burns, Gail E., and Melinda Kanner. "Women, Danger, and Death: The Perversion of the Feminine Principle in Stephen King's Fiction." *Sexual Politics and Popular Culture.* Ed. Diane Raymond. Bowling Green, OH: The Popular Press, 1990. 158–172.

"The Buzz." *The Advocate.* 4 Apr. 1995.

Campbell, Joseph. *The Hero with a Thousand Faces.* Cleveland and New York: World Publishing Company, 1956.

Carrie. Dir. Brian De Palma. Screenplay by Lawrence D. Cohen. Perf. Sissy Spacek, Piper Laurie, Amy Irving. United Artists, 1976.

Cocks, Geoffrey. *The Wolf at the Door: Stanley Kubrick, History, and the Holocaust.* New York: Peter Lang, 2004.

Collings, Michael. *Stephen King as Richard Bachman*. Mercer Island, WA: Starmont House, 1985.

Cruz, Gilbert. "Q & A: Talking with Stephen King." *Time Magazine*. 28 Nov. 2007. http://www.time.com/time/arts/article/0,8599,1687229,00.html.

Davis, David. "Ten-Gallon Hero." *The Western: A Collection of Critical Essays*. Ed. James K. Folsom. Englewood Cliffs, NJ: Prentice Hall, 1979.

Dickerson, Mary Jane. "Stephen King Reading William Faulkner: Memory, Desire, and Time in the Making of *IT*." *The Dark Descent: Essays Defining Stephen King's Horrorscape*. Ed. Tony Magistrale. Westport, CT: Greenwood Press, 1992. 171–186.

Dolan, Colleen. "The Feminist King: *Dolores Claiborne*." *The Films of Stephen King*. Ed. Tony Magistrale. New York: Palgrave, 2008. 153–164.

Dolores Claiborne. Dir. Taylor Hackford. Screenplay by Tony Gilroy. Perf. Kathy Bates, Jennifer Jason Leigh, Christopher Plummer. Castle Rock Entertainment, Columbia Pictures, 1995.

Dreamcatcher. Dir. Lawrence Kasdan. Screenplay by William Goldman. Perf. Morgan Freeman and Jason Lee. Castle Rock Entertainment, Village Roadshow Productions, 2003.

Dyson, Cindy. "Biography of Stephen King." *Bloom's BioCritiques: Stephen King*. Ed. Harold Bloom. Philadelphia: Chelsea House, 2002. 1–47.

Edmundson, Mark. *Nightmare on Main Street: Angels, Sadomasochism, and the Culture of the Gothic*. Boston: Harvard UP, 1997.

Eyes Wide Shut. Dir. Stanley Kubrick. Screenplay by Stanley Kubrick and Frederic Raphael. Perf. Tom Cruise and Nicole Kidman. Hobby Films, Warner Brothers, 1999.

Fiedler, Leslie. *Love and Death in the American Novel*. 1960. New York: Dell, 1975.

Findley, Mary. "The Prisoner, the Pen, and the Number One Fan: *Misery* as a Prison Film." *The Films of Stephen King*. Ed. Tony Magistrale. New York: Palgrave, 2008. 91–100.

1408. Dir. Mikael Hafstrom. Screenplay by Matt Greenberg and Scott Alexander. Perf. John Cusack and Samuel L. Jackson. Dimension Films, Paramount Pictures, 2007.

Forster, E. M. *Aspects of the Novel*. 1927. Orlando, FL: Harcourt Publishing, 1955.

Frank, Frederick S. "Proto-Gothicism: The Infernal Iconography of Walpole's *Castle of Otranto*." *Orbis Litterarum* 41 (1986): 199–212.

Friday the 13th. Dir. Sean S. Cunningham. Screenplay by Victor Miller. Perf. Ari Lehman. Georgetown Productions Pictures, 1980.

Grand Torino. Dir. Clint Eastwood. Screenplay by Nick Schenk. Perf. Clint Eastwood. Village Roadshow Pictures, Warner Brothers, 2008.

The Green Mile. Dir. Frank Darabont. Screenplay by Frank Darabont. Perf. Tom Hanks, Michael Clarke Duncan, David Morse. Castle Rock Entertainment, Warner Brothers, 1999.

Guran, Paula. "Interview with Jeanne Cavelos." *Dark Echo*. April 2002. http://www.darkecho.com/darkecho/archives/cavelos.html.

Hardy, Thomas. *Tess of the D'Urbervilles*. 1891. Ed. Scott Elledge. New York: Norton, 1965.

Hatlen, Burton. "Beyond the Kittery Bridge: Stephen King's Maine." *Fear Itself: The Horror Fiction of Stephen King*. Ed. Tim Underwood and Chuck Miller. New York: New American Library, 1982. 45–60.

Heldreth, Leonard G. "Viewing 'The Body': King's Portrait of the Artist as a Survivor." *The Gothic World of Stephen King*. Ed. Gary Hoppenstand and Ray B. Browne. Bowling Green, OH: The Popular Press, 1987. 64–74.

Hicks, Heather J. "Hoodoo Economics: White Men's Work and Black Man's Magic in Contemporary American Film." *Camera Obscura* 18 (2003): 27–55.

Hohne, Karen A. "In Words Not Their Own: Dangerous Women in Stephen King." *Misogyny in Literature*. Ed. Katherine Ann Ackley. New York: Garland, 1992. 327–345.

Indick, Ben P. "King and the Literary Tradition of Horror and the Supernatural." *Fear Itself: The Horror Fiction of Stephen King*. Ed. Tim Underwood and Chuck Miller. New York: New American Library, 1982. 175–190.

Jackson, Shirley. *The Haunting of Hill House*. New York: Penguin, 1959.

Jameson, Fredric. *Signatures of the Visible*. New York: Routledge, 1990.

Keesey, Douglas. "'The Face of Mr. Flip': Homophobia in the Horror of Stephen King." *The Dark Descent: Essays Defining Stephen King's Horrorscape*. Ed. Tony Magistrale. Westport, CT: Greenwood Press, 1992. 187–202.

Kent, Brian. "Canaries in a Gilded Cage: Mental and Marital Decline in *McTeague* and *The Shining*." *A Casebook on* The Stand. Ed. Tony Magistrale. Mercer Island, WA: Starmont House, 1992. 139–154.

———. "Christian Martyr or Grateful Slave? The Magical Negro as Uncle Tom in Frank Darabont's *The Green Mile*." *The Films of Stephen King*. Ed. Tony Magistrale. New York: Palgrave, 2008. 115–128.

———. "Stephen King and His Readers: A Dirty, Compelling Romance." *A Casebook on The Stand*. Ed. Tony Magistrale. Mercer Island, WA: Starmont House, 1992. 37–68.

King, Stephen. *Apt Pupil. Different Seasons*. New York: Viking, 1982.

———. *The Body. Different Seasons*. New York: Viking, 1982.

———. "The Bogeyboys." Keynote Address, Vermont Library Conference. May 26, 1999. http://www.stephenking.de/interviews/interview6.html.

———. *Carrie*. New York: Doubleday, 1974.

———. *Danse Macabre*. New York: Berkley, 1981.

———. *The Dark Half*. New York: Viking, 1989.

———. *The Dark Tower: The Gunslinger*. West Kingston, RI: Donald M. Grant, 1982.

———. *The Dark Tower II: The Drawing of the Three*. New York: New American Library, 1987.

———. *The Dark Tower III: The Waste Lands*. New York: New American Library, 1993.

———. *The Dark Tower IV: Wizard and Glass*. New York: Penguin Putnam, 1997.

———. *The Dark Tower V: The Wolves of Calla*. New York: Simon and Schuster, 2003.

———. *The Dark Tower VI: Song of Susannah*. New York: Scribner, 2004.

———. *The Dark Tower VII: The Dark Tower*. New York: Simon and Schuster, 2004.

———. *Dolores Claiborne*. New York: Viking, 1993.

———. *Duma Key*. New York: Scribner, 2008.

———. *Gerald's Game*. New York: Viking, 1992.

———. "The Gingerbread Girl." *Esquire Magazine*. July 2007.

———. *The Girl Who Loved Tom Gordon*. New York: Scribner, 1999.

———. *IT*. New York: Viking, 1994.

———. *Lisey's Story*. New York: Scribner, 2006.

[Richard Bachman, pseud.]. *The Long Walk*. New York: New American Library, 1979.

———. *Misery*. New York: Viking, 1987.

———. "National Book Award Acceptance Speech." 24 Mar. 2008. http://www.nationalbook.org/nbaacceptspeech_sking.html.

———. *Needful Things*. New York: Viking, 1991.

———. *Night Shift*. New York: Doubleday, 1978.

———. "On Impact." *The New Yorker*. 19 June 2008.

———. "On *The Shining* and Other Perpetrations." *Whispers* 17/18 (1982): 11–16.

———. *Pet Sematary*. New York: Doubleday, 1983.

———. "The Raft." *Skeleton Crew*. New York: G.P. Putnam's Sons, 1985.

[Richard Bachman, pseud.]. *Rage*. New York: New American Library, 1977.

[Richard Bachman, pseud.]. *Roadwork*. New York: New American Library, 1988.

———. *Rose Madder*. New York: Viking, 1995.

[Richard Bachman, pseud.]. *The Running Man*. New York: New American Library, 1982.

———. *'Salem's Lot*. New York: New American Library, 1975.

———. *The Shawshank Redemption. Different Seasons*. New York: Viking, 1982.

———. *The Shining*. New York: Doubleday, 1977.

———. *The Stand*. New York: Doubleday, 1978. 1990.

[With Peter Straub.] *The Talisman*. New York: Viking and G.P. Putnam's Sons, 1987.

[Richard Bachman, pseud.]. *Thinner*. New York: New American Library, 1984.

———. *The Tommyknockers*. New York: G.P. Putnam's Sons, 1984.

———. "Why I Was Bachman." *The Bachman Books: Four Early Novels*. New York: New American Library, 1985.

Lant, Kathleen Margaret, and Teresa Thompson. "Introduction." *Imagining the Worst: Stephen King and the Representation of Women*. Ed. Kathleen Margaret Lant and Teresa Thompson. Westport, CT: Greenwood Press, 1998. 3–8.

Lukács, Georg. *The Theory of the Novel*. Trans. Anna Bostock. Boston: MIT Press, 1971.

Madden, Edward. "Cars Are Girls: Sexual Power and Sexual Panic in Stephen King's *Christine*." *Bloom's Modern Critical Views: Stephen King*. Ed. Harold Bloom. New York: Chelsea House, 2007. 177–194.

Magistrale, Tony. *Hollywood's Stephen King*. New York: Palgrave, 2003.

———. *Stephen King: The Second Decade, Danse Macabre to The Dark Half*. Boston: Twayne, 1992.

Magistrale, Tony, and Sidney Poger. *Poe's Children: Connections between Tales of Terror and Detection.* New York: Peter Lang, 1999.

The Magnificent Seven. Dir. John Sturgis. Screenplay by William Roberts. Perf. Yul Brynner, Steve McQueen, James Coburn. United Artists, 1960.

Making "The Shining." Dir. Vivian Kubrick. Perf. Jack Nicholson, Shelley Duvall, Danny Lloyd, Scatman Crothers. Eagle Film SS, 1980.

Manchel, Frank. "What about Jack? Another Perspective on Family Relationships in Stanley Kubrick's *The Shining.*" *Discovering Stephen King's The Shining.* Ed. Tony Magistrale. San Bernardino, CA: The Borgo Press, 1998. 82–94.

Maximum Overdrive. Dir. Stephen King. Screenplay by Stephen King. Perf. Emilio Estevez. Dino De Laurentiis Productions, 1986.

McCarthy, Cormac. *No Country for Old Men.* New York: Alfred A. Knopf, 2005.

———. *The Road.* New York: Alfred A, Knopf, 2006.

Misery. Dir. Rob Reiner. Screenplay by William Goldman. Perf. Kathy Bates and James Caan. Castle Rock Entertainment, Columbia Pictures, 1990.

Mustazza, Leonard. "The Red Death's Sway: Setting and Character in Poe's 'Masque of the Red Death' and King's *The Shining.*" *The Shining Reader.* Ed. Tony Magistrale. Mercer Island, WA: Starmont House, 1991. 105–120.

Night of the Living Dead. Dir. George A. Romero. Screenplay by George A. Romero and John A. Russo. Perf. Duane Jones. Image Ten and Laurel, 1968.

Nilsen, Sarah. "White Soul: The 'Magical Negro' in the Films of Stephen King." *The Films of Stephen King.* Ed. Tony Magistrale. New York: Palgrave, 2008. 129–140.

The Outer Limits. [Television Series.] ABC-TV, 1963–1965.

Pharr, Mary. "Partners in the *Danse*: Women in Stephen King's Fiction." *The Dark Descent: Essays Defining Stephen King's Horrorscape.* Ed. Tony Magistrale. Westport, CT: Greenwood Press, 1992. 19–32.

Pet Sematary. Dir. Mary Lambert. Screenplay by Stephen King. Perf. Dale Midkiff, Fred Gwynne, Denise Crosby. Paramount Pictures, 1990.

The Quick and the Dead. Dir. Sam Raimi. Screenplay by Simon Moore. Perf. Sharon Stone, Gene Hackman. TriStar Pictures, 1995.

Reading Stephen King: Issues of Censorship, Student Choice, and Popular Literature. Ed. Brenda Miller Power, Jeffrey D. Wilhelm, and Kelly Chandler. Urbana, IL: National Council of Teachers of English, 1997.

Reesman, Jeanne Campbell. "Riddle Game: Stephen King's Metafictive Dialogue." *The Dark Descent: Essays Defining Stephen King's Horrorscape.* Ed. Tony Magistrale. Westport, CT: Greenwood Press, 1992. 157–170.

———. "Stephen King and the Tradition of American Naturalism in *The Shining.*" *The Shining Reader.* Ed. Tony Magistrale. Mercer Island, WA: Starmont House, 1991. 121–138.

Reino, Joseph. *Stephen King: The First Decade.* Boston: G.K. Hall, 1988.

Russell, Sharon A. *Stephen King: A Critical Companion.* Westport, CT: Greenwood Press, 1996.

Senf, Carol. "*Gerald's Game* and *Dolores Claiborne*: Stephen King and the Evolution of an Authentic Female Narrative Voice." *Imagining the Worst: Stephen King and the*

Representation of Women. Ed. Kathleen Margaret Lant and Teresa Thompson. Westport, CT: Greenwood Press, 1998. 91–110.

The Shawshank Redemption. Dir. Frank Darabont. Screenplay by Frank Darabont. Perf. Tim Robbins, Morgan Freeman, Bob Gunton. Castle Rock Entertainment, Columbia Pictures, 1994.

The Shining. Dir Stanley Kubrick. Screenplay by Stanley Kubrick and Diane Johnson. Perf. Jack Nicholson, Shelley Duvall, Danny Lloyd. Warner Brothers, 1980.

The Shinning. The Simpson's Treehouse of Horror, #6. [Animated Television Program.] Dir. Jim Reardon. Teleplay by Jim Reardon, Greg Daniels, Dan McGrath, David Cohen. Fox Television, 1994.

Singer, Mark. "What Are You Afraid Of?" *The New Yorker*. 7 Sept. 1998.

Smith, Greg. "The Literary Equivalent of a Big Mac and Fries?: Academics, Moralists, and the Stephen King Phenomenon." *The Midwest Quarterly* 43 (2002): 329–345.

Sperb, Jason. *The Kubrick Façade: Faces and Voices in the Films of Stanley Kubrick*. Lanham, MD: Scarecrow Press, 2006.

Stand by Me. Dir. Rob Reiner. Screenplay by Raynold Gideon and Bruce E. Evans. Perf. Wil Wheaton, River Phoenix, Corey Feldman, Kiefer Sutherland. Columbia Pictures, Act III Productions, 1986.

Stanton, Michael N. *Hobbits, Elves, and Wizards: Exploring the Wonders and Worlds of J.R.R. Tolkien's The Lord of the Rings*. New York: Palgrave, 2001.

Stephen King's Rose Red. Dir. Craig R. Baxley. Teleplay by Stephen King. Perf. Nancy Travis and Robert Blanche. Greengrass Productions, Victor Television Productions, Mark Carliner Productions, 2002.

Stephen King's The Shining. Dir. Mick Garris. Teleplay by Stephen King. Perf. Rebecca De Mornay, Steven Weber, Courtland Mead. Lakeside, Warner Brothers Television, ABC-TV, 1997.

Stephen King's Storm of the Century. Dir. Craig R. Baxley. Teleplay by Stephen King. Perf. Tim Daly, Colm Feore, Debrah Farentino. Greengrass Productions, Victor Television Productions, Mark Carliner Productions, Walt Disney Television, ABC-TV, 1999.

Strengell, Heidi. *Dissecting Stephen King: From the Gothic to Literary Naturalism*. Madison: University of Wisconsin Press, 2005.

Terrell, Carroll E. *Stephen King: Man and Artist*. Orono, ME: Northern Lights Publishing, 1990.

Thoens, Karen. "*It*, A Sexual Fantasy." *Imagining the Worst: Stephen King and the Representation of Women*. Ed. Kathleen Margaret Lant and Teresa Thompson. Westport, CT: Greenwood Press, 1998. 127–142.

Thoreau, Henry David. *Civil Disobedience*. 1849. *The Portable Thoreau*. Ed. Carl Bode. New York, Viking, 1947. 109–137.

Tolkien, J. R. R. *The Lord of the Rings*. New York: Ballantine, 1965.

Twain, Mark. *The Adventures of Huckleberry Finn*. 1855. Ed. Gerald Graff and James Phelan. New York: Bedford-St. Martin's, 1995.

The Twilight Zone. [Television Series.] Created by Rod Serling. CBS-TV, 1959–1964.

Underwood, Tim, and Chuck Miller, eds. *Bare Bones: Conversations on Terror with Stephen King*. New York: McGraw-Hill, 1988.

The Unforgiven. Dir. Clint Eastwood. Screenplay by David Webb Peoples. Perf. Clint Eastwood, Gene Hackman, Morgan Freeman. Warner Brothers, 1992.

Warren, Bill. "The Movies and Mr. King: Part II." *Reign of Fear: The Fiction and Films of Stephen King.* Ed. Don Herron. Lancaster, PA: Underwood Miller, 1988. 123–148.

The Wild One. Dir. Lasio Benedek. Screenplay by Ben Maddow and John Paxton. Perf. Marlon Brando. Columbia Pictures, 1953.

Winter, Douglas E. *Stephen King: The Art of Darkness.* New York: New American Library, 1984.

Yarbro, Chelsea Quinn. "Cinderella's Revenge—Twists on Fairy Tales and Mythic Themes in the Work of Stephen King." *Fear Itself: The Horror Fiction of Stephen King.* Ed. Tim Underwood and Chuck Miller. New York: New American Library, 1982. 61–71.

Index

About the Author

TONY MAGISTRALE is Professor of English and Chair of the English department at the University of Vermont where he has taught courses in writing and American literature since 1983, when he returned to the United States after a Fulbright post-doctoral fellowship at the University of Milan, Italy. He has lectured at many universities in North America and Western Europe, including the University of Augsburg, Germany, where he continues to serve as Visiting Professor in American Studies. He obtained a PhD at the University of Pittsburgh in 1981. Over the past three decades, Magistrale's twenty books and many articles have covered a broad area of interests. He has published on the writing process and international study abroad, and he has published his own poetry. Several of his books have centered on defining and exploring Anglo-American Gothicism, from its origins in eighteenth-century romanticism to its contemporary manifestations in popular culture, particularly in the work of Edgar Allan Poe, the history of the horror film, and Stephen King.